How to

COMPOSE BETTER PHOTOS

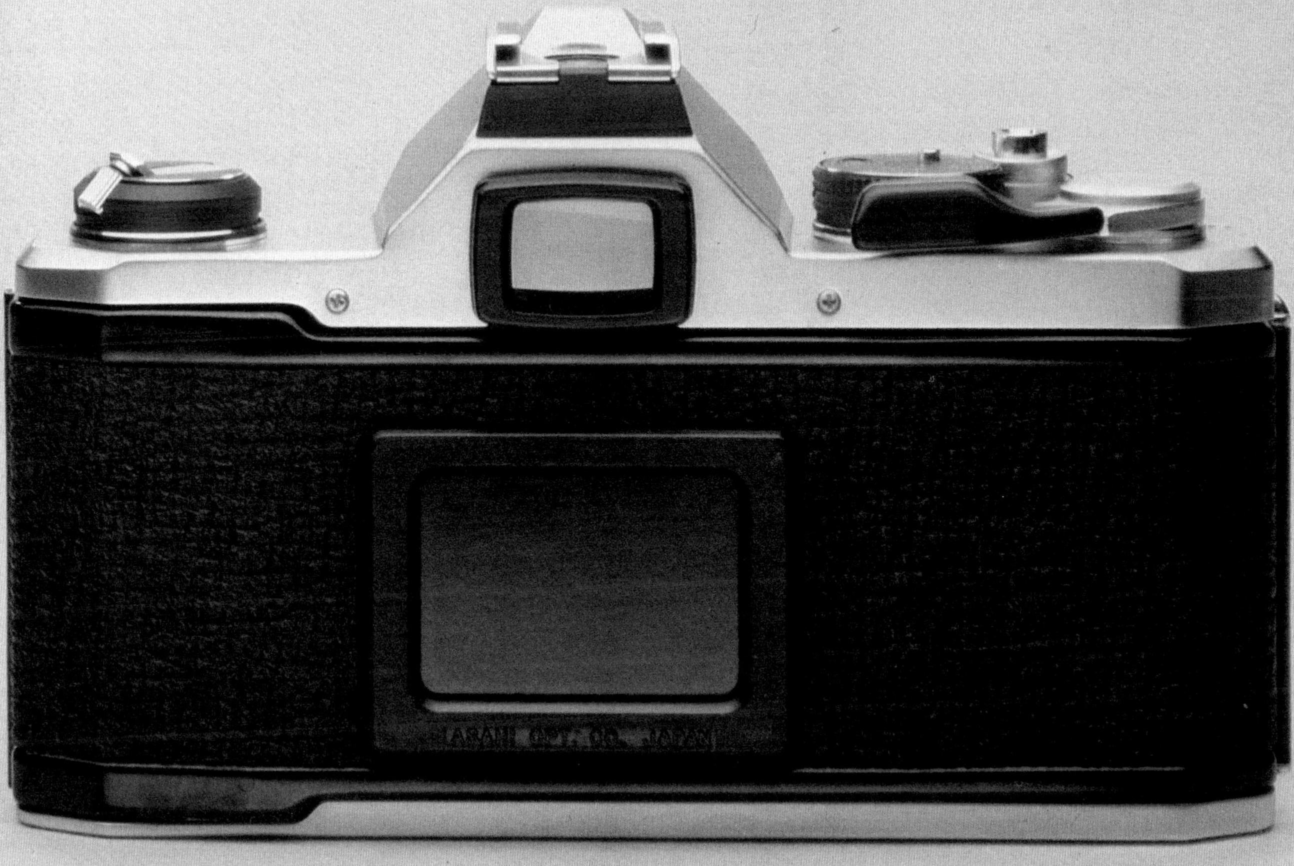

Executive Editor: Carl Shipman
Editors: David A. Silverman, Theodore DiSante
Art Director: Don Burton
Book Assembly: George Haigh, Pat O'Dell
Typography: Cindy Coatsworth, Joanne Nociti, Michelle Claridge

Notice: This material was first published in England in the magazine You and Your Camera, produced by Eaglemoss Publications Limited. It has been adapted and re-edited for North America by HPBooks. The information contained in this book is true and complete to the best of our knowledge. All recommendations are made without any guarantees on the part of Eaglemoss Publications Limited or HPBooks. The publishers disclaim all liability incurred in connection with the use of this information.

Published by H.P. Books, P.O. Box 5367, Tucson, AZ 85703 602/888-2150
ISBN: 0-89586-111-9 Library of Congress Catalog No. 81-82063

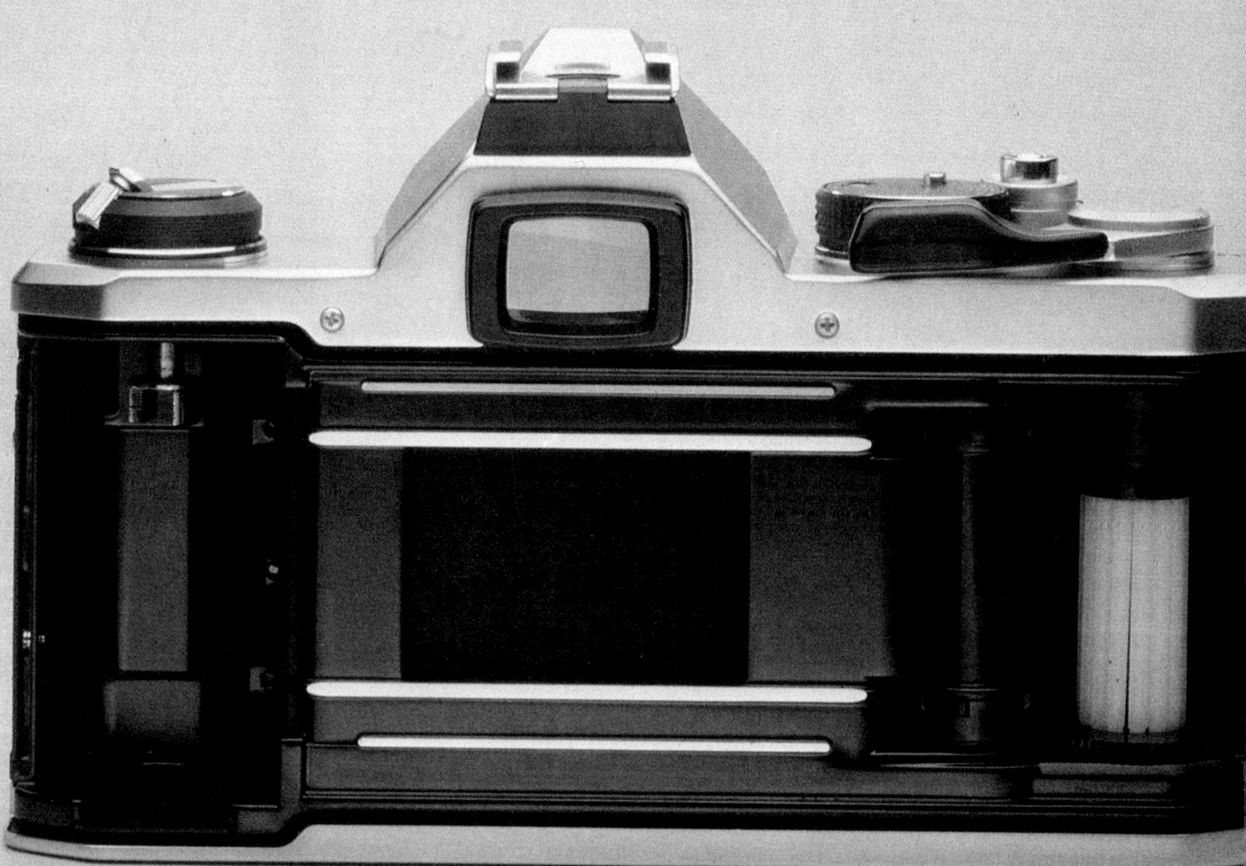

How to COMPOSE BETTER PHOTOS

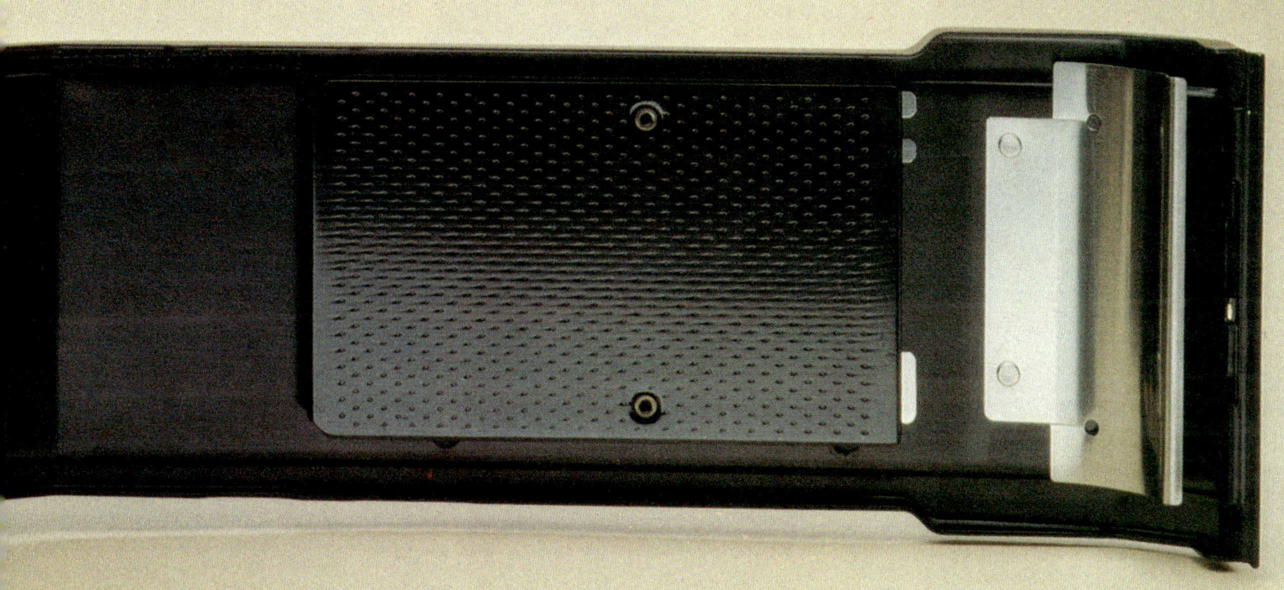

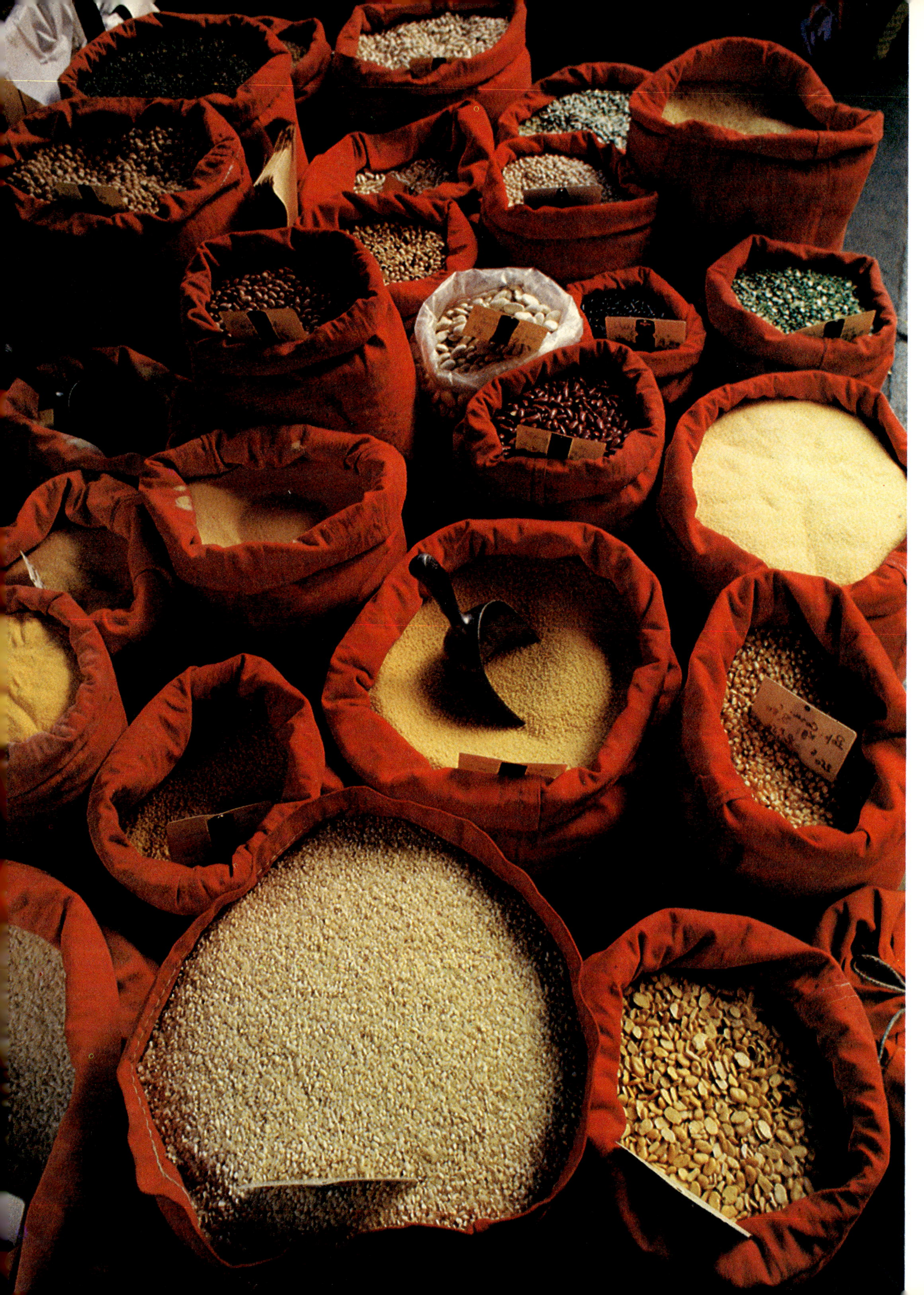

Contents

Composing in the Viewfinder

The panoramic view on the right is very much as people see it—but we subconsciously focus on certain details as our eyes scan across the landscape. What each person notices is very much a personal choice—it may be the form of a particular tree, the pattern made by branches, or the position of a figure.

When you take a photograph you make two decisions—*what* to include and *when* to press the shutter button. For both, you should consider how to compose the picture—in other words, how to show the subject in the most effective way.

Good composition may mean simplifying your photograph by changing viewpoint—moving higher, lower or to one side. Certainly it means thinking about the direction and quality of the light. Composition makes the difference between a photograph that is muddled or boring, and one that looks right.

HOW TO SEE BETTER PICTURES

Some people have a natural ability to see good composition right away, but most of us have to keep looking and experimenting until we start seeing well-composed photographs. Remember, this is something anyone can do, no matter how simple or elaborate the camera.

Photography is concerned with showing how the world appears as shown in a rectangular or square area on a flat piece of photographic paper. The question is, which parts of the scene or view should you include or leave out? This depends not only on the main center of interest, but also on the visual appeal of shapes, colors, patterns and textures. Moving around while looking through the viewfinder helps you emphasize important aspects and isolate them from the overall view.

Look also at the way objects may be "cut" by the edges of the picture. The hard lines at the edges of the viewfinder give a definite border to what you select. In a photograph you might cut part of your subject, or you can use this border to contain entire subject. This is another difference between seeing the scene as the human eye sees it and composing it for a photograph.

To become more aware of composition, it is helpful to make a cardboard viewing frame. Then look through it at familiar objects, such as parts of your home, people's faces or landscapes. By imposing this frame on what you see, you'll start to discover interesting "pictures" you may not have noticed before.

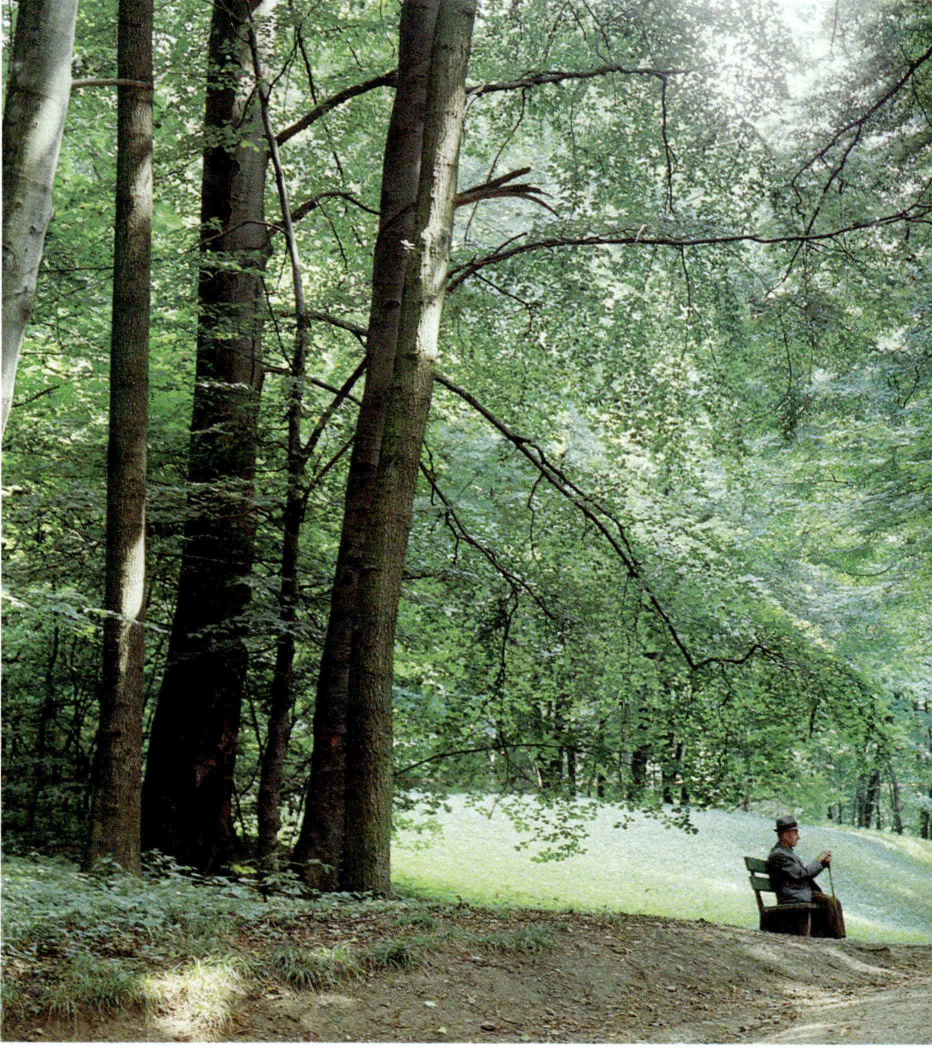

▲▶ You can choose which part of a general view to include in the picture. With a static scene such as a landscape, you have time for careful composition in the viewfinder. Experiment by changing camera position and moving closer to parts of the scene to find out how this affects what you see in the viewfinder. Photographing people in a landscape gives a sense of scale and often contributes to the balance and interest of the composition.

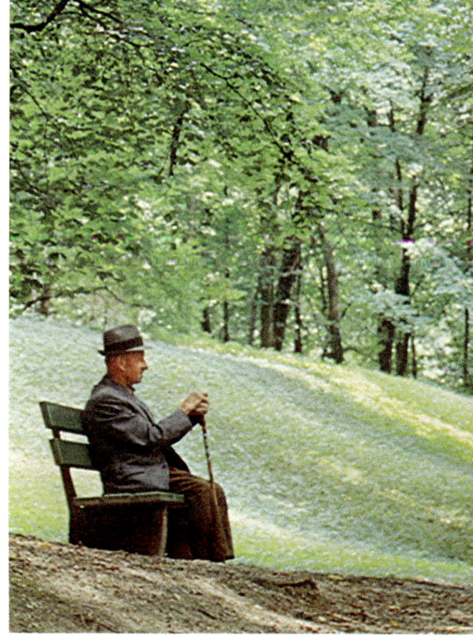

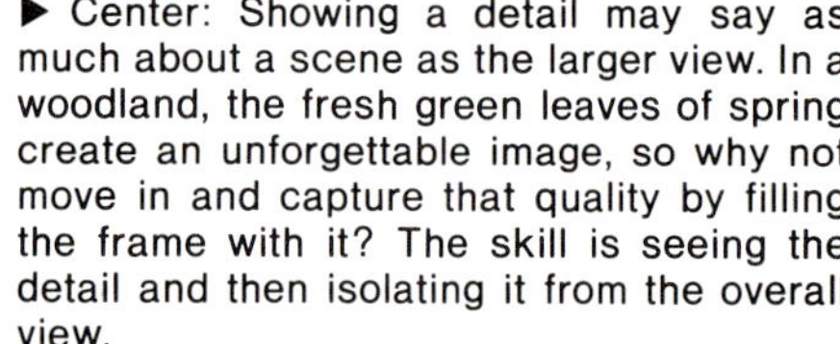

▶ Center: Showing a detail may say as much about a scene as the larger view. In a woodland, the fresh green leaves of spring create an unforgettable image, so why not move in and capture that quality by filling the frame with it? The skill is seeing the detail and then isolating it from the overall view.

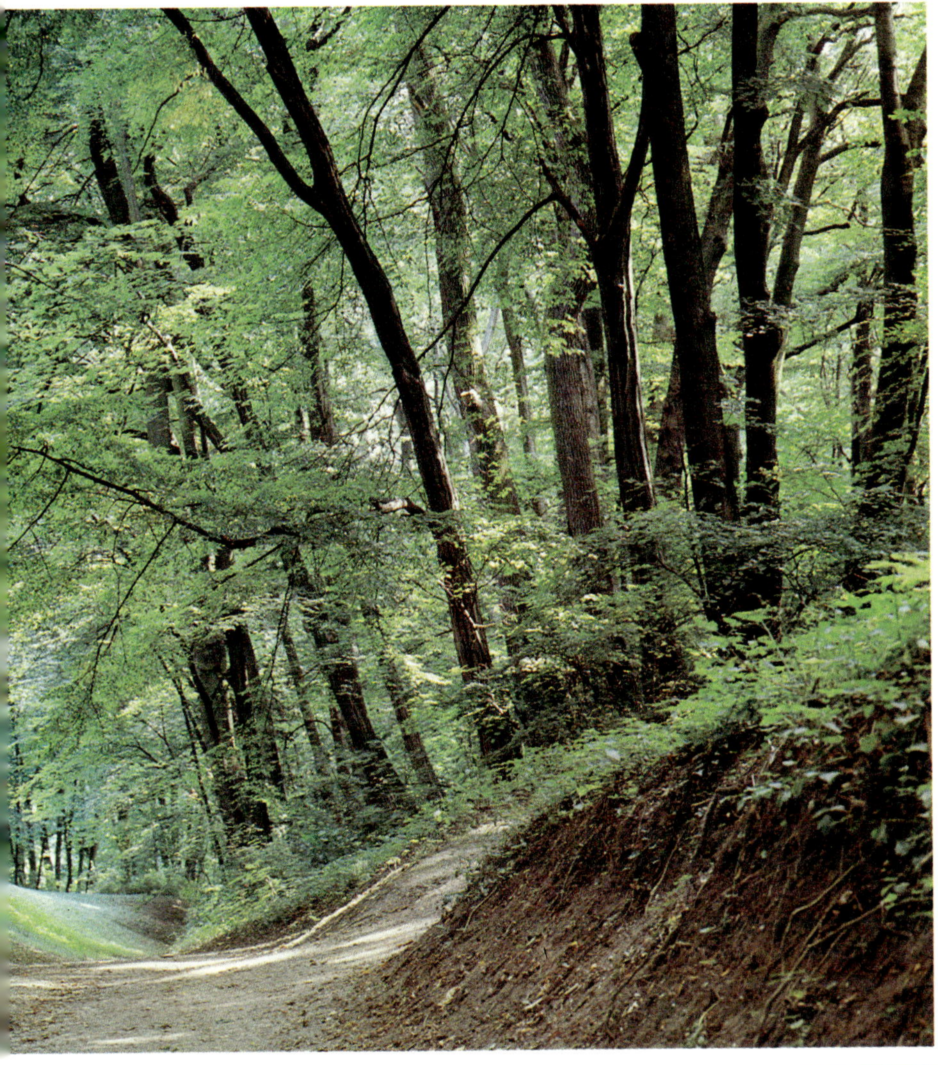

▼ Tall trees are best represented in a vertical format. By moving in close, you can emphasize the soaring quality of the trees, patterns of light and shade, and rough texture of bark against a lacy canopy of leaves. You can later strengthen the vertical shape as shown here by trimming the print, or *cropping,* to make a narrower shape than the original film format.

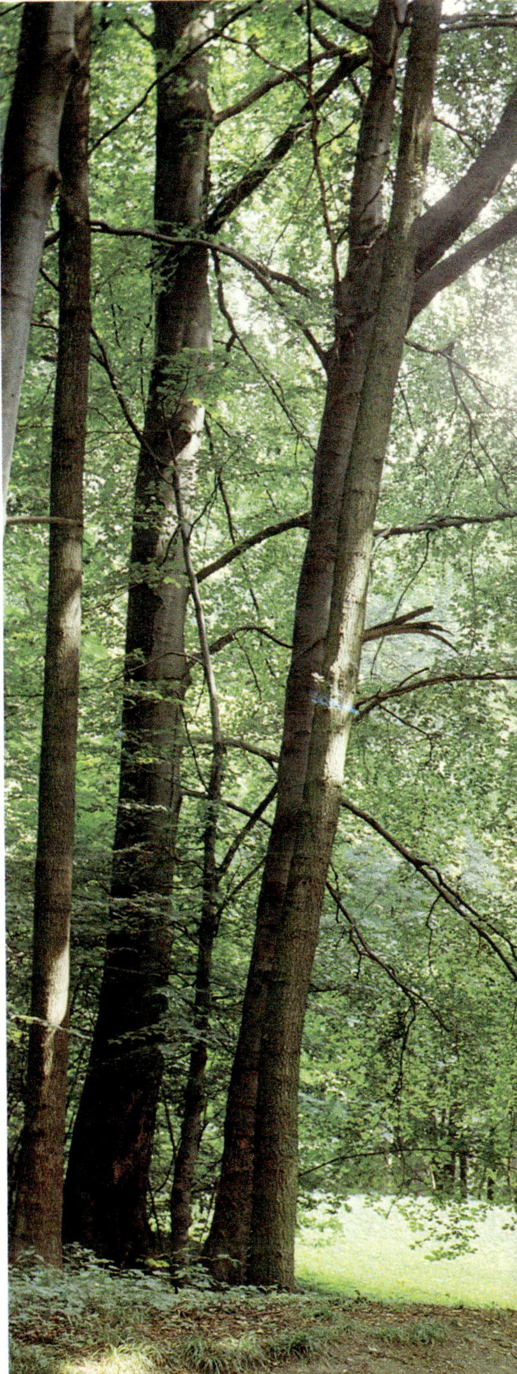

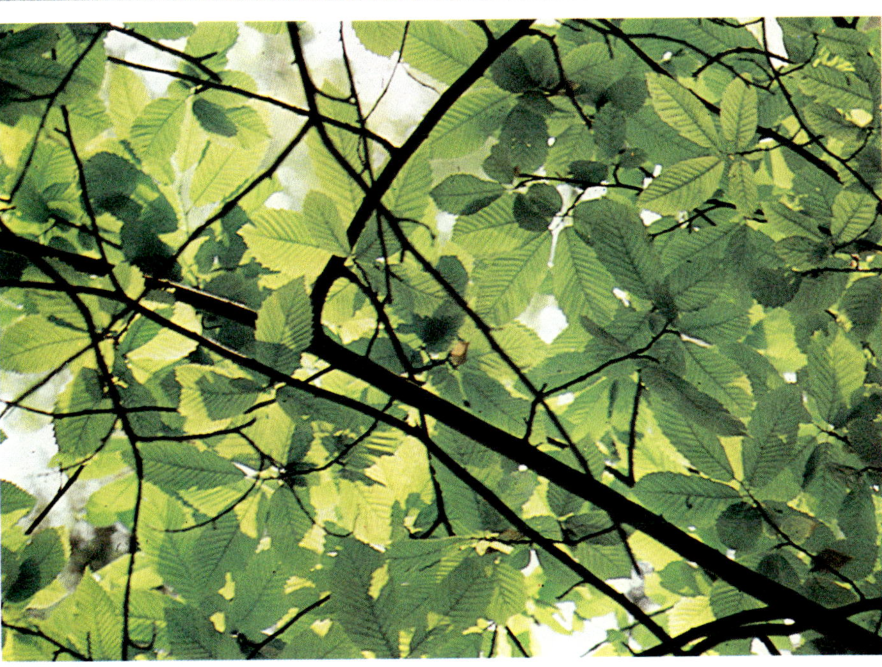

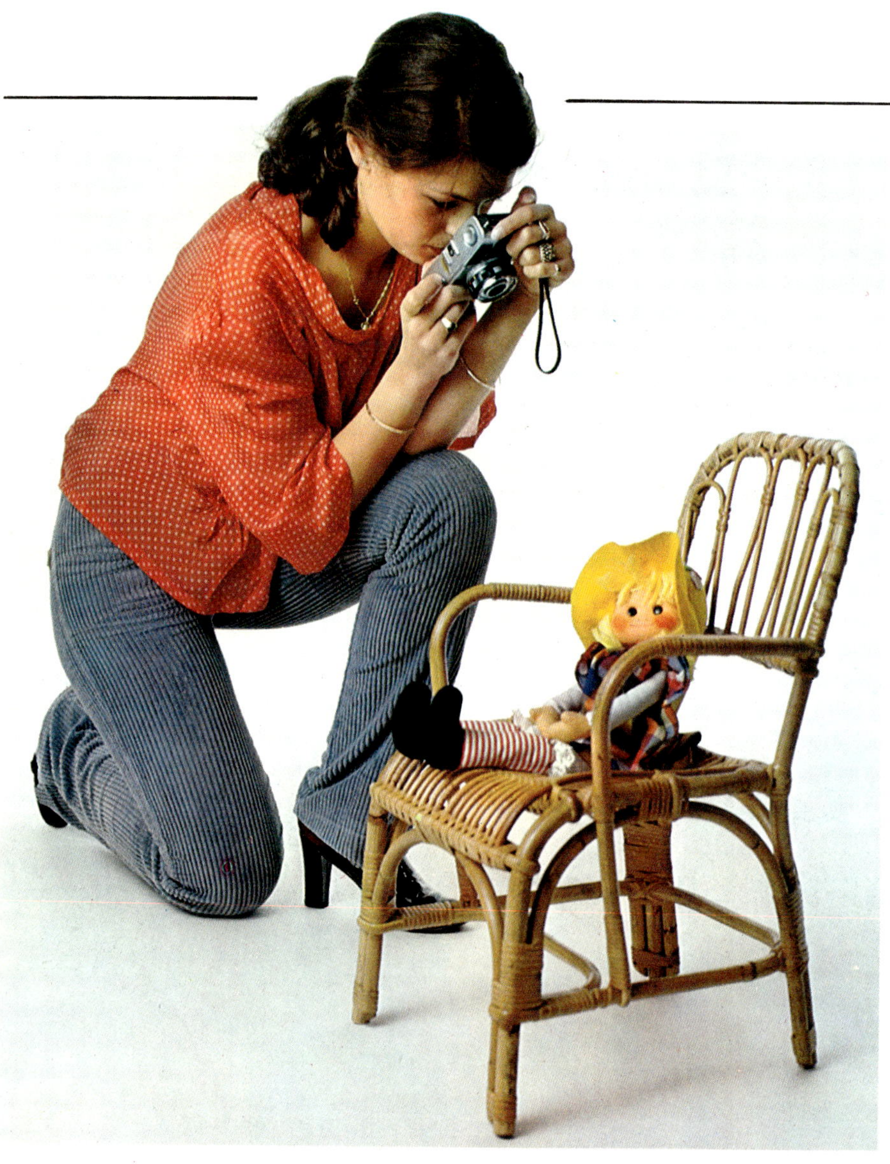

USING A VIEWFINDER

Some people find the camera viewfinder awkward and inhibiting—a mechanical block between them and the subject. Using a cardboard viewing frame to find an image you like can help you compose better.

Whether you use a viewing frame or the camera viewfinder, this section will help you explore the effects of changing viewpoint. Following sections show how to compose more complicated photographs of subjects, people, buildings and landscapes.

Start by looking at just one simple object and *seeing* it as divided into three main elements—the *subject*, the *rectangle or square* imposed by the picture format and the *spaces around the subject.*

As you look at the subject, notice the importance of the spaces surrounding it—both the shapes they make and the way the shadows fall. The strength, position and shape of the shadows help define the subject's three-dimensional form.

CHOOSING A TEST SUBJECT

This will depend on how close the camera lens can get to the subject. Check the minimum focusing distance of the lens, then pick something that fills the viewfinder. If you can get as close as 18 inches (45cm), you might choose a cup and saucer. If the minimum distance is about three feet (90cm), choose something larger with an interesting shape, such as a lamp or a watering can.

Try to choose a neutral background that does not interfere with your perception of

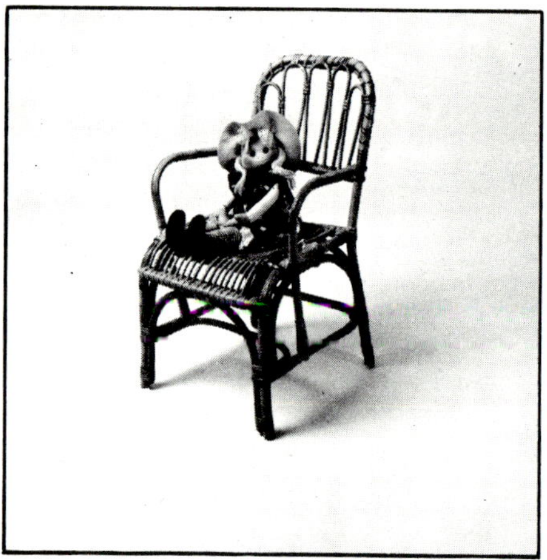

LONG VIEW
Start by looking at the subject from as far away as possible. Then keep moving in, searching for the right balance between the subject and the space around the subject. A long view has a different mood than a close-up.

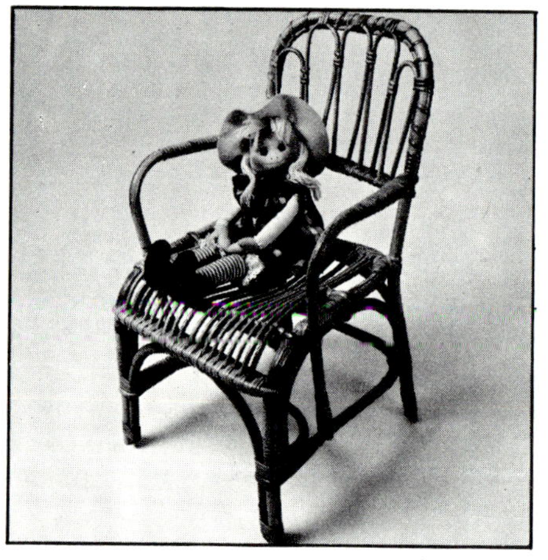

CLOSE-UP
Move in until the subject fills the frame. Visualize this with both horizontal and vertical formats. The closer you get, the more you become aware of shape, and how light and shadow give the subject form.

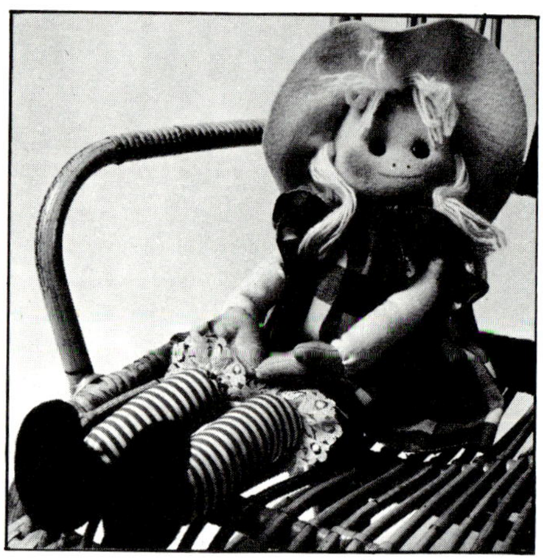

DETAIL
Move as close as your camera lens will allow. While looking through the viewfinder, move the camera to try different compositions. Interesting lines, textures and patterns may emerge.

the subject. You may be able to isolate the subject from distracting surroundings by placing the subject on or in front of a large piece of background paper, in an empty room, on a white sheet or on your lawn. Position the subject so it is lit by natural light from the side. Unless you are experienced with electronic flash, don't use it at this point. The light has such short duration that you can't be sure what effect it will create.

With a simple subject like a chair, you have two choices in finding a point of view—either move the subject or move the camera. It's a good idea to get into the habit of moving the camera rather than the subject. Thus, when you photograph an immovable object such as a tree or building, you will be accustomed to finding the best viewpoint by moving yourself rather than the subject.

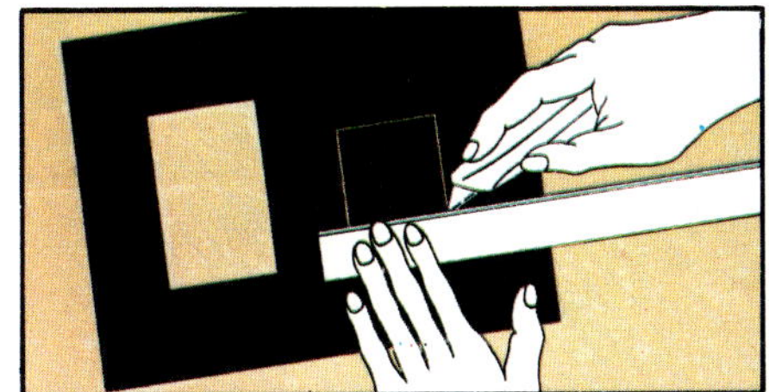

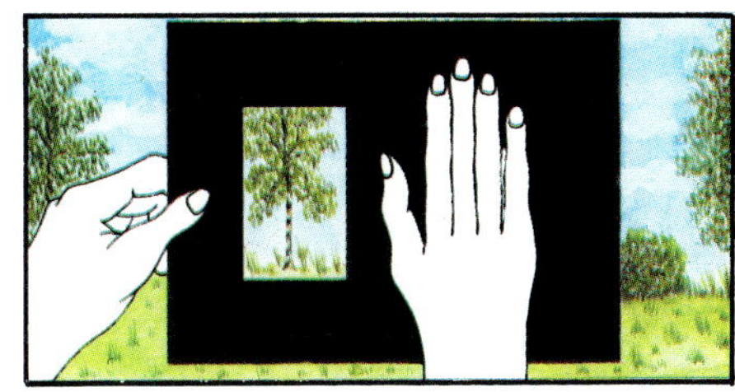

THE VIEWING FRAME

This will help you see better pictures. You can use a plastic slide mount, but a larger, black cardboard frame is easier to handle and helps isolate the subject better. To make a cardboard frame, you need a steel ruler, a piece of matte black cardboard, a sharp knife and a pencil.

On the black side of the card, in separate areas, draw a rectangle in the proportion of 2:3, such as 2x3 inches (5x7.5cm), and a square with 1 inch (25mm) sides. Cut on the black side of the card along the edge of the ruler so the edges are clean.

View from the black side. Close one eye and look through the frame at the subject, moving the frame toward and away from you until the subject is framed in a pleasing way. Everyday objects make effective pictures when they are well composed, and background clutter is minimized.

THE FORMAT

There are two photographic formats—square and rectangular. The size of the rectangle varies, but the 2:3 proportion applies closely to 35mm and 110-size film formats. If you have viewing frames in both shapes, you can compare the effects of the square and rectangular formats—a point to consider if you buy another camera with a different format. Some people are devoted to one format and find it hard to work with the other. Start by looking at the subject from the same viewpoint through one frame and then the other. Of course, you should try the rectangular format both vertically and horizontally.

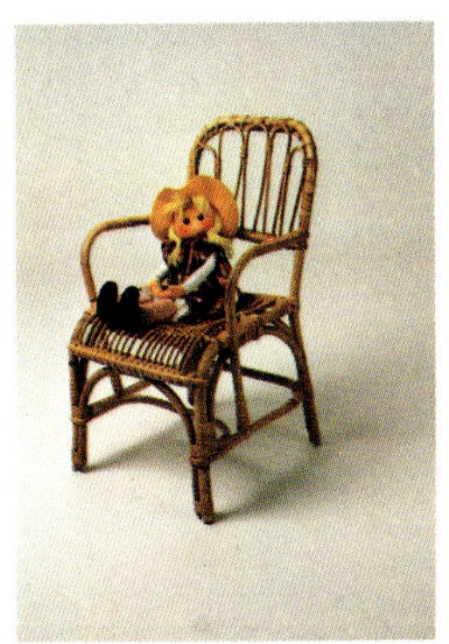

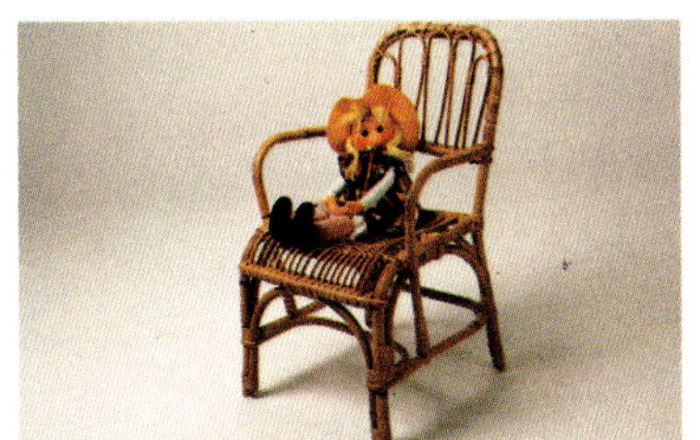

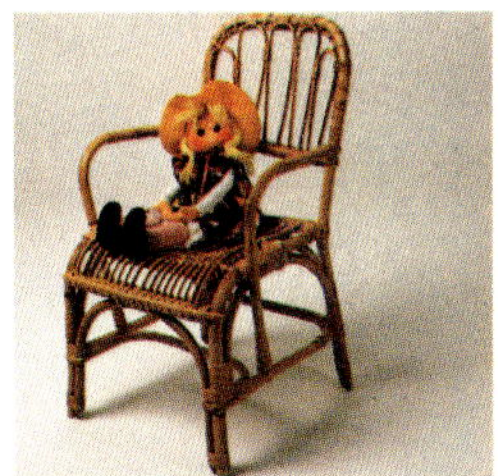

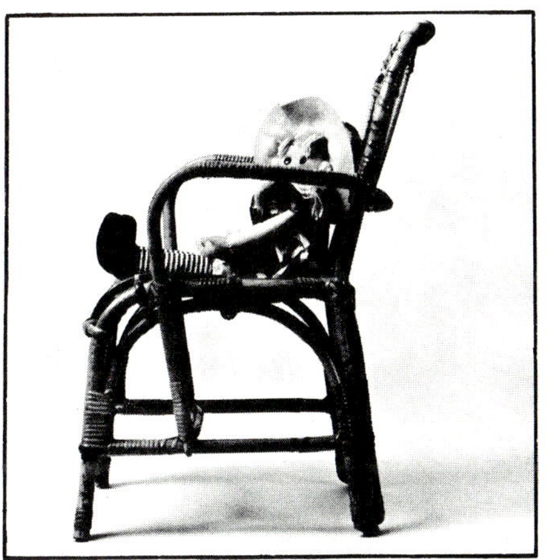

LOW LEVEL VIEW

Now try a lower viewpoint: Does the subject look best from ground level or a little higher? Is the subject identifiable? Should you move around to find a better vantage point?

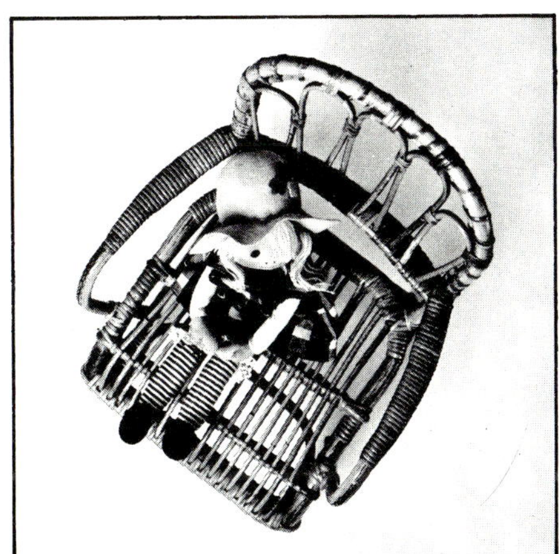

FROM ABOVE

Use a chair or stepladder to look straight down at the subject. Shapes and outlines change form and the ground or floor becomes the background. This view gets immediate attention because it is unusual.

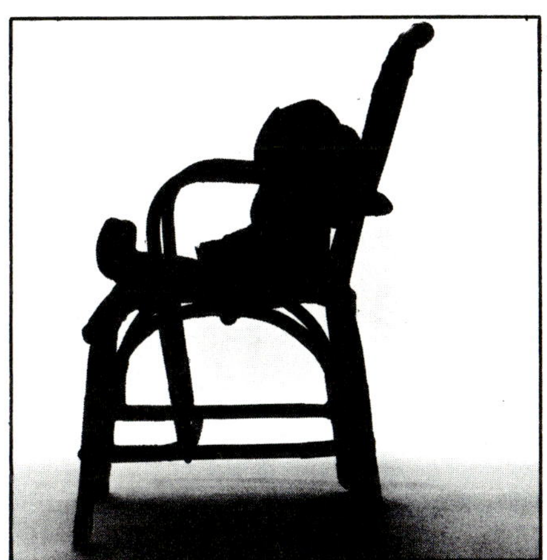

SILHOUETTE

Arrange the lighting so the background is brighter than the subject and then adjust the viewpoint until you see the most satisfactory silhouette. Notice how this simplifies the photograph by presenting only the essential shapes.

Where to Put the Horizon

In photography, as in painting, the horizon is an important element for emphasizing the subject and balancing the picture as a whole. The horizon also gives a sense of scale to a landscape, whether it is a towering mountain range or a smooth, glassy sea. The way you balance the composition adds to the visual impact of what you are trying to convey.

HORIZONTAL OR VERTICAL?

Most cameras produce images in a rectangular format. This gives you a choice between composing *horizontal* or *vertical* photographs.

Horizontal photographs have the horizon parallel to the long side of the picture. This emphasizes the space from left to right. The viewer's gaze follows along the horizon the same way you scan words on a page. This gives horizontal photographs a sense of "wide open spaces," but you need to include some foreground objects to give the picture a feeling of scale and perspective.

Vertical photographs can convey a feeling of depth, depending on how the horizon is handled. You tend to "read" the scene from the foreground back, and then up to the sky. With a high viewpoint, you can normally include a lot of detail in this type of composition because the landscape appears to extend from the viewer's feet up to the horizon and sky.

When photographing a landscape, practice composing both horizontally and vertically through the viewfinder or viewing frame.

WHERE TO PUT THE HORIZON

The classic "comfortable" position for the horizon is a third of the way down the frame. But if you want to create a more dramatic effect, position the skyline higher, lower or in the middle.

▶ Locating the horizon one-third of the way from the top of the picture gives a comfortable, but rather predictable, result.

The four photographs at the bottom of these pages show the effects of positioning the horizon. From left to right:

With no horizon, the subject is isolated and given prominence.

With the horizon in view, the subject is placed in its setting.

A larger sky area is often dramatic, but this halfway split can be an uneasy compromise.

A low horizon makes full use of the sky's dramatic potential without detracting from the subject.

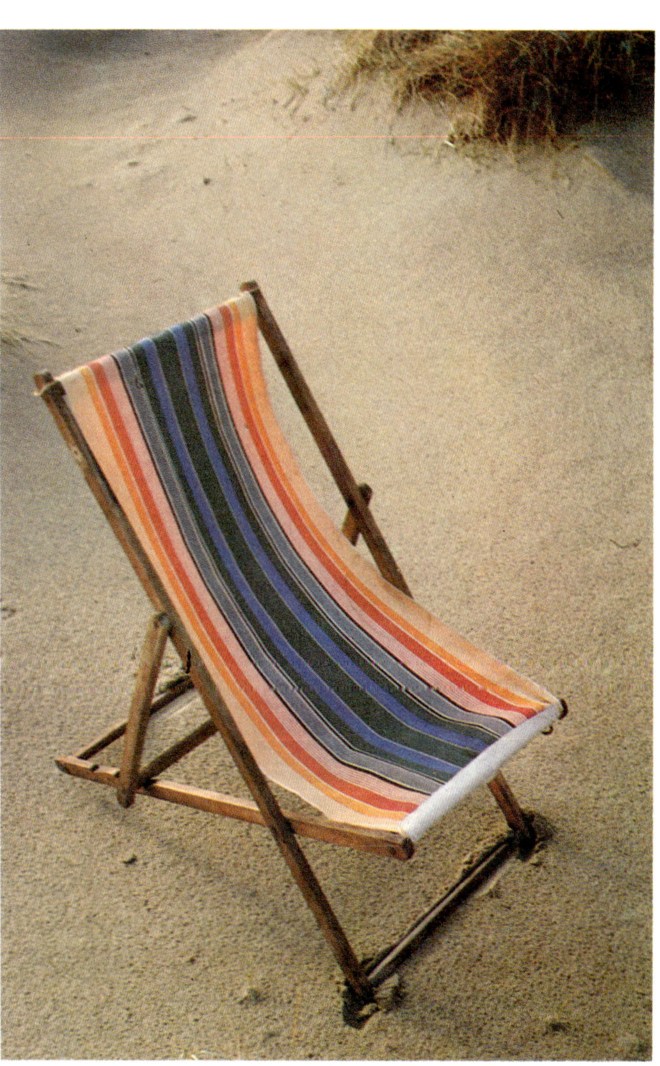

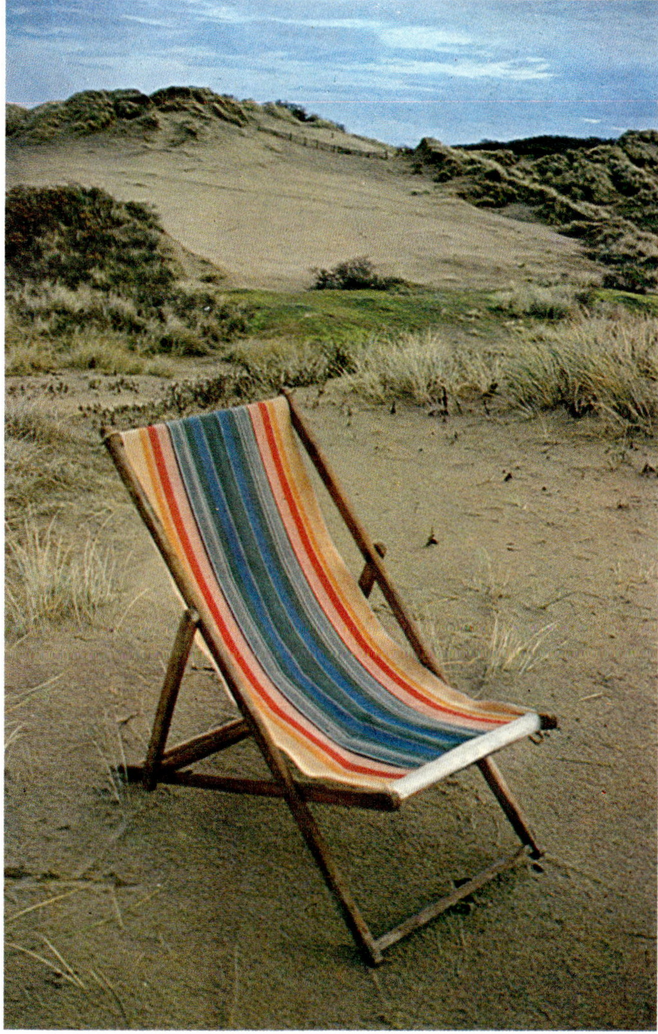

1/3

2/3

THE CLASSIC SOLUTION

Most Western painters from the Renaissance up to the end of the 19th century were preoccupied with breaking landscapes down into foreground, middle distance, background and sky. One of the formulas they developed, based on a ratio of one-third sky to two-thirds land, is still useful in composing photographs. No one quite knows why, but this proportion gives a harmonious, satisfying balance to most pictures. Whenever the photographer breaks away from this classic formula, he probably—either consciously or unconsciously—intends to create a more emphatic picture.

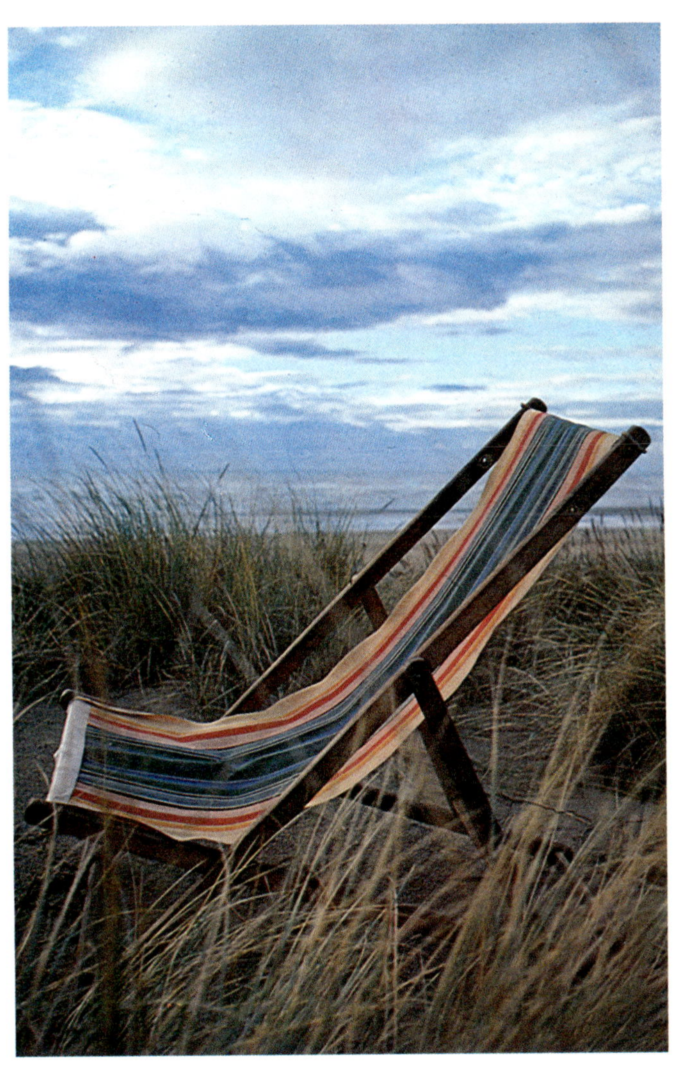

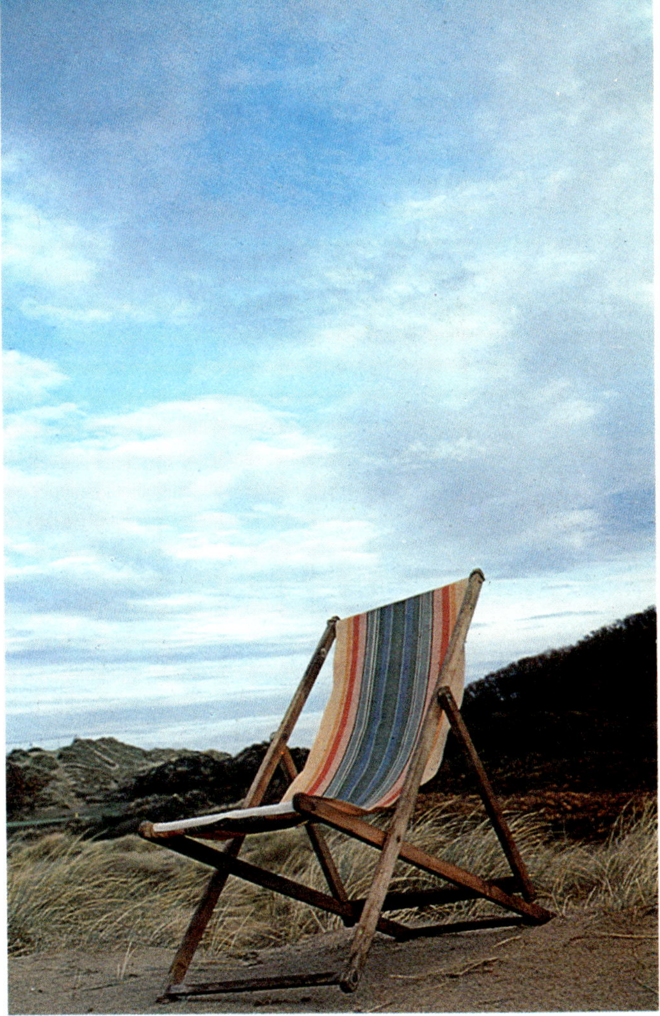

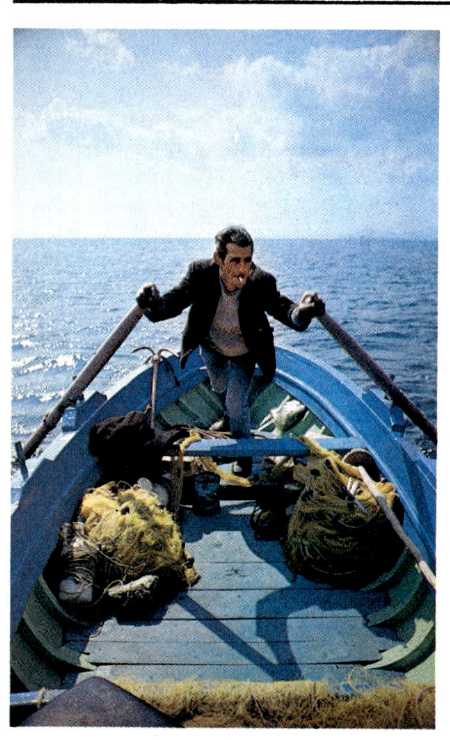

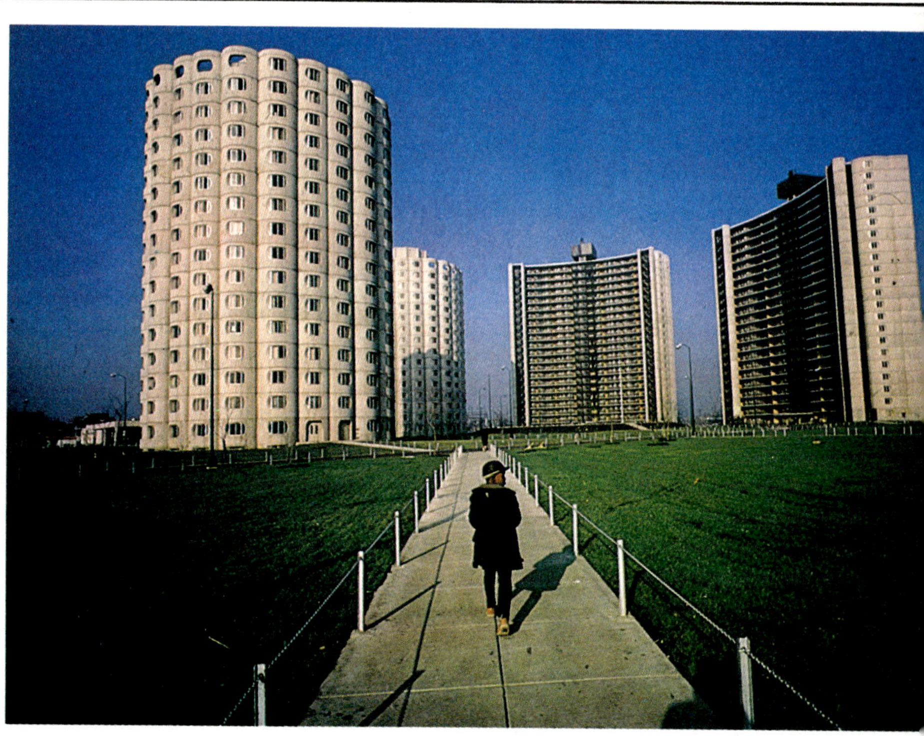

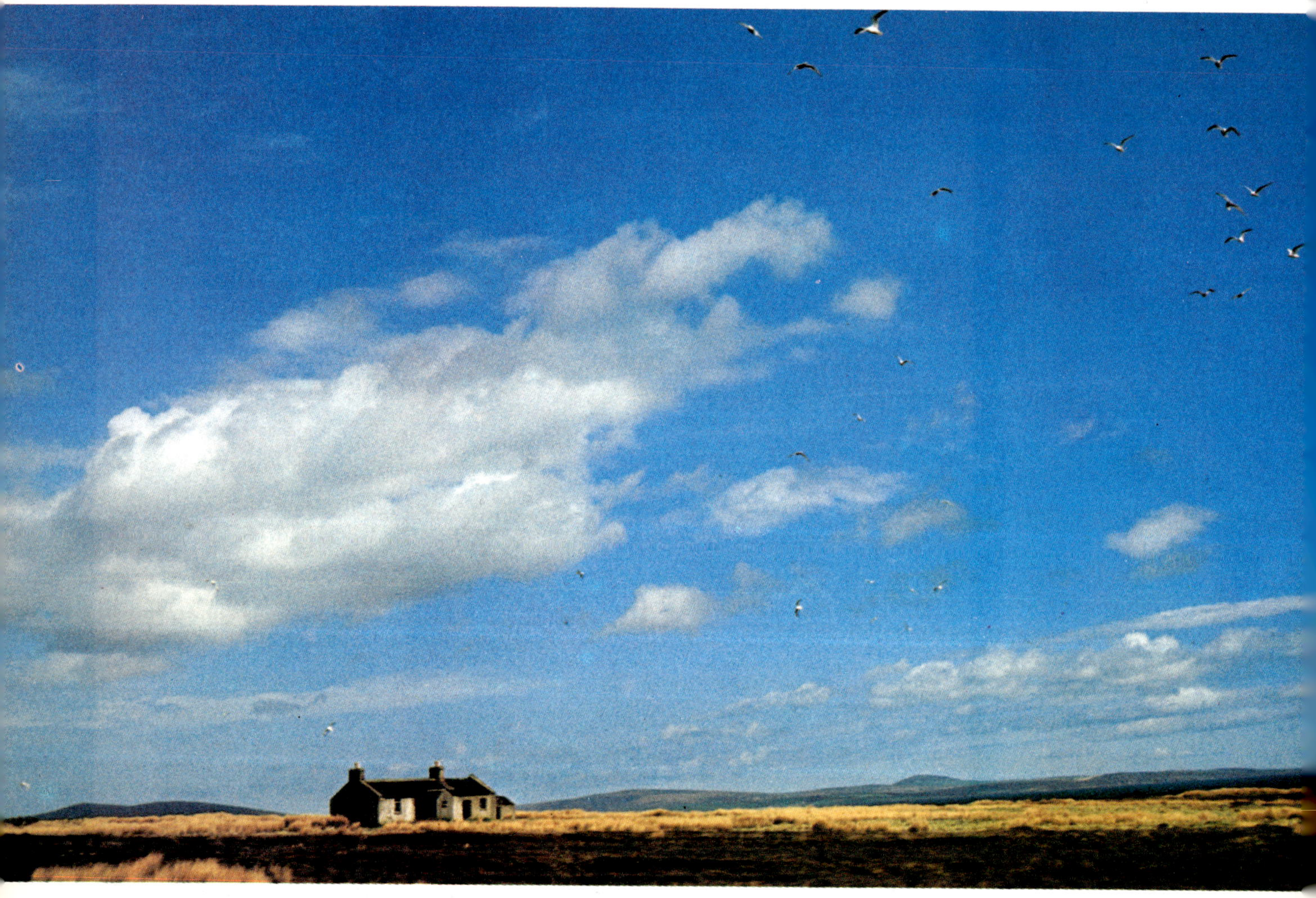

◀ Far left: Here you see a centered subject and classic horizon. Emphasis would differ with a lower horizon. Photo by Spike Powell.

◀ The centrally placed horizon combines with bold vertical and horizontal lines to give balance to this urban landscape. Photo by John Bulmer.

▶ Here foreground is the subject; the horizon simply acts as the end of the picture. Photo by Barry Lewis.

▼ In this landscape, the low horizon places the emphasis on the sky. The house is balanced by the cloud mass. Photo by John Bulmer.

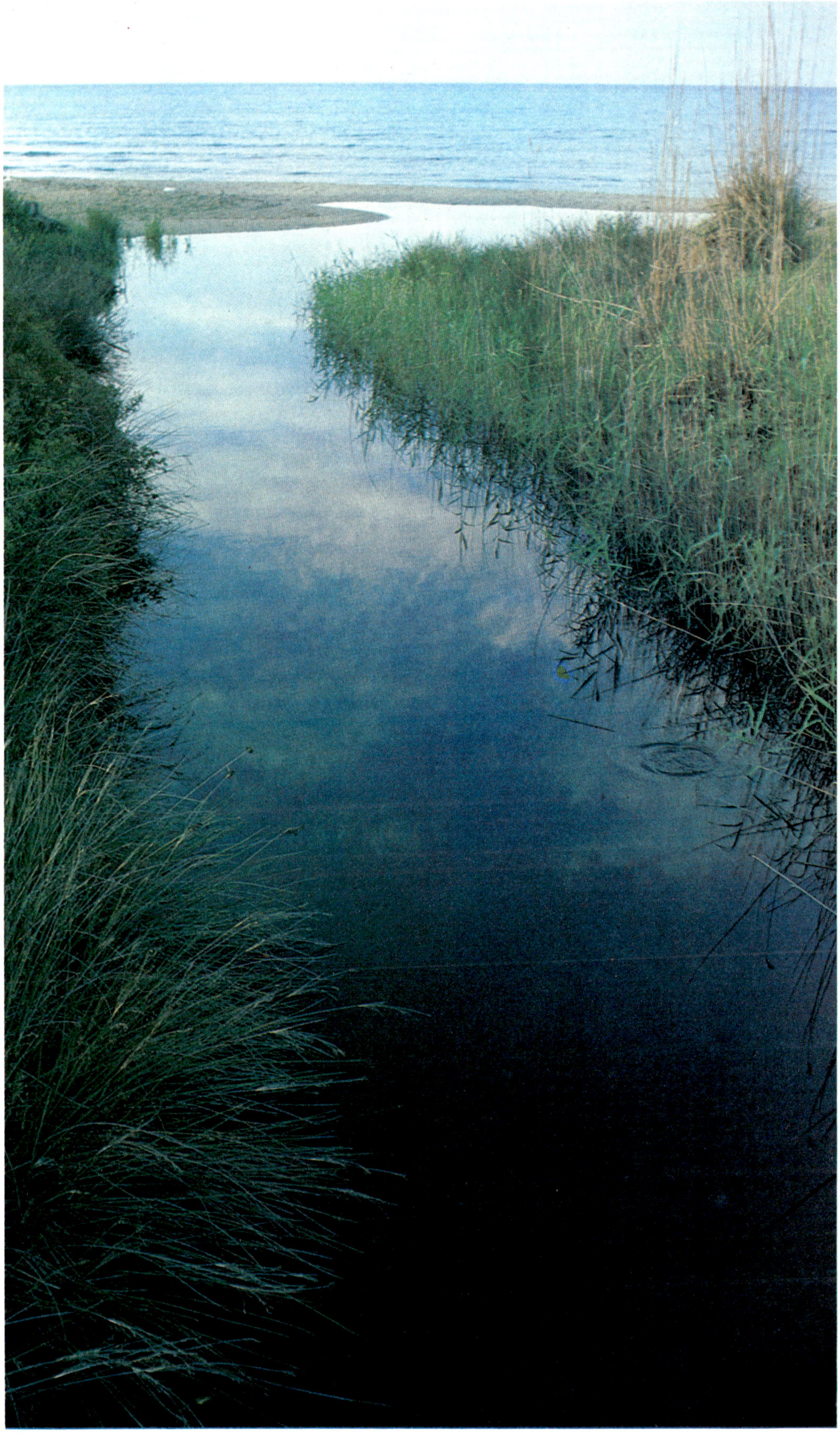

Using the Background

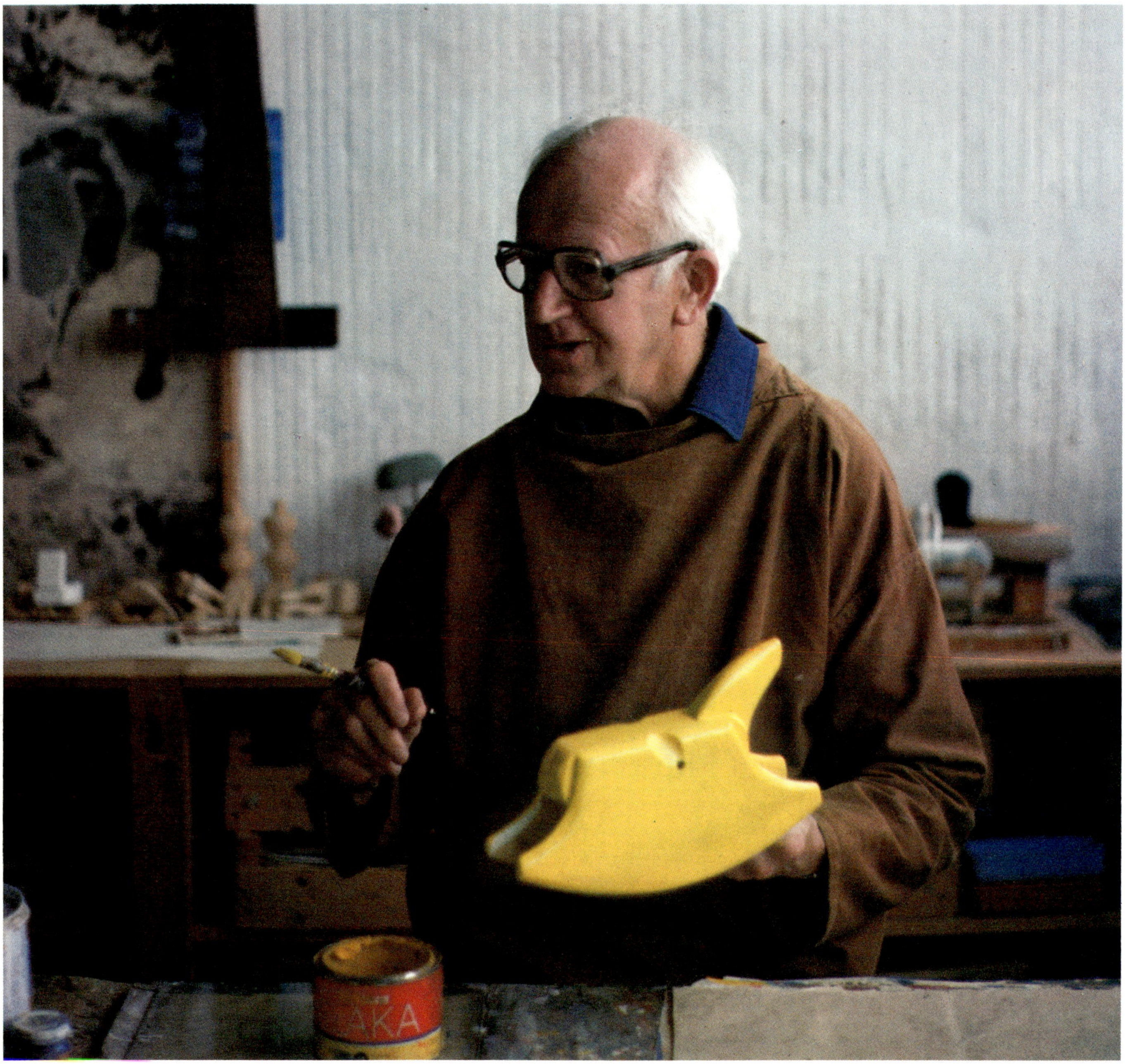

Many amateur photographers concentrate their attention on the subject, with little thought for the background. Yet the background can be of vital importance—a cluttered or intrusive one can ruin a perfectly good photograph. When the background adds something to the subject, it can make the overall image very special.

Watch for three main things about the background—*false attachments, competitive elements* and *intrusive light or color.*

FALSE ATTACHMENTS

When people appear to have lamp posts sprouting from their heads, or branches growing out of their ears, these are "false attachments." It is easy to miss these when looking through the viewfinder. If you do notice it, move the camera until the "attachment" separates from the subject.

COMPETITIVE BACKGROUNDS

These include the kind of general confusion or jumble that you should be able

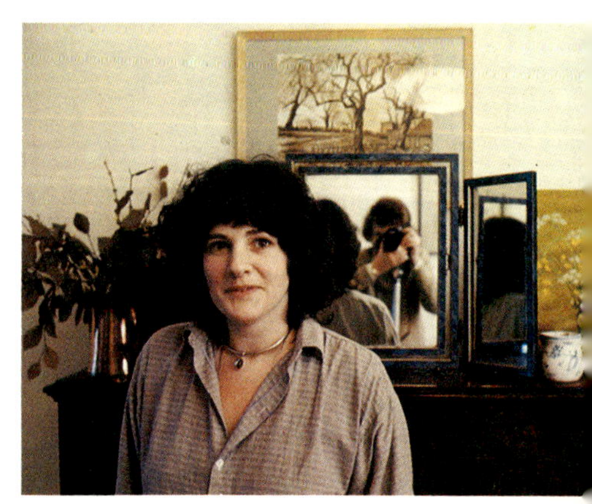

◀ The small picture at the bottom of page 14 shows what can happen if the background is left to take care of itself—the girl disappears into the muddle and the photographer has inadvertently included his own reflection in the mirror. In the larger photograph on the same page, Homer Sykes moved the toymaker away from the messy part of the background and asked him to stand so his head was clear of the paraphernalia on the shelf.

▶ If you are using large depth of field, look carefully at the background. The chimney growing out of the subject's head is typical of the "false attachments" hidden in many backgrounds. A slight shift of camera position would have avoided this.

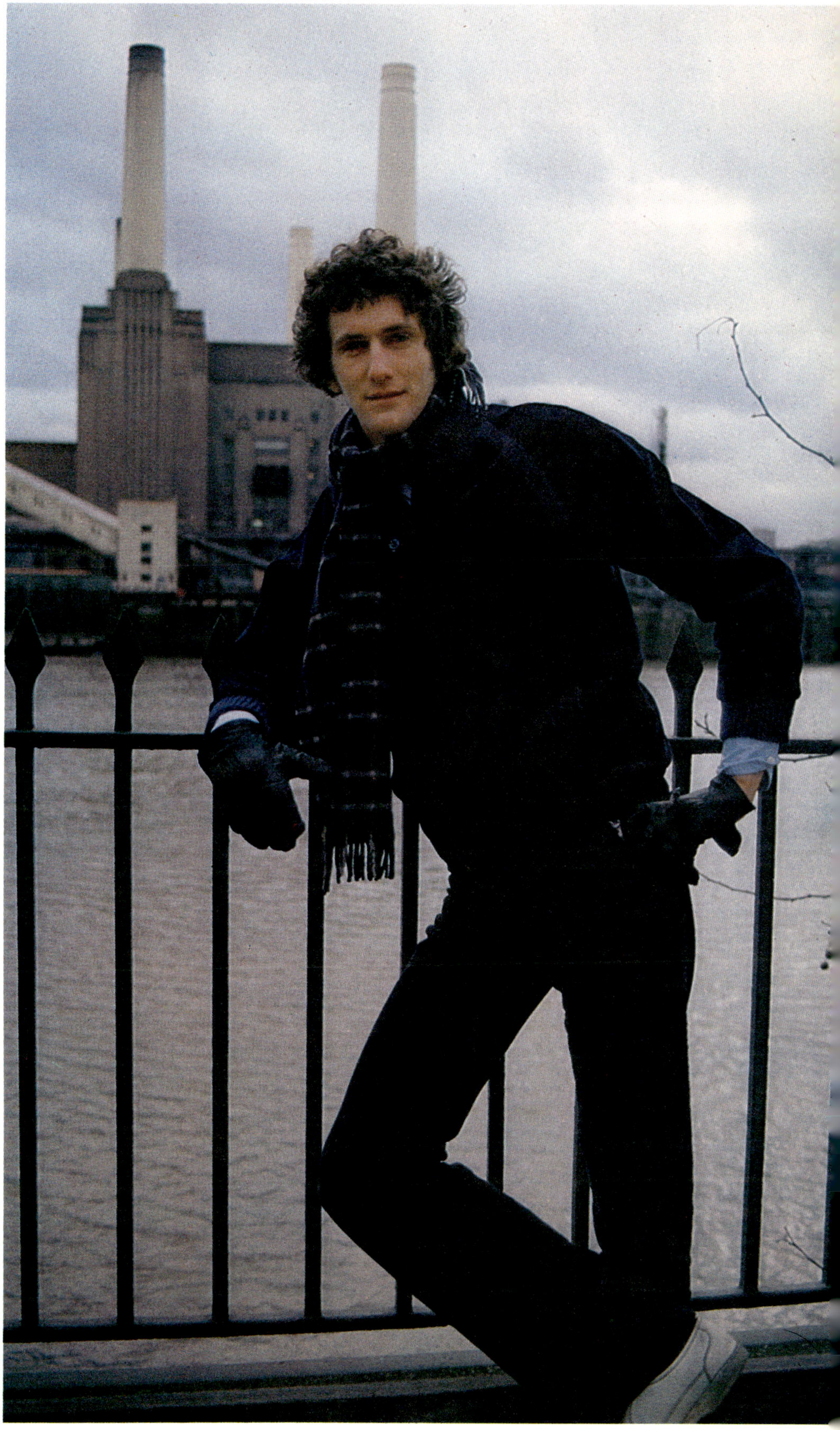

▼ Subjects with complicated patterns or shapes can merge into a patterned background and become confusing. Put the wallpaper out of focus by using a large aperture; the flowers then stand out from the background. Check the depth-of-field scale and viewfinder image to make sure you have the zone of sharpness you need. Photo by Colin Barker.

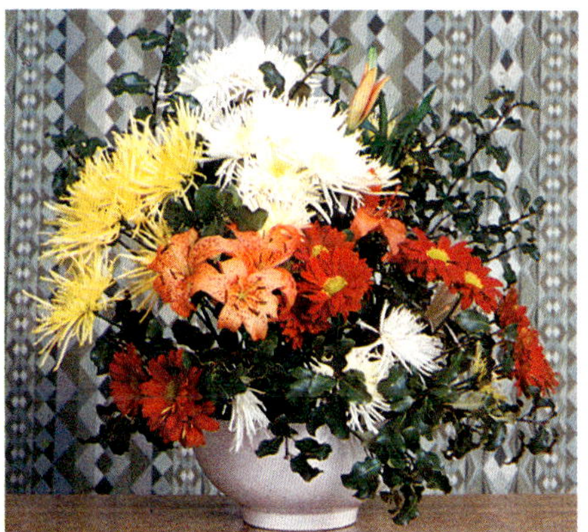

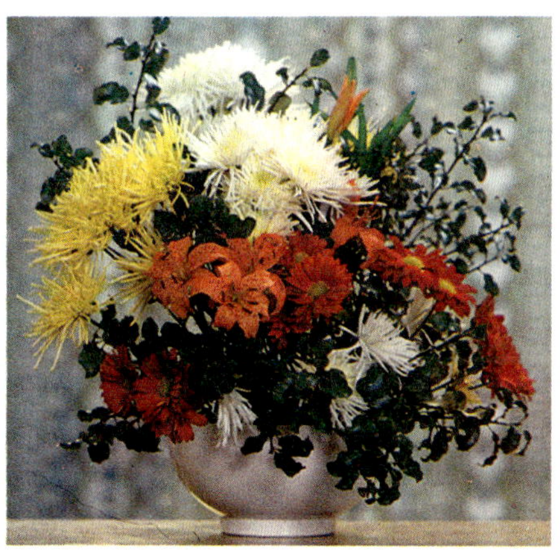

to eliminate. If you cannot rearrange the background, you will have to move the subject, but there are many cases where you do not have such control over the subject, such as in candid photography or when you are photographing something immovable like a statue or a building. In such instances, try altering the viewpoint. This may also help to solve tonal problems, such as when a statue seems to merge into the trees behind it instead of standing out.

INTRUSIVE LIGHT OR COLOR

Light or color can also distract from the main subject. In a scene there might be a strong light source that draws your eye away from the main subject. Or perhaps an area of strong color, such as a bright curtain, dominates the scene when the subject is wearing muted, delicate colors. Here again, the answer may be to move either the subject or the camera. Alternatively, you can put the background out of focus by reducing depth of field.

Become aware of these distractions. Do this *before* you take the picture. To handle backgrounds successfully so they contribute to the overall effect of the photograph, consider them as part of the picture you see in the viewfinder. The background should not be an afterthought, but an integral part of the composition.

▼ The two photos below show how an intrusive spot of color in the background distracts the viewer from the subject. Although the background is intentionally out of focus, the bright yellow spot commands your attention first. Omit the splash of yellow and you are attracted straight to the subject. Photo by Homer Sykes.

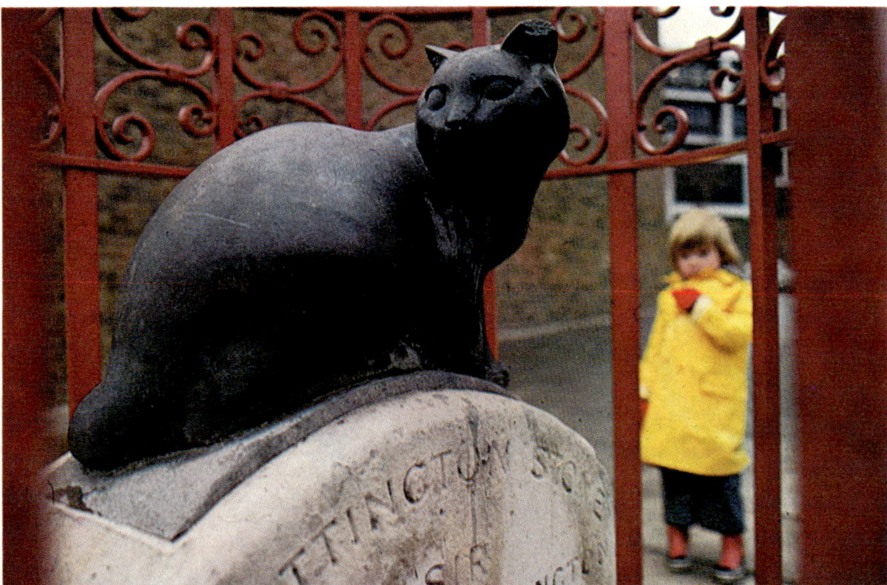

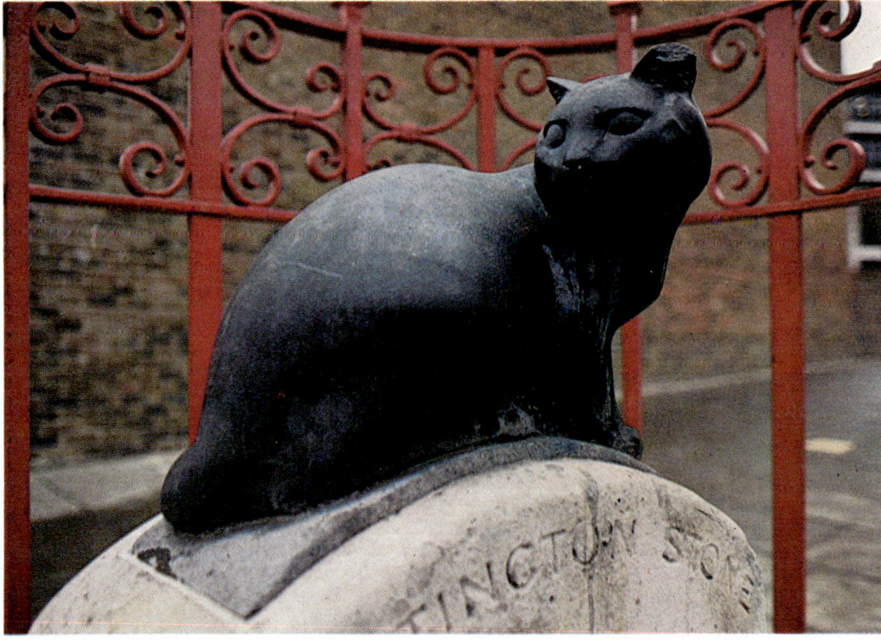

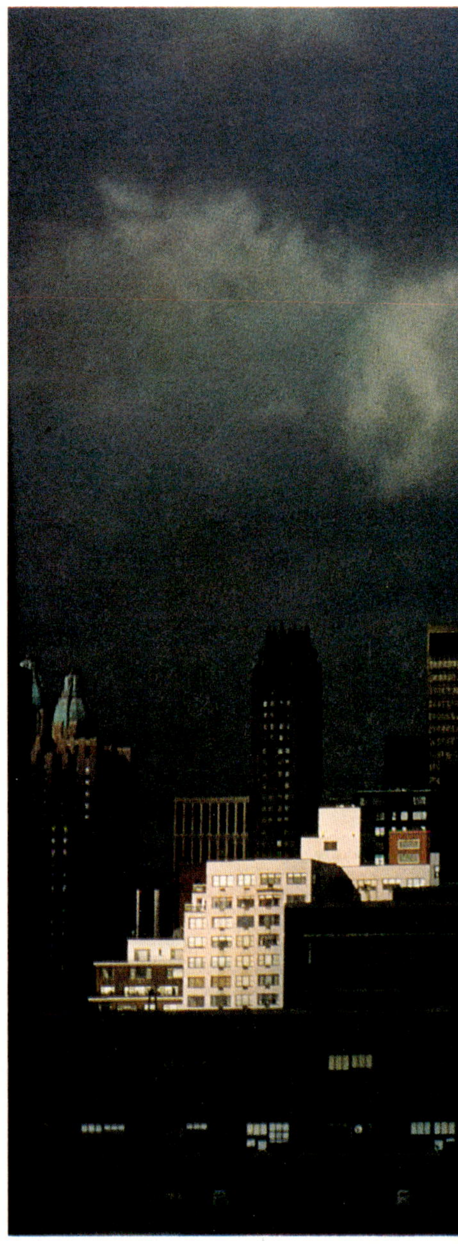

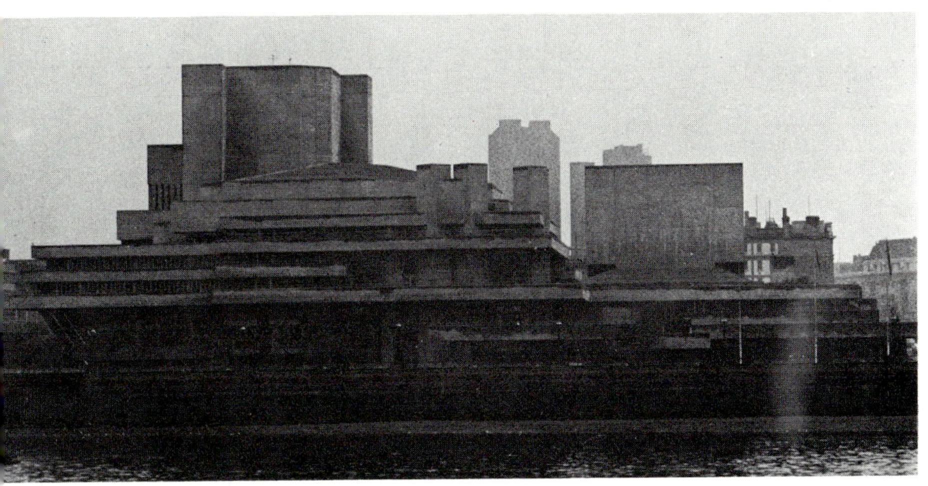

◀ The combination of a gray subject and poor light means that the subject merges into the background and details are obscured.

▼ Poor lighting caused the subject to disappear into the background in this photo of the New York skyline. However, in the middle, the sunlight has highlighted a group of buildings and lifted them out of the monotone of the background. Photo by Tomas Sennett.

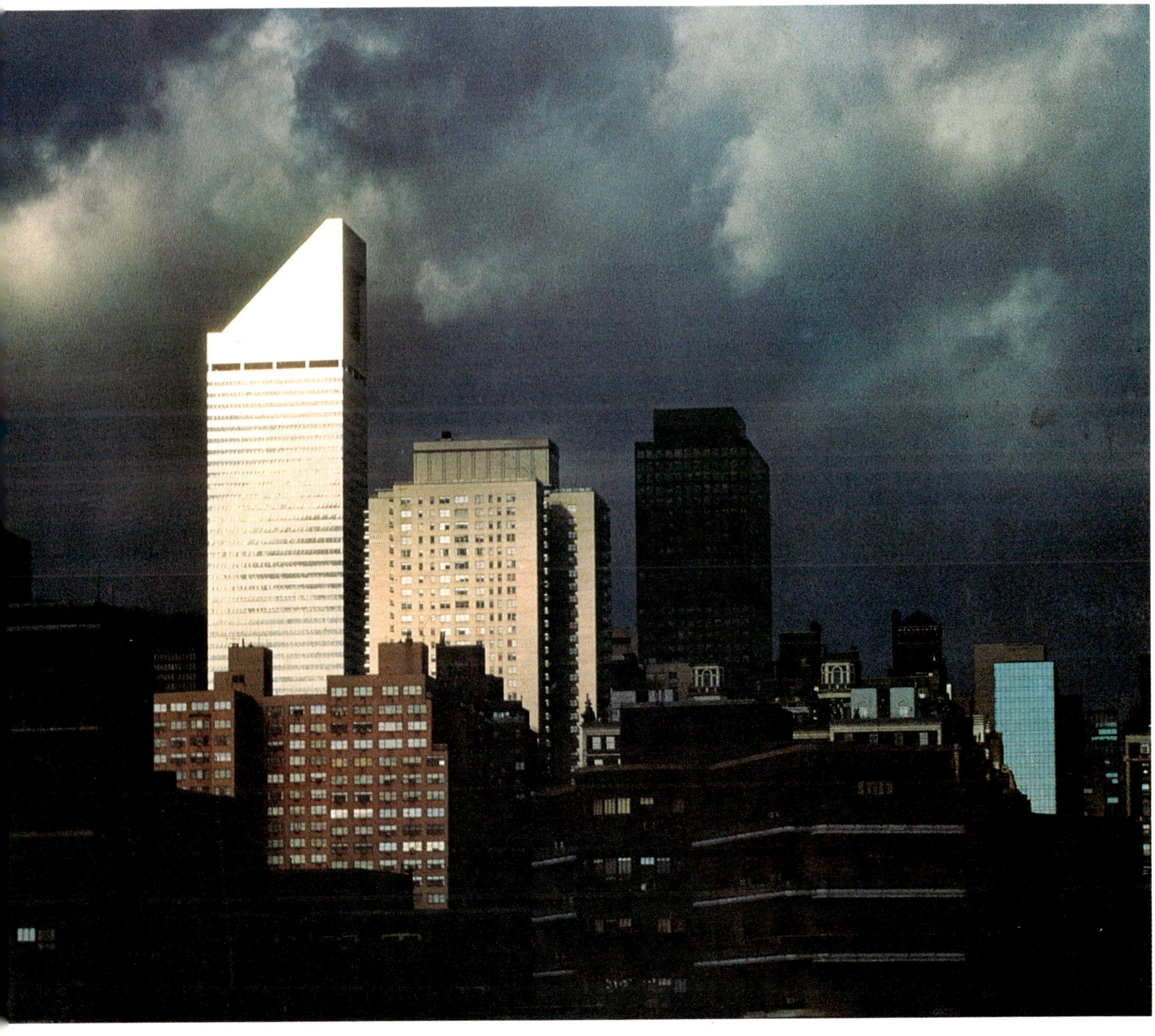

Using the Foreground

It is too easy to think carefully about the background before taking a picture—and then leave the foreground to take care of itself. Often the result is that distracting foreground objects seem to appear from nowhere to upset the balance of the picture. You have to decide whether the foreground is important and, if so, how much of it should appear in the photograph. Many successful photographs have no foregrounds, but these are usually of subjects fairly close to the camera.

USING THE FOREGROUND

Constructive use of the foreground is an important compositional tool. It can add emphasis and balance, and tell more about the subject. If the perfect foreground is not immediately obvious, it may be simply a question of altering the viewpoint to include a wall, a hedge or some other object close to the camera.

You can also use foreground to give more information about the subject, especially when photographing people. This technique of *environmental portraiture* is done by including plants and flowers in a photograph of a florist or a stack of books with an author.

CREATING DEPTH

Proper use of foreground can also introduce an impression of depth and scale to photographs. This is especially important in landscape photography, where foreground makes the picture start right at your feet, rather than in the middle distance. If you include a ridge of grass at the front of a seascape with a distant fishing boat, the viewer subconsciously relates one to the other and perceives both distance and relative size.

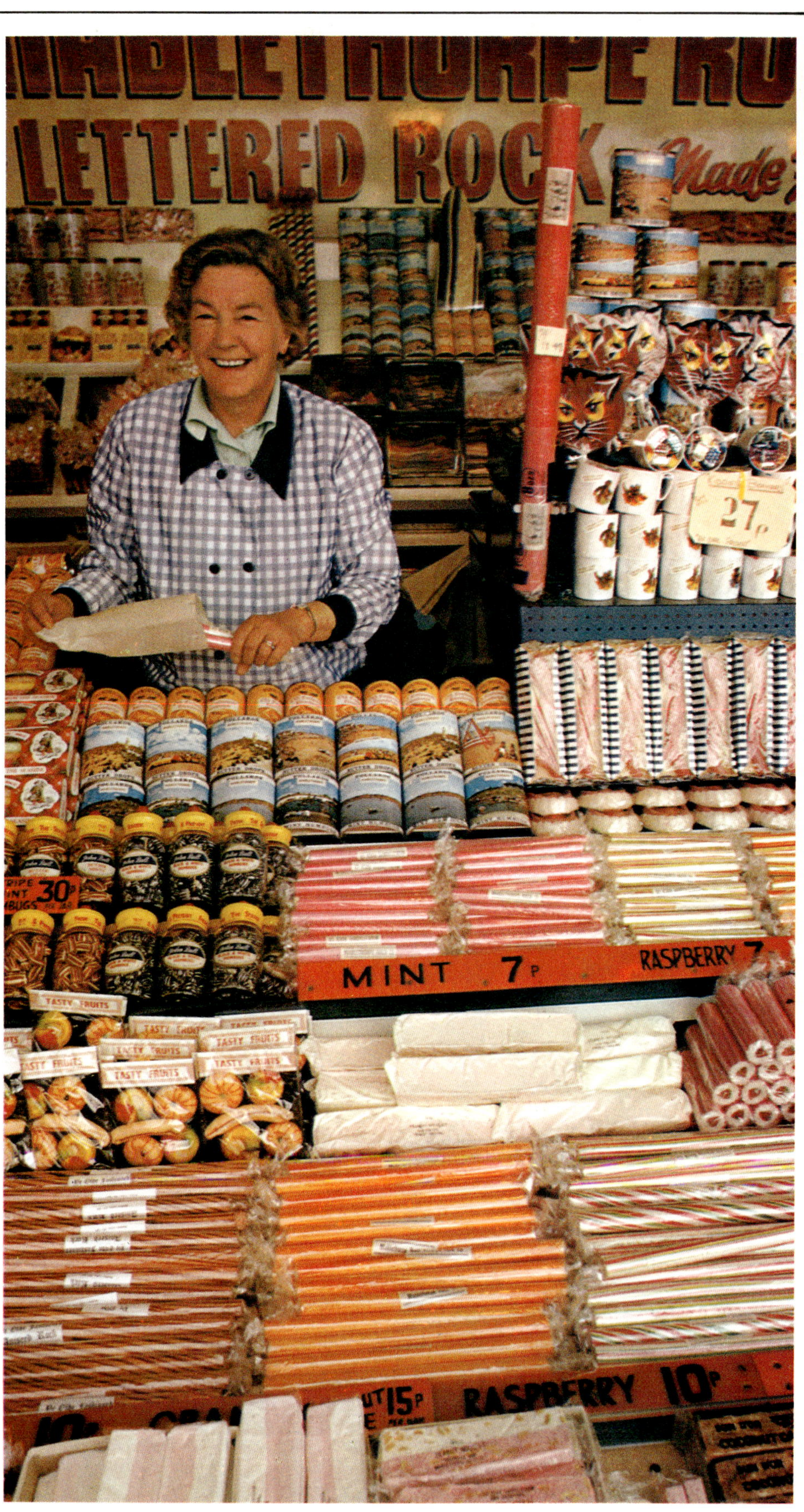

▶ This photograph succeeds because of its composition. The sharp foreground tells a story and builds up the striking pattern of shapes and colors. Photo by Patrick Thurston.

▶ Far right: Notice how this use of foreground brings the viewer "into the picture." Jon Gardey included the foreground to emphasize the feeling of distance. The extreme depth of field also contributes to this impression. Cover the lower half of this photo with your hand and notice how the feeling changes.

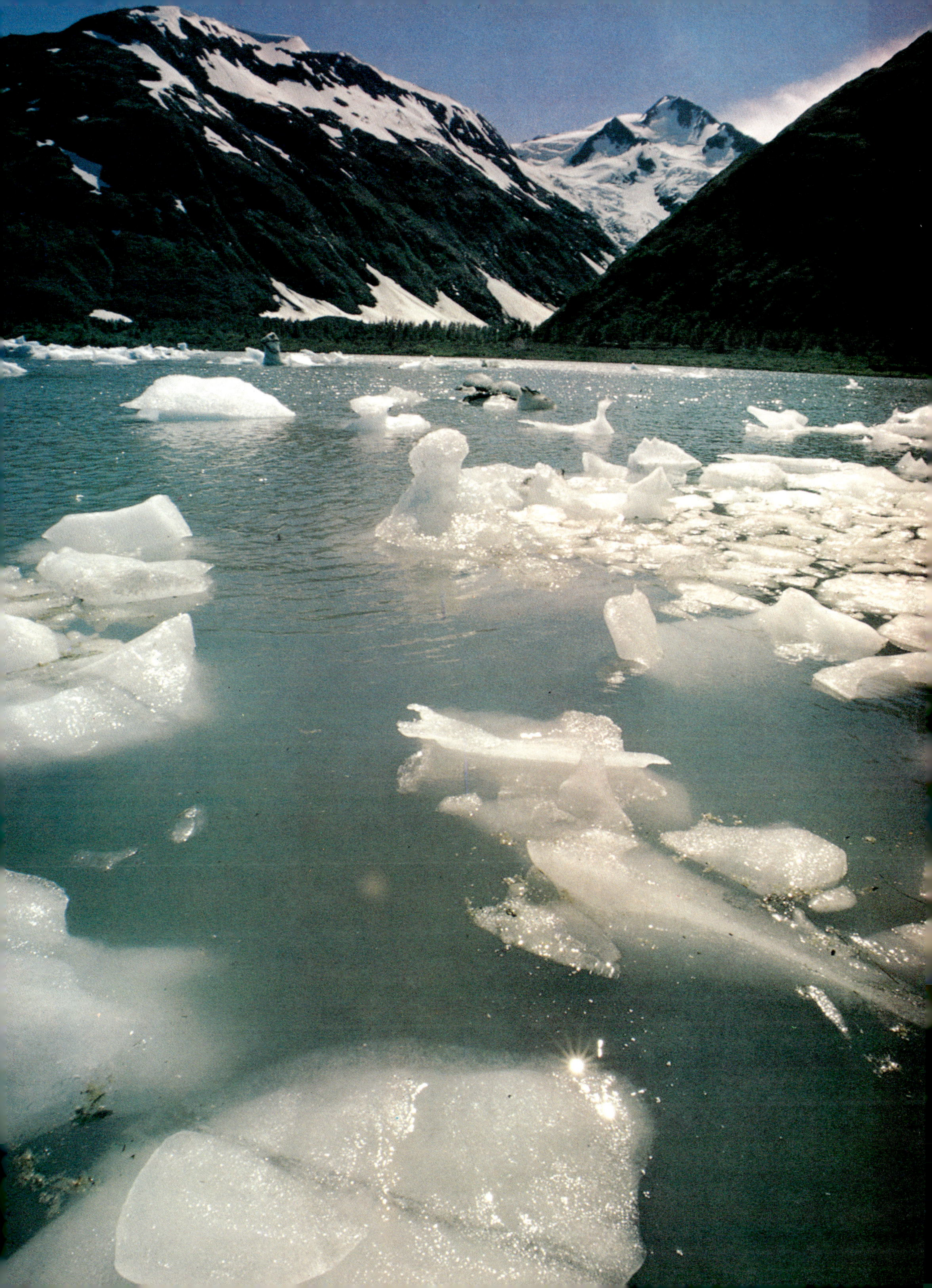

FRAMING WITH FOREGROUND

The foreground does not always have to be confined to the bottom of the picture. It can also create a complete or partial frame for the subject. Doorways, arches or windows are obvious foreground frames. Outdoors, a branch or a pattern of leaves at the top of a picture can be used to block large expanses of uninteresting sky and create a more intimate view. Often these are most effective as silhouettes, showing no detail or texture. This technique also works well with part of the foreground area out of focus, thus preventing the foreground from dominating the picture.

LOSING THE FOREGROUND

There is always the possibility that a prominent foreground will take over or dominate the picture and become distracting. In this case, objects close to the camera appear more defined and larger than distant objects. In the photograph of the ice-filled lake on the preceding page, if you include a boat in the foreground, it might take over and become the main subject. Always be sure of what you want in the photograph.

There are three ways to "lose" the foreground:

1) Change camera position.
2) Use a lens of longer focal length that takes in less of the scene.
3) Reduce depth of field to put the foreground out of focus.

If something in the foreground threatens to become a distraction, you may choose to have it out of focus by using a larger aperture, rather than leave it out of the picture. However, be sure it does not turn into a distracting blur. With many SLR cameras you can use the depth-of-field preview button to see how sharp the foreground will be.

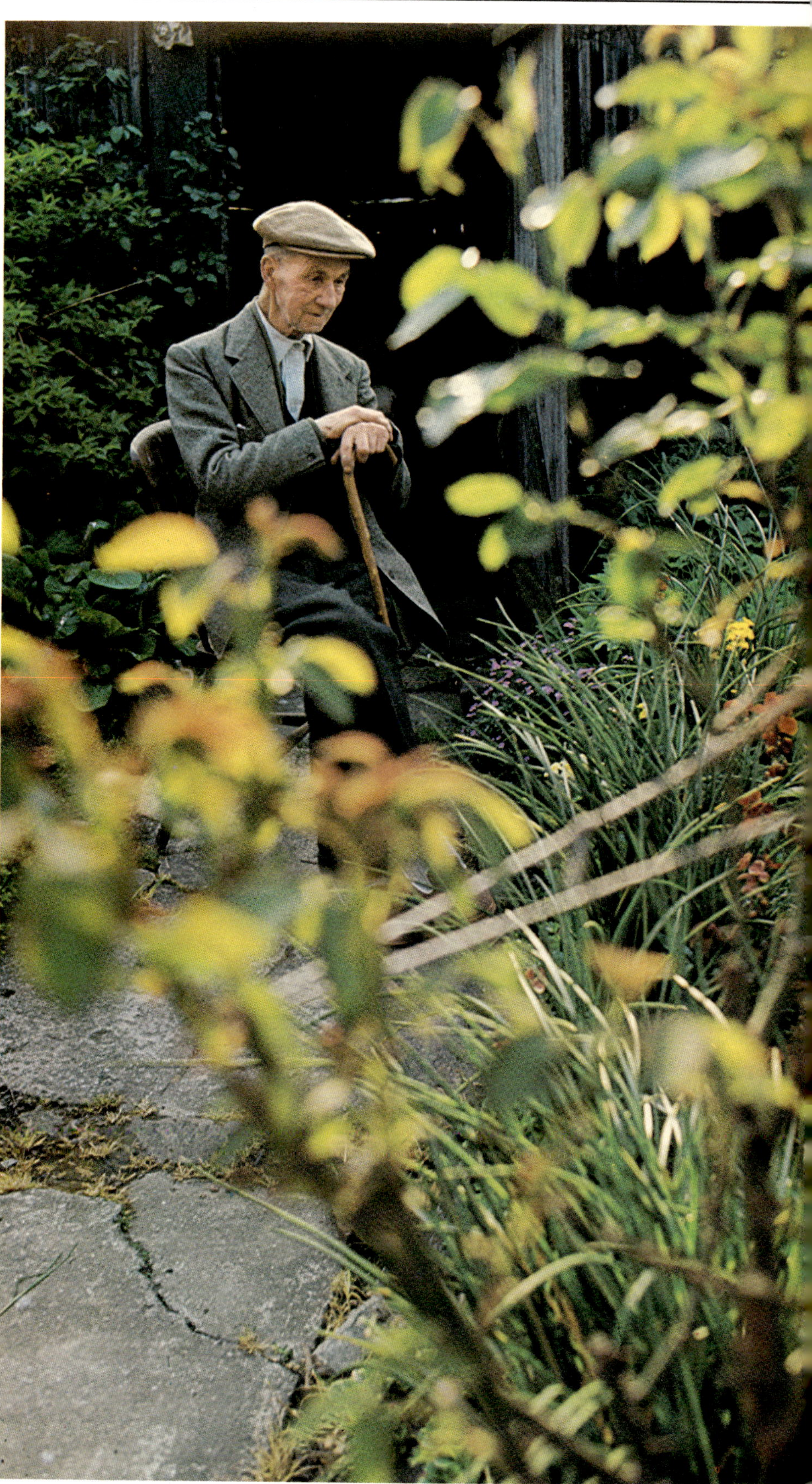

▶ Out-of-focus foliage in the foreground acts as a frame and adds color. This technique can be effective when photographing people, houses and even landscapes, when the subject might otherwise look isolated. Photo by John Bulmer.

▶ Opposite: Imagine this scene without the arch. Take advantage of things like archways, doorways and foliage as simple but interesting frames to provide a reference point for the viewer. Photo by Robin Laurance.

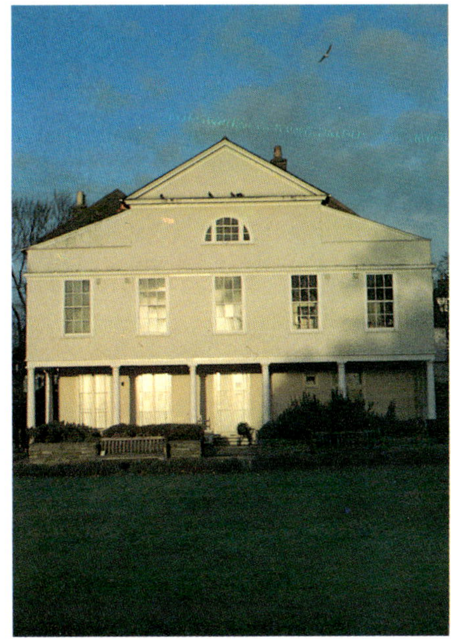

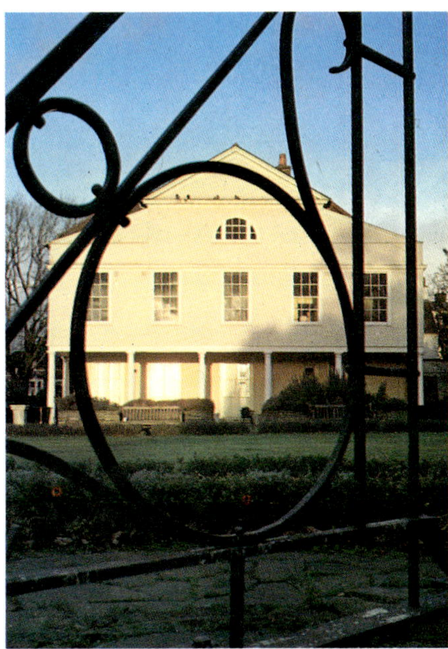

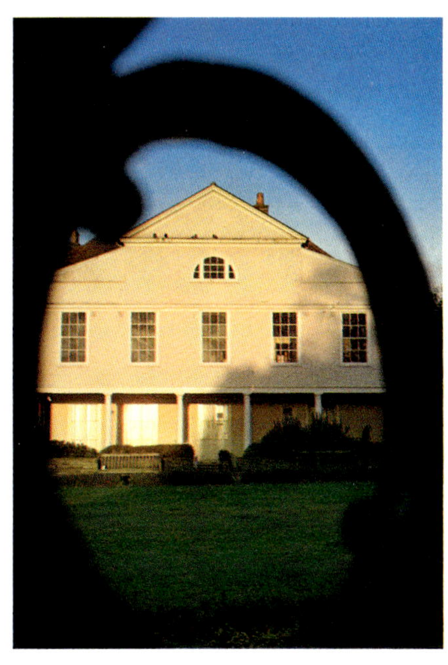

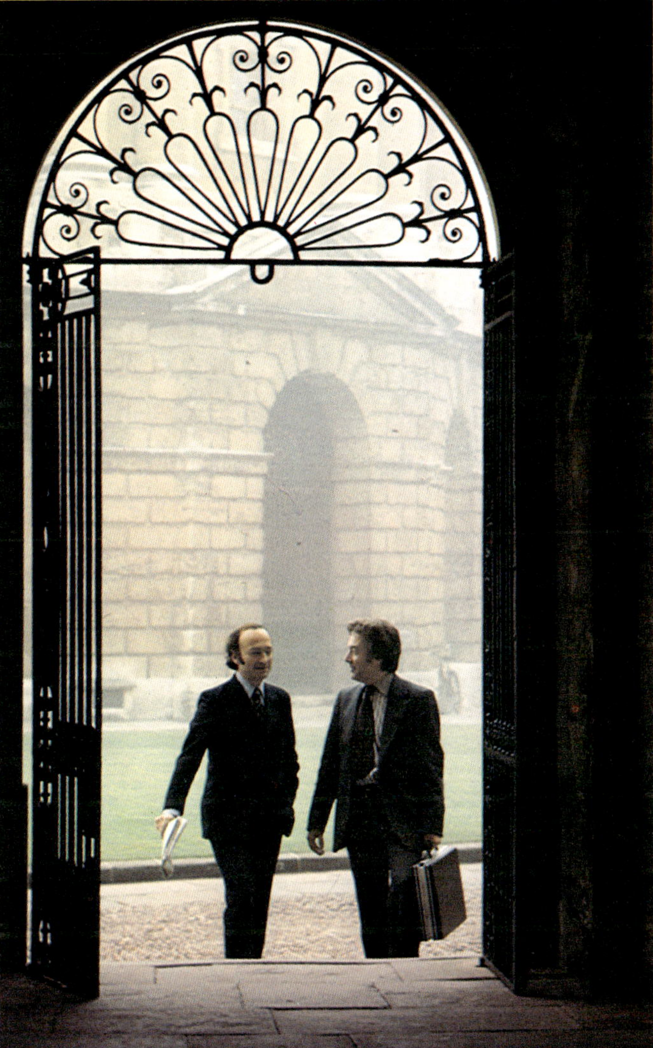

▲ Any clearly shaped object—a gate, window frame, rigging on a boat—can be used as a frame. Here, the house alone looks bare and boring. In the center picture, the gate is too distracting. In the photo at right, the simple, slightly out-of-focus shape does not interfere with the view of the house. Photo by Barry Lewis.

▼ If the wall had been left out of this picture, the stretch of grass in the foreground would have dominated the scene. Including the soft colors of the lichen-covered wall makes an effective "starting point" for the image without overwhelming the horse and the view. Photo by John Bulmer.

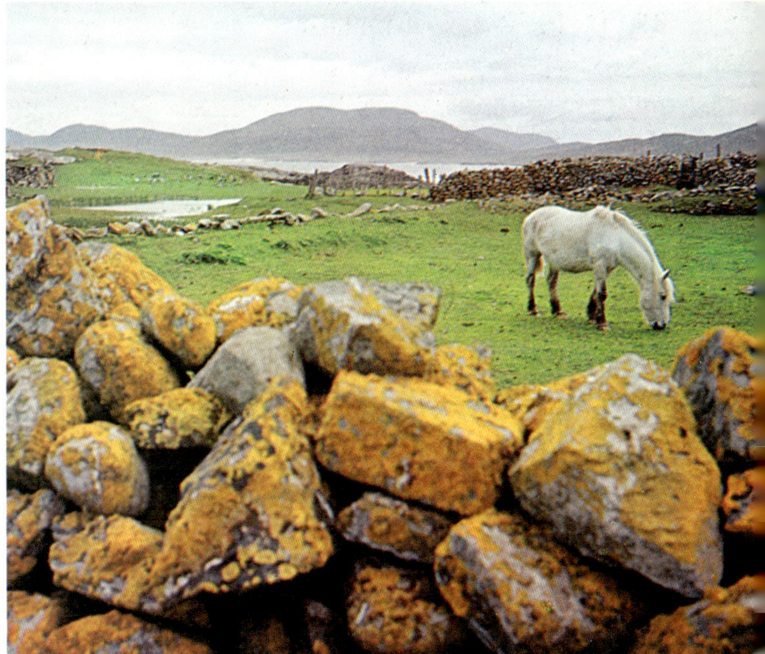

Where to Put the Subject

For many experienced photographers, deciding where to position the subject in the frame is instinctive. But for the beginner, this consideration needs as much attention as the horizon, background and foreground. Guidelines are useful for beginners, but you should soon let yourself react to the subject and not feel inhibited by rules.

The most obvious position for the subject is in the center of the frame, where there is no danger of cutting off the tops of heads or other parts of the subject.

However, a centrally placed subject often results in a dull image. It also means that you may not be filling the frame enough, with the result that the subject is too small in the final print or slide and is dominated by a background that adds little to the photograph.

Even so, a centrally placed subject can work particularly well when the picture has strong geometric lines. This is especially true when the geometric balance is important, such as when photographing architecture.

Most people find they prefer to look at a point just above the geometric center, so consider positioning the most important part of the subject in that area. Then compare the effects of placing it in the geometric center, and in the top or bottom half, to see which is most effective for the particular subject.

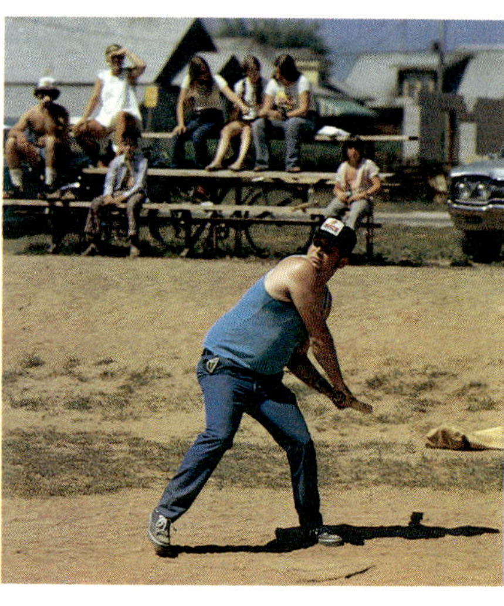

▼ The center of the frame is often the most satisfactory location for a round subject. With this much detail, the photo doesn't need any compositional device to hold interest. Photo by Eric Crichton.

▶ This is a strongly geometric composition—rectangular door, triangular ladder and the man centered. The facial expression and the position of the subject's hand add a touch of vitality. Photo by Martin Parr.

▲ Centering the subject tends to make a scene static. But if the subject is shown doing something actively, the photo has a dynamic feeling. Photo by Robert Estall.

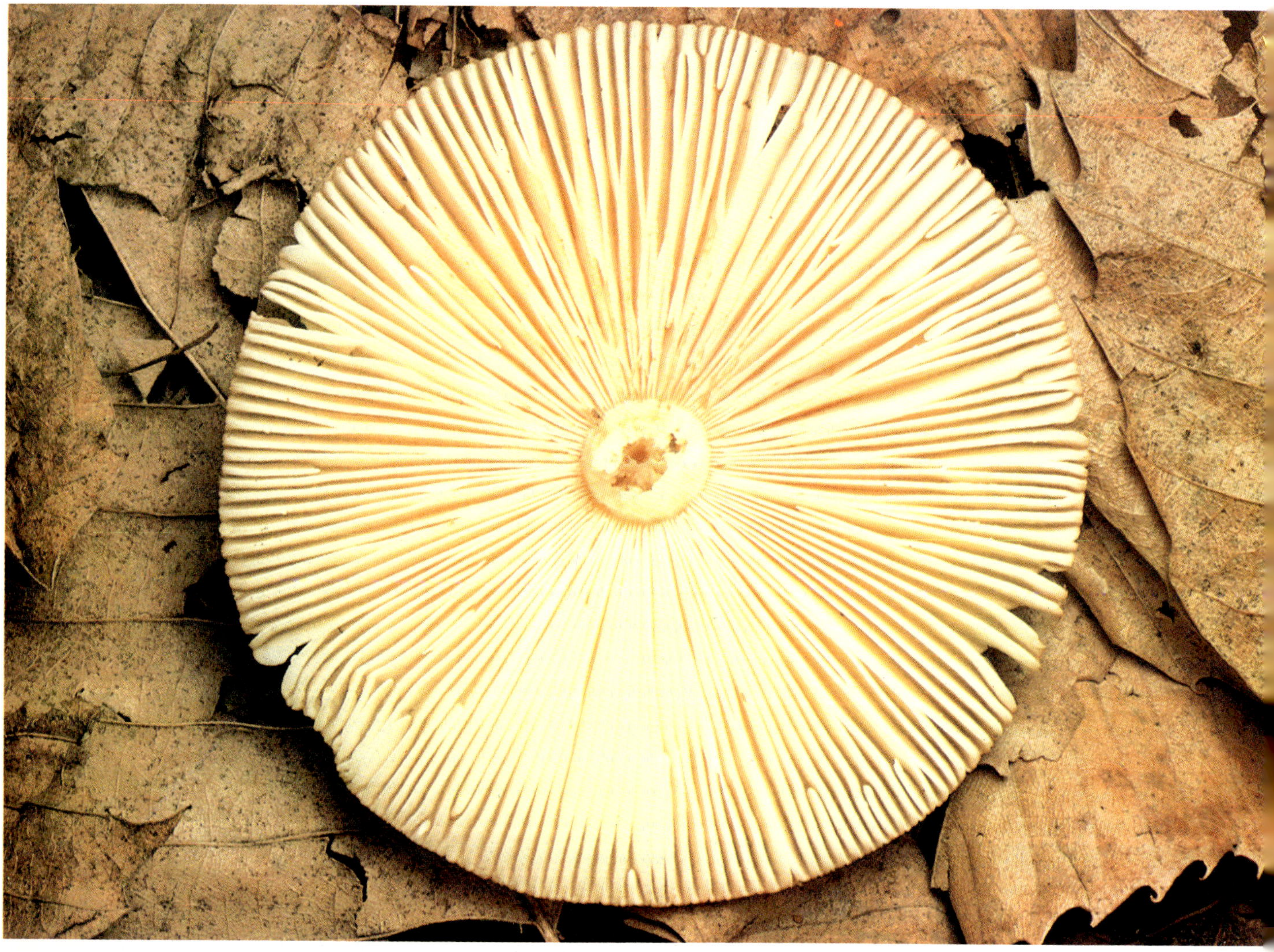

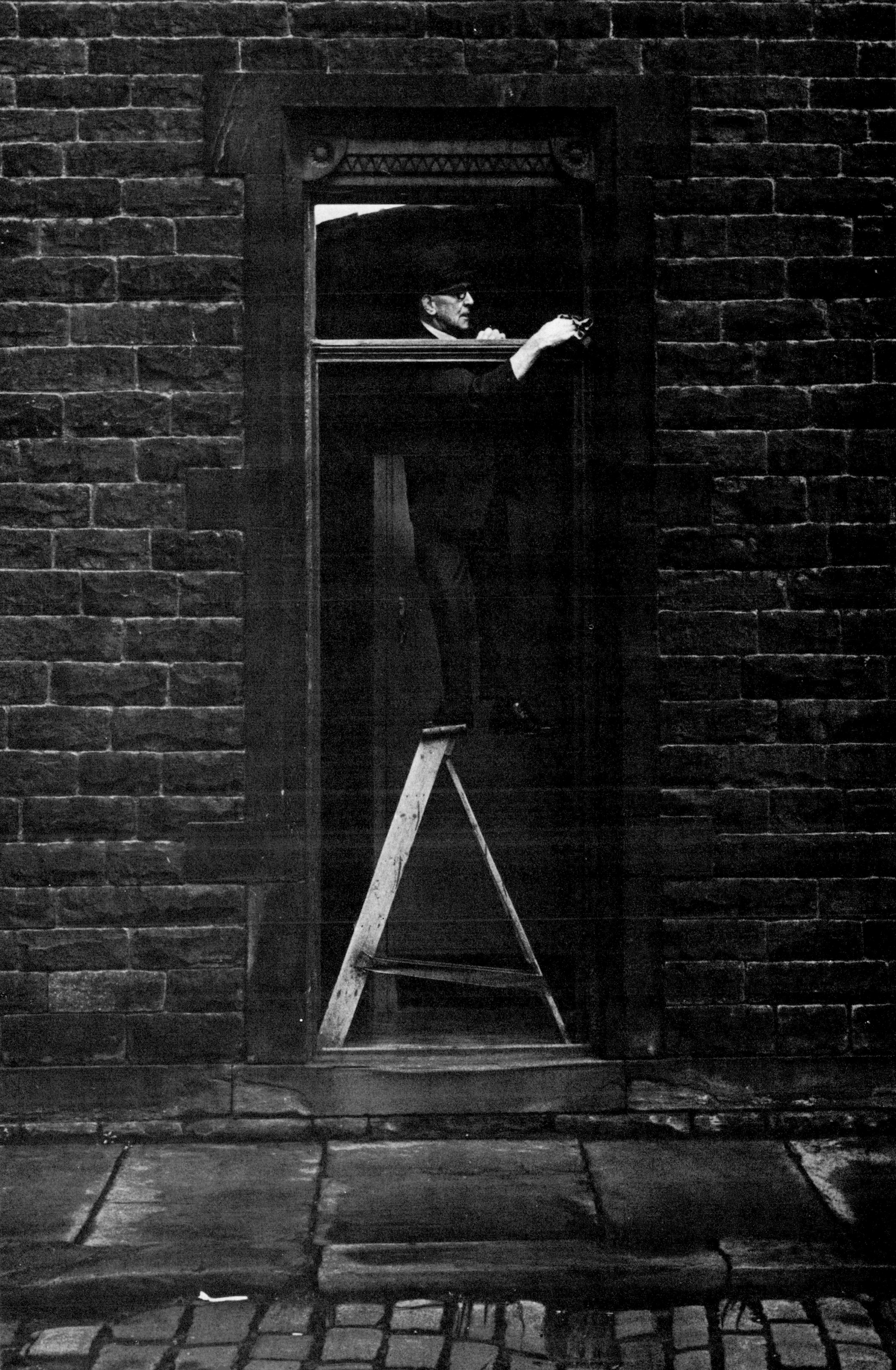

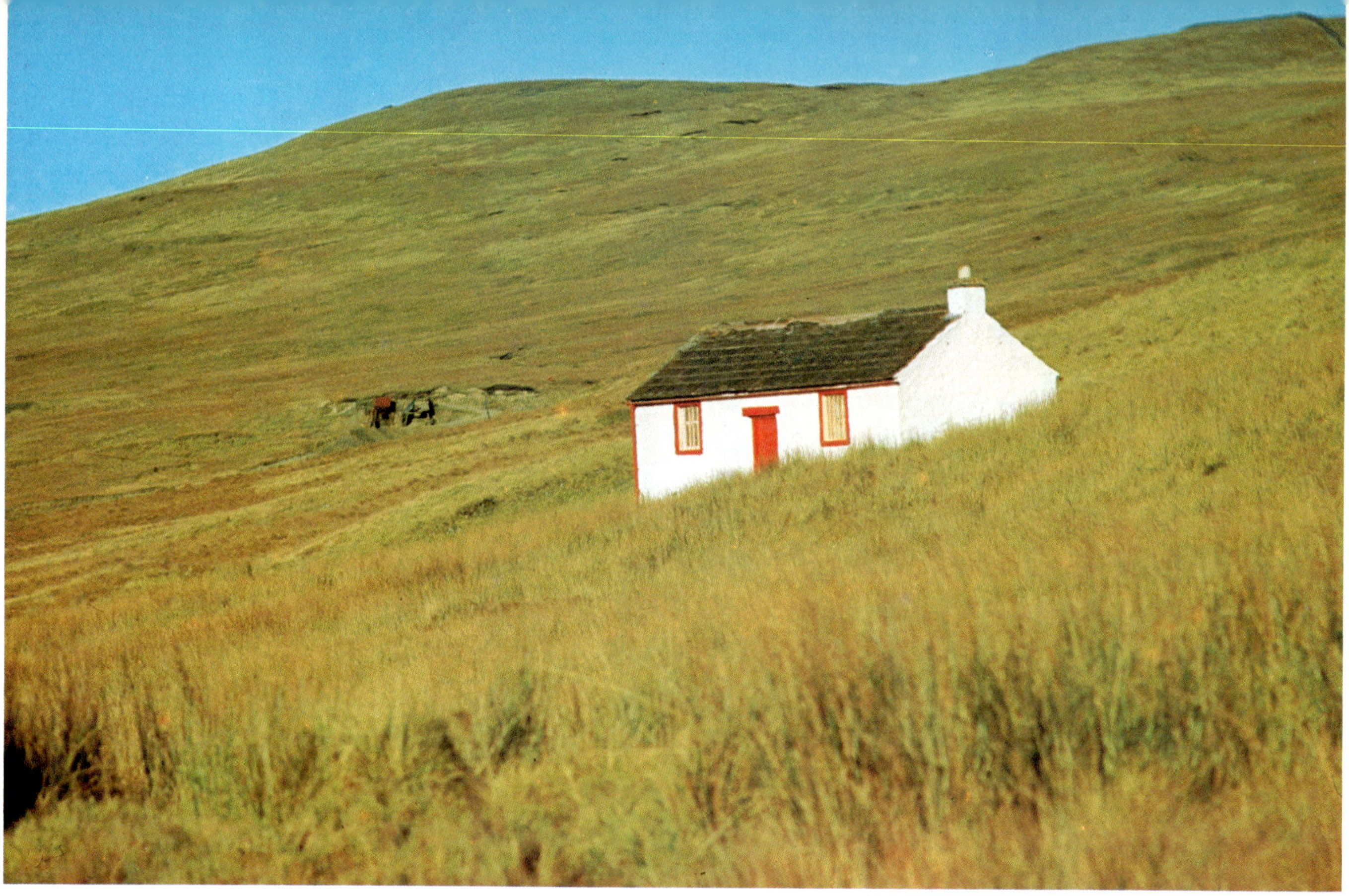

THE INTERSECTION OF THIRDS

The traditional way to produce a balanced, satisfying composition is to use the *intersection of thirds.* Painters have used this formula for centuries, and some photographers find it helpful too. See the accompanying drawings. Don't apply this to *every* picture or you will soon find the results boring and repetitive.

If you have a subject such as a tree, person or chair, start by positioning it on one of the two vertical grid lines. This location often results in a more satisfactory composition.

Next, imagine that the scene is divided into horizontal *and* vertical thirds. The intersection of the lines produces four *ideal* points on which to position the subject.

▲ The photographs on these two pages are balanced differently to suit either the shape or mood of the subject. Landscapes are easy to experiment with because they do not move. This house is positioned on a vertical third. Visualize how the picture would look with the house a little higher or lower, or positioned on a different intersection. Photo by John Bulmer.

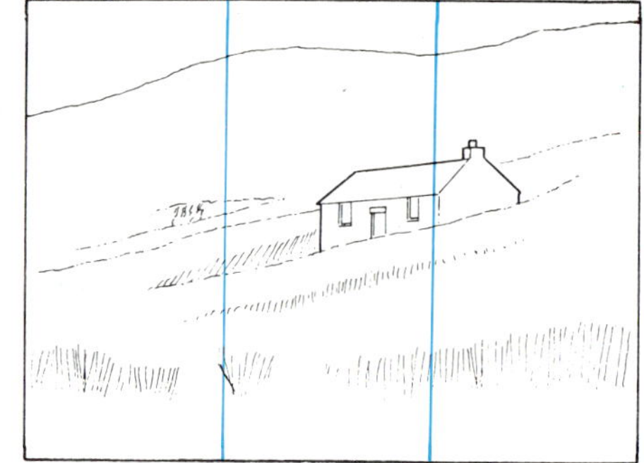

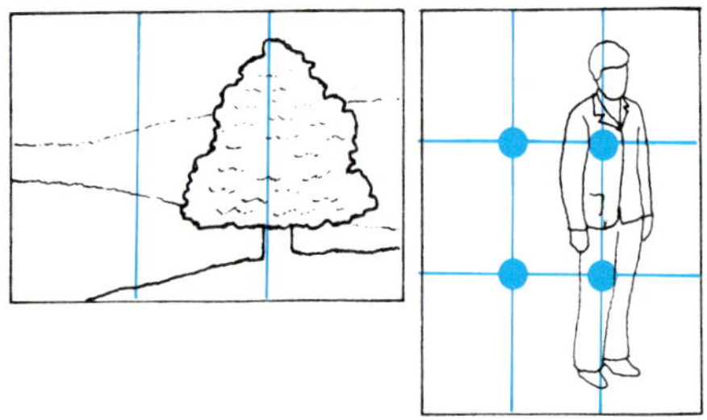

The diagrams above show the vertical thirds and the four intersections of thirds.

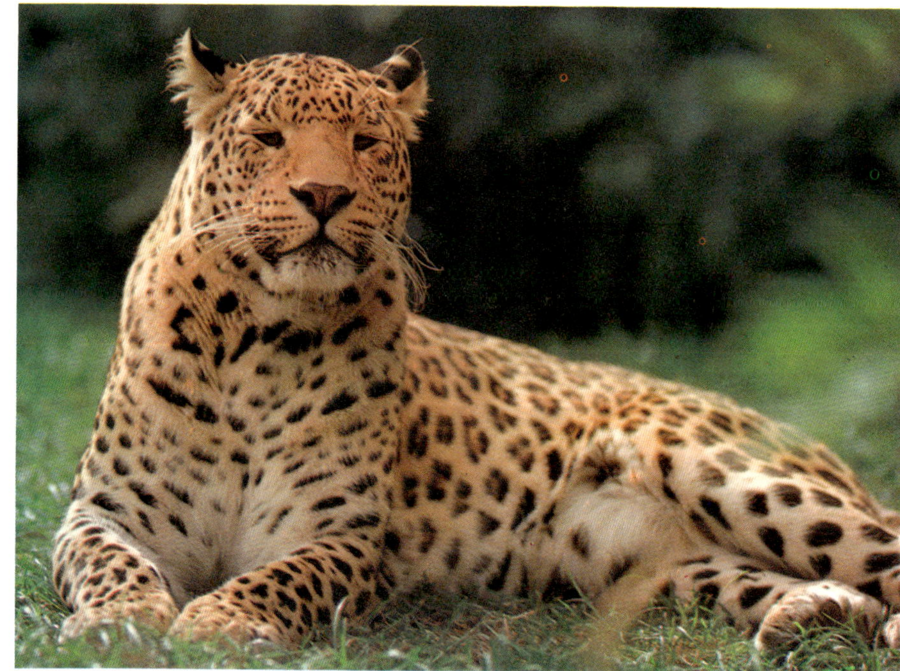

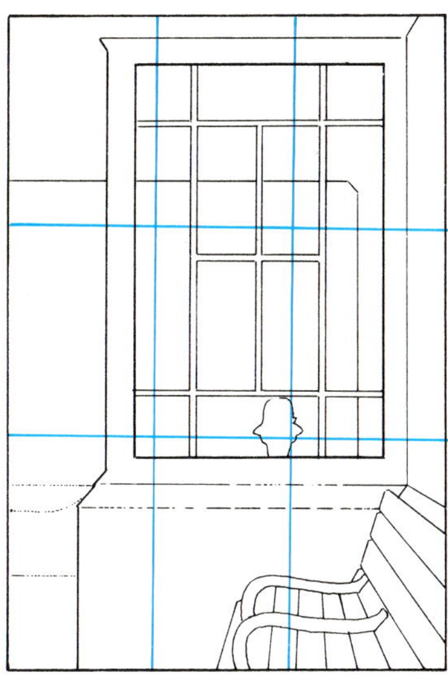

▶ When composing the picture in the viewfinder, try altering camera position. With a still subject, take more than one photograph and try arranging the composition differently. Here, Bryn Campbell used the strong rectangular shapes to dominate the image. But your attention is immediately drawn to the placement of the head.

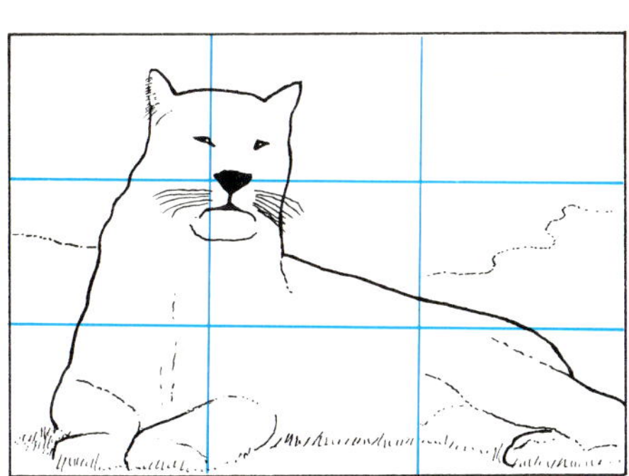

◀ The position of this animal, combined with the rule of thirds, makes a photo with impact. The head and shoulders dominate the compositon. A lower placement of the head would have included distracting background, producing a weaker picture. Photo by Eric Stoye.

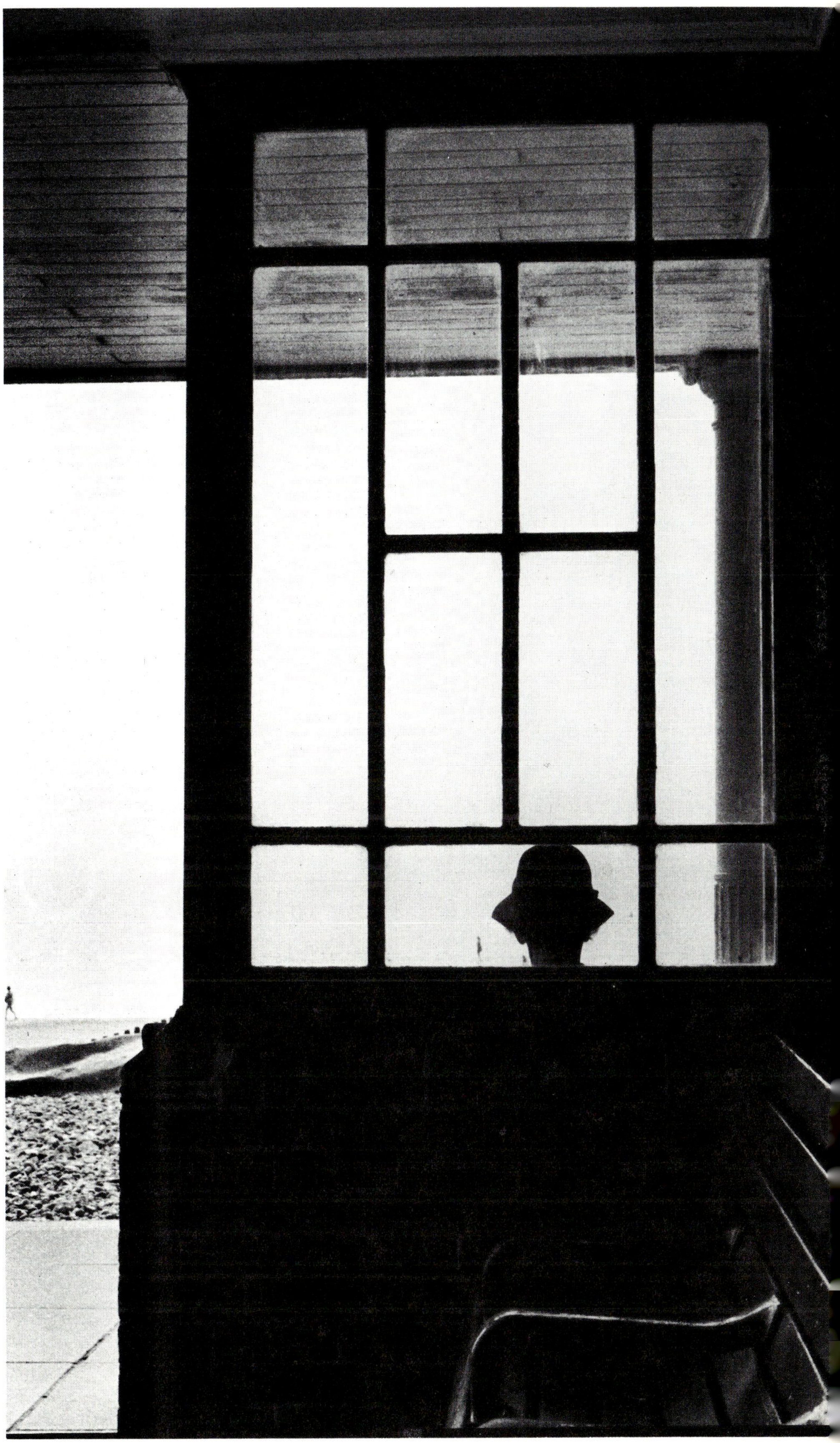

EMPHATIC ALTERNATIVES

Placing a subject off center in any direction is one of many ways to create emphasis in a photograph—to make the viewer look straight at the subject. At first glance, Tomas Sennett's photograph of the family group on the facing page might seem totally unbalanced, with the figures pushed to the side of the frame. But in fact, the group is carefully balanced by the expanse of sea, which also places them in natural surroundings.

Similarly, Roland Michaud's image of the Tibetan monk positioned on one side of the frame is a satisfying, well-balanced composition because the subject is looking *into* the picture. By closing in on the head, the photographer leaves no doubt where the center of interest lies.

If you place a subject off center, what happens to the "space" created? In many cases, like the two pictures just discussed, the space becomes a balancing factor in the composition. You can also use it to add information about the subject.

ROOM TO MOVE

There is another important reason for not composing some pictures too tightly. A moving subject seldom looks right if placed in the middle of the frame. Patrick Ward's photograph of the man on a bicycle needs the space on the right. It is not only a question of balance, but also that a moving subject needs space to "move into." This is especially worth remembering in sports photography, although it is often difficult to achieve because your attention is on the action.

Another effect of leaving plenty of space around the subject is to emphasize loneliness or isolation. In such cases, that space is as vital as the subject itself. The photograph of the tractor plowing would be less effective if it had been taken closer—the space emphasizes the scale of the open landscape.

TRY IT ANOTHER WAY

Not every subject should be placed off center. The important thing is to try several alternatives before taking the picture. If you can't move the subject, move the camera. If there is time, make more than one exposure, varying the camera viewpoint or changing the position of the subject. If you can't move yourself or the subject but you can change lenses, try using a lens of different focal length to alter the angle of view.

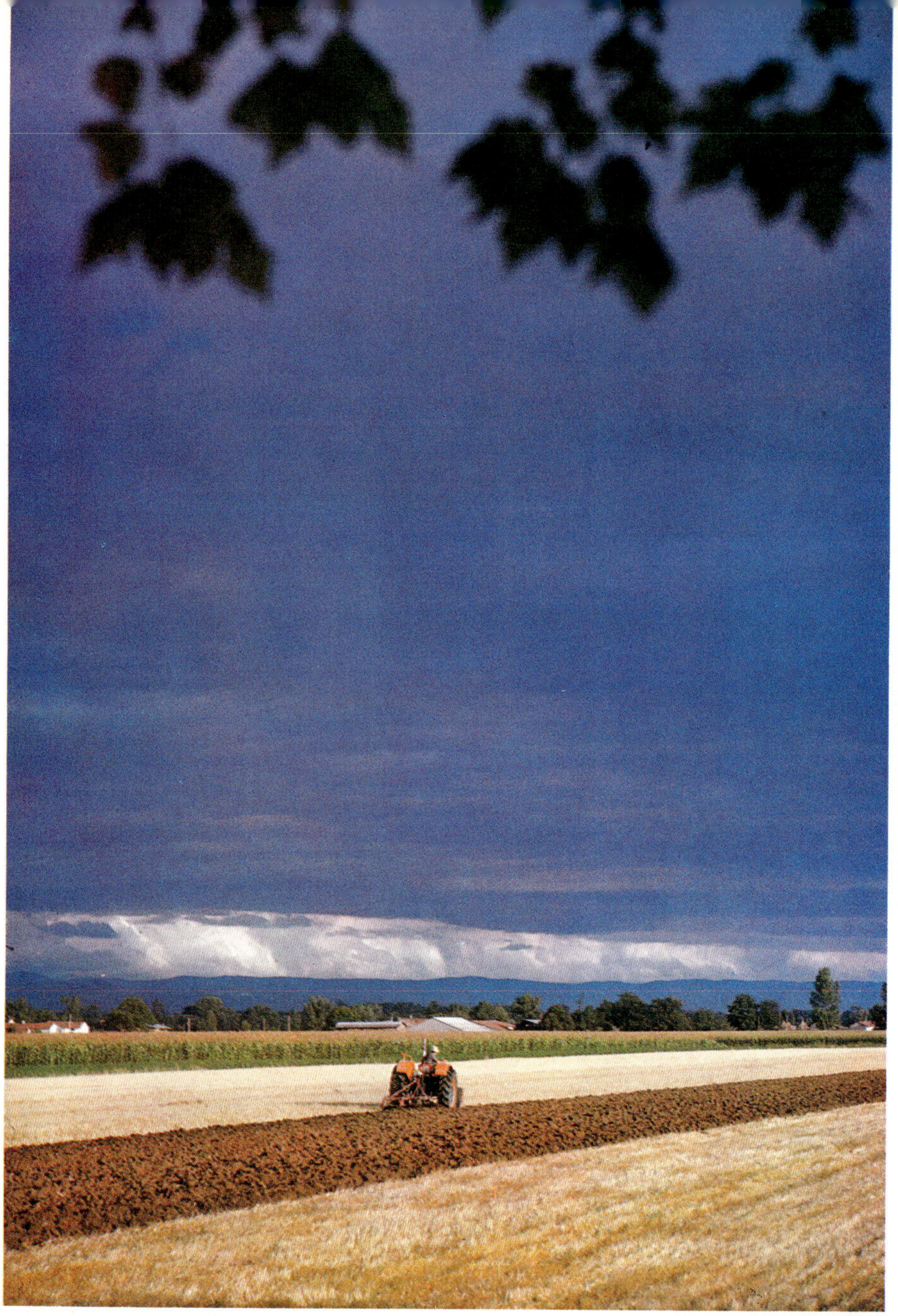

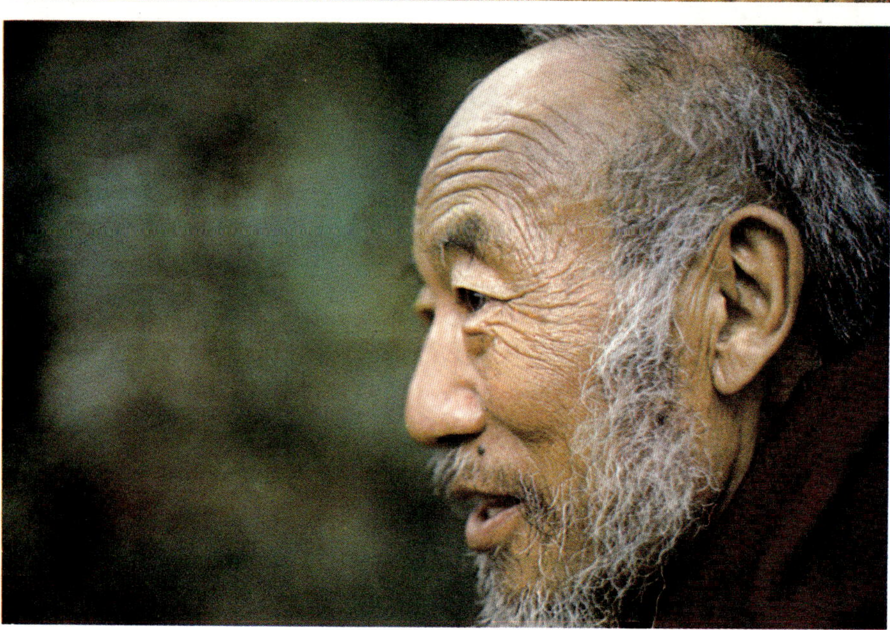

Emphasis is a way of making people notice a picture. This can be achieved by the way the picture is composed or by the way shapes, pattern and color are used. Placement of the subject is one of the most obvious ways of drawing attention. The photographs on these two pages seem to break rules—but all succeed in holding our attention.

◀ Emphasizing the sense of wide-open space with a vast sky.

◀ Emphasizing the monk's gaze by leaving space in front of him.

▶ Emphasizing the importance of the sea in these people's lives.

▼ Emphasizing movement by leaving space for the bicycle to "move into."

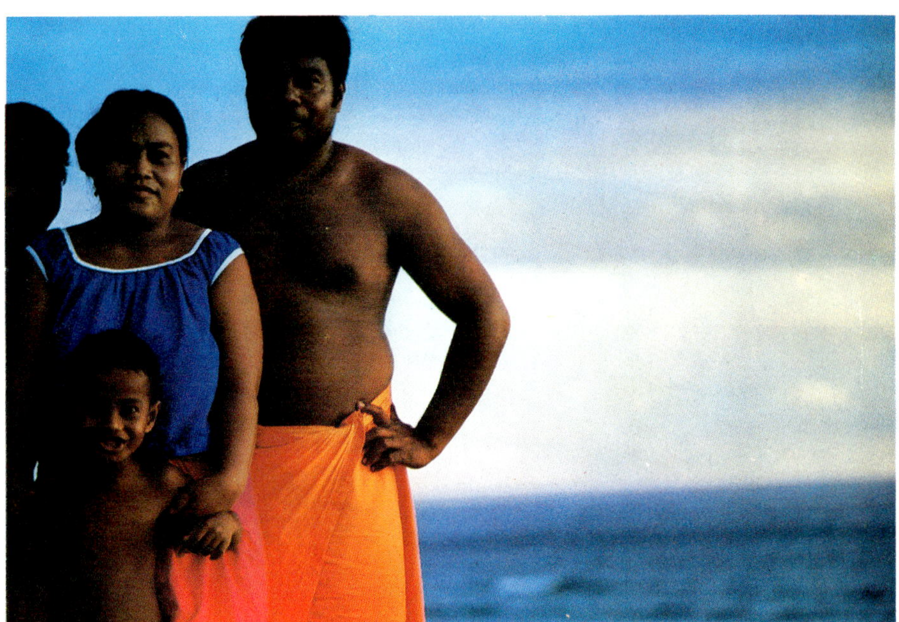

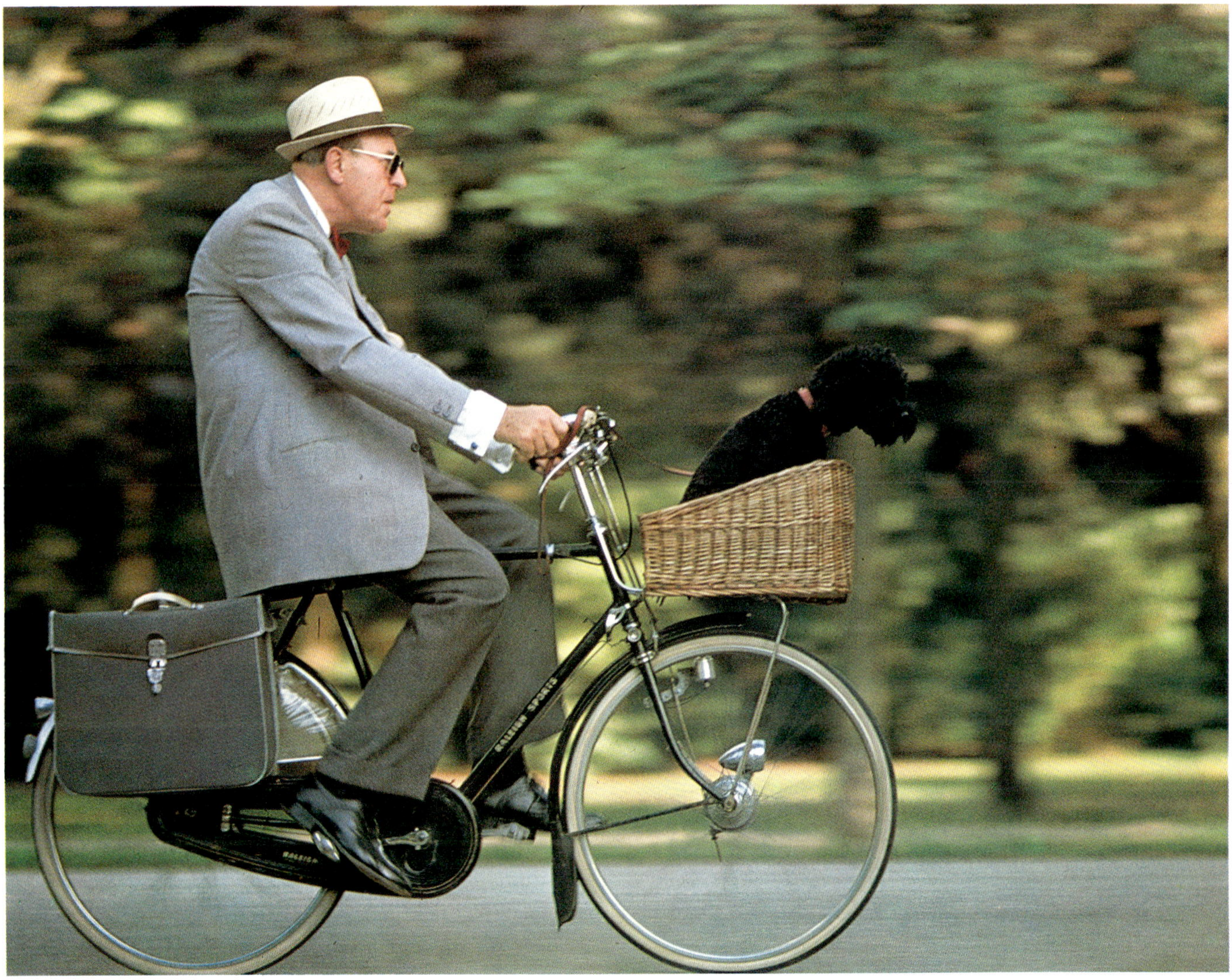

The Edges of the Picture

Once you have decided where to place the subject, plan how the content of the picture will relate to the edges of the frame. This involves more than just glancing at the edges of the viewfinder to be sure the image is correctly framed. The common mistake of cutting off heads or feet often results from taking the picture too quickly or being too close to the subject. But apart from such elementary mistakes, how should you decide to crop or frame the picture in the viewfinder?

A good way to discover the different ways of framing is to use a pair of right-angled strips of cardboard when looking at photographs. Place them over the print and move them to vary the composition. To produce the same effect in the camera, move the camera closer to or farther from the subject and change the direction of view. The best way to test this method is to choose a static subject such as a landscape or building. Remember that the simpler the picture, the more likely it is to be strong and effective.

Another way of giving emphasis is by looking at the same subject several different ways. Very tight cropping around a portrait will draw the viewer's eye to the face, or even part of the face, and can strengthen a weak or uninteresting picture. It is a way of leading the viewer straight to the essential point you are trying to make, or of excluding confusing foreground or background detail to make the photograph more explicit.

USE THE EDGES

There is no hard and fast rule of composition that says the edge of the frame must not "cut" into the subject. Often a single detail of a subject or scene can be as strong a way of portraying it as showing the entire subject. Just as in placing the subject, it is a question of the emphasis you desire. There is nothing wrong with getting very close to some subjects.

On the other hand, a building may not look right if you are too close. Move back and allow a little more space around the edges and it looks better. If you move back even farther, the distracting elements on either side may begin to compete with the subject. The picture then ends up with no clear center of interest.

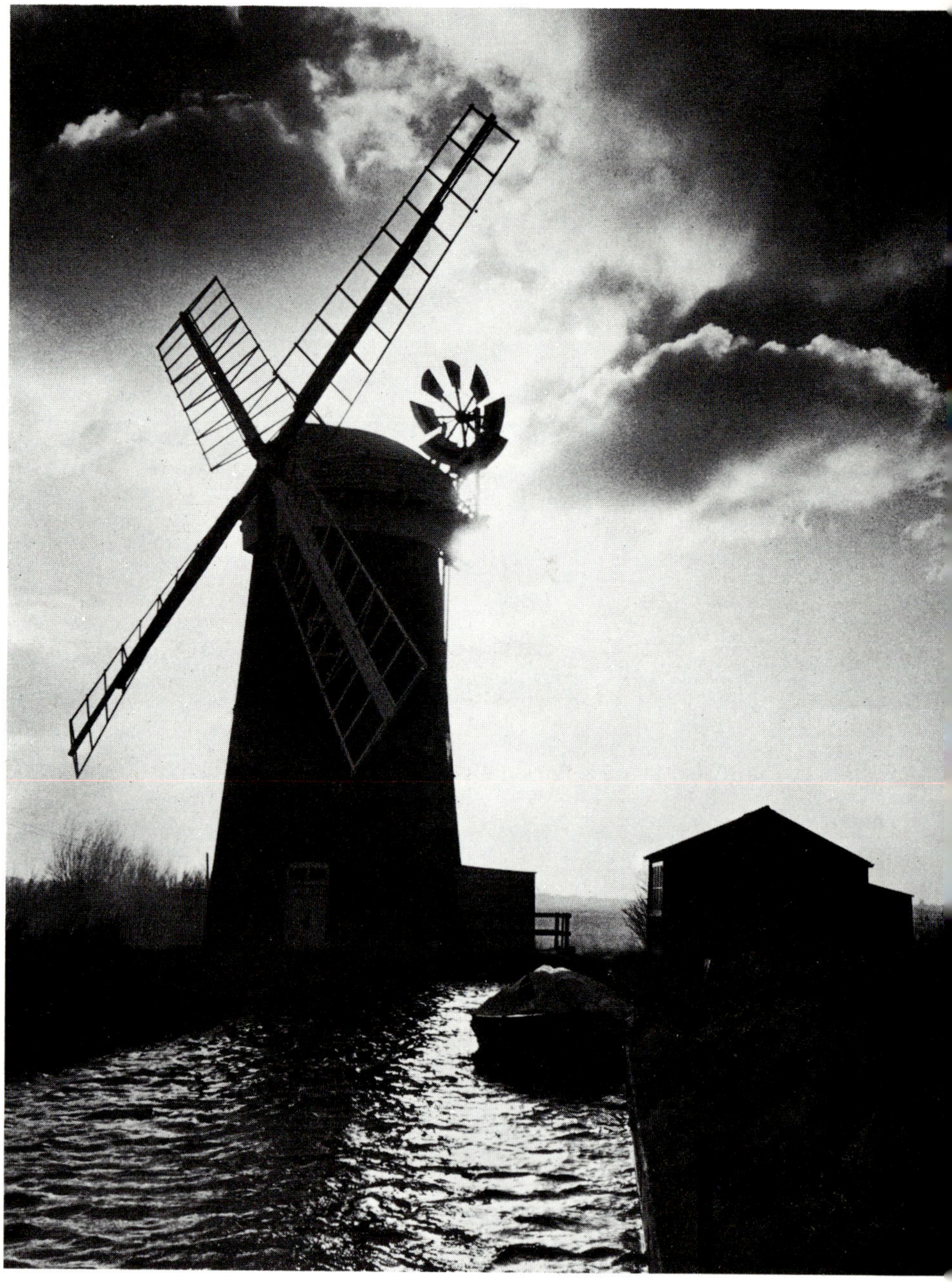

LOOK AT THE TOP
The photograph on the right shows the windmill with the top cut off. Compare it with the picture above that completes the shape, giving "breathing space" to the mill and including enough of the canal in front and the shed on the right to balance the weight of the windmill. Think of these points when photographing any building. Photo by Bill Coleman.

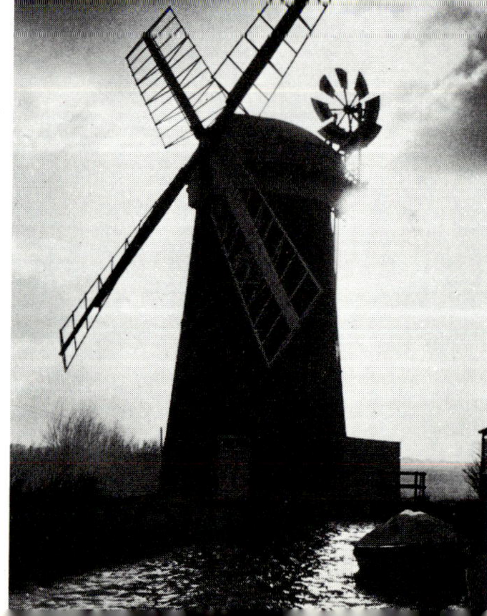

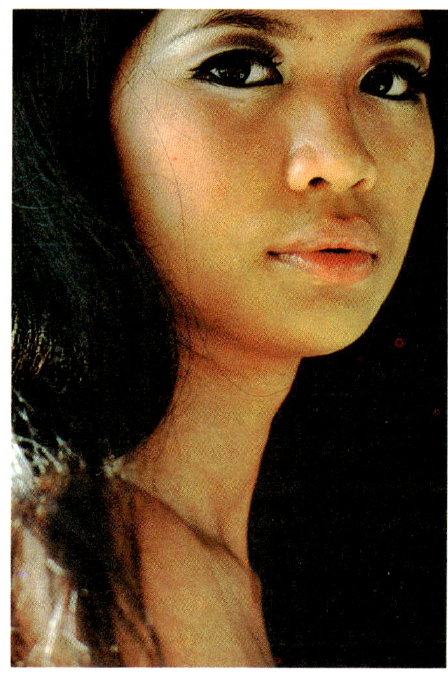

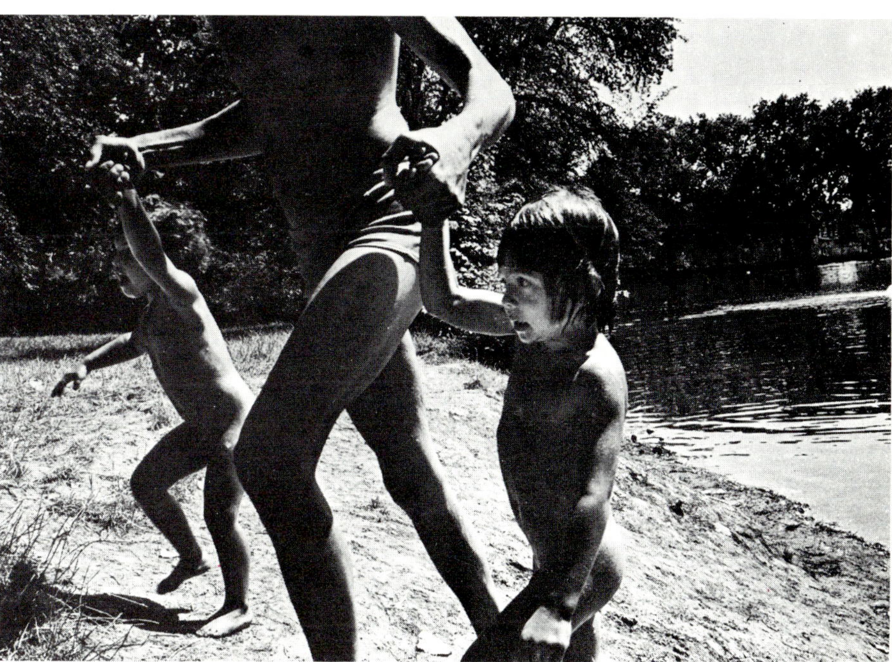

▲ If you are going to "cut off" part of a subject, it is often most effective to do it emphatically. Tomas Sennett used a telephoto lens to avoid distortion and yet get close enough to the subject to create the effect he wanted.

▲ Ask yourself *what* you really want to emphasize. Here, William Wise emphasizes the children. If he had included the father's face, the children would have become less significant and the photo would tell another story.

▼ Obviously, photographer Thomas Hopker was amused by the symmetry of these figures and the repetition of colors and poses. Cropping the heads accentuates the point.

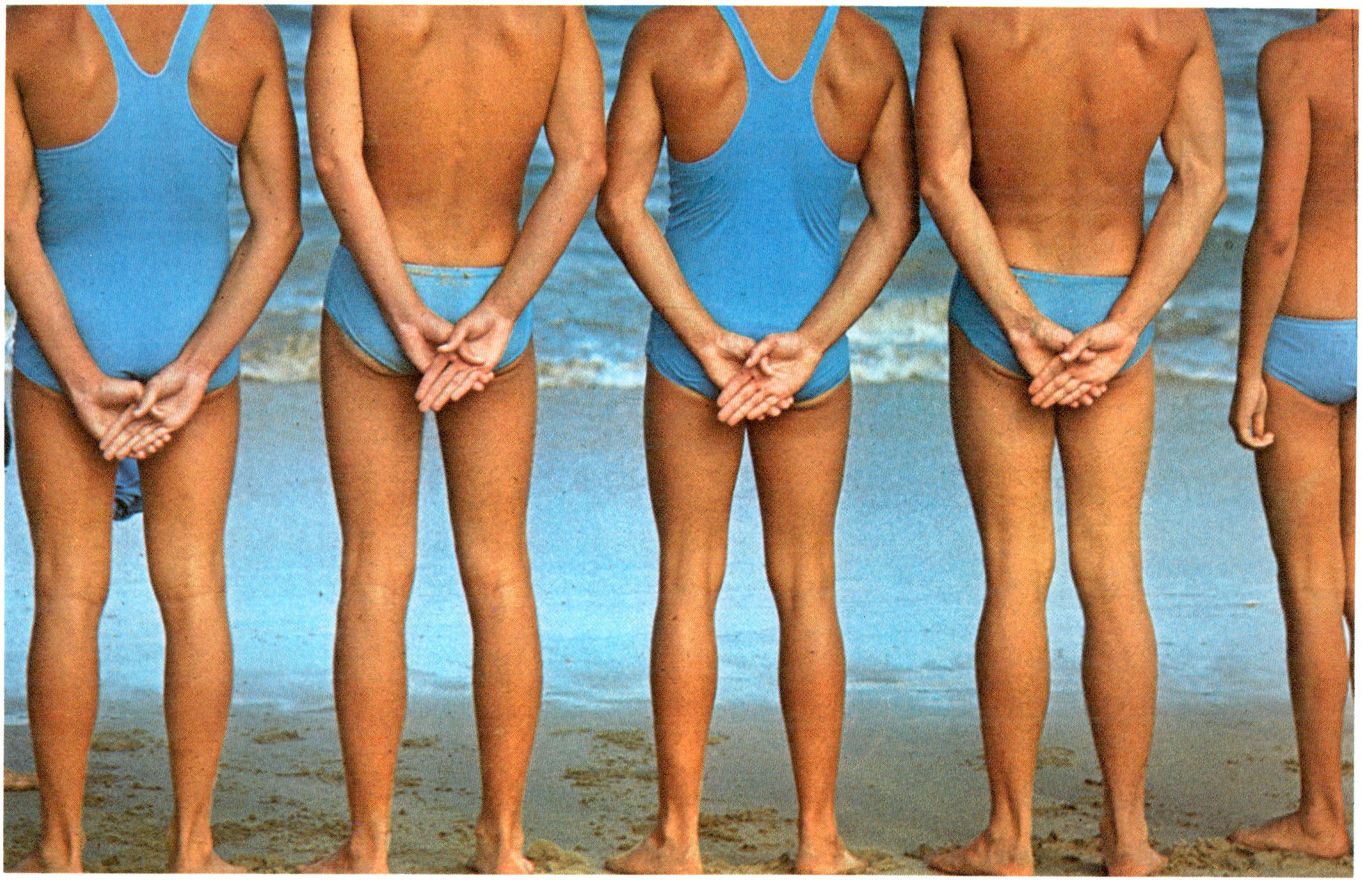

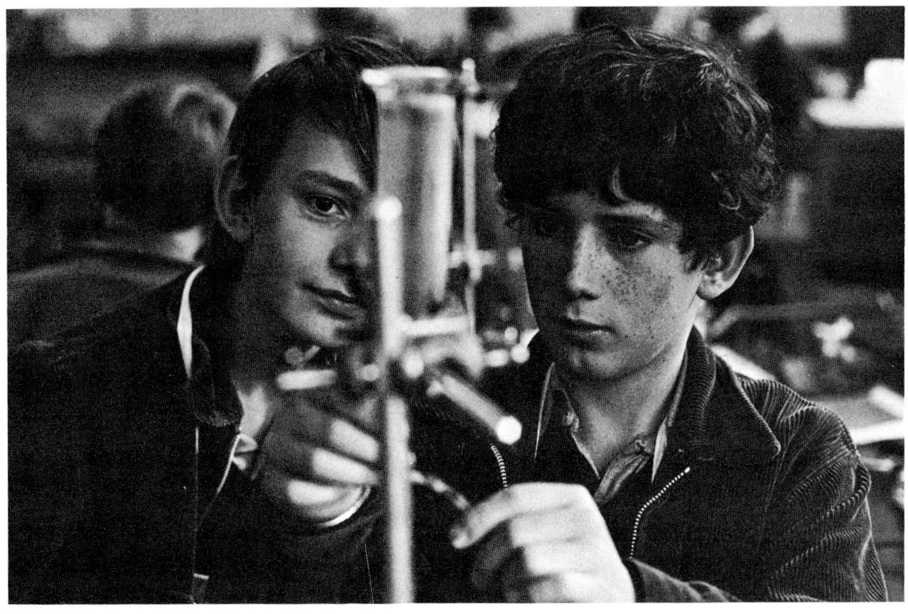

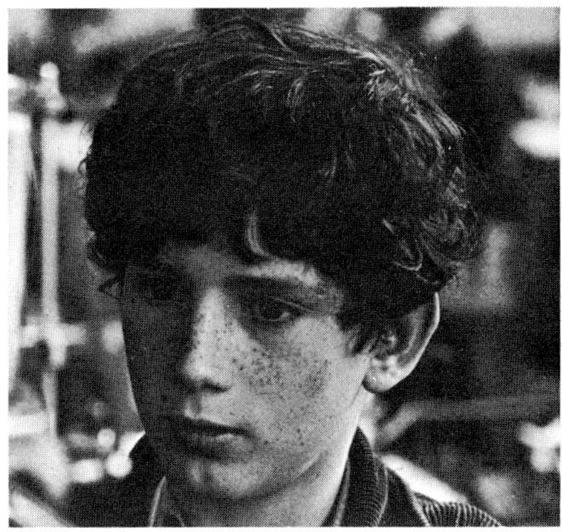

CHANGING THE MEANING
Cropping excludes distracting detail, but can also produce a misleading picture. The boy looks like he's daydreaming in the close-up. In the full frame, he is actually absorbed in an experiment.

MAKING A POINT

How you frame a photograph can establish its meaning or accentuate a specific point. A close crop on the face of the boy shows simply that—a boy's face, out of context. The longer view places the subject in appropriate surroundings, at work in a school laboratory, absorbed in an experiment. The emphasis is changed from a straightforward portrait to one that tells a story.

SIDES OF THE PICTURE
One of the hardest decisions to make is how much detail to leave in at the sides. The maxim, "when in doubt, leave it out," doesn't always apply, as in this photograph. The bank on the right tells you clearly that this is a river scene and not a sea view.

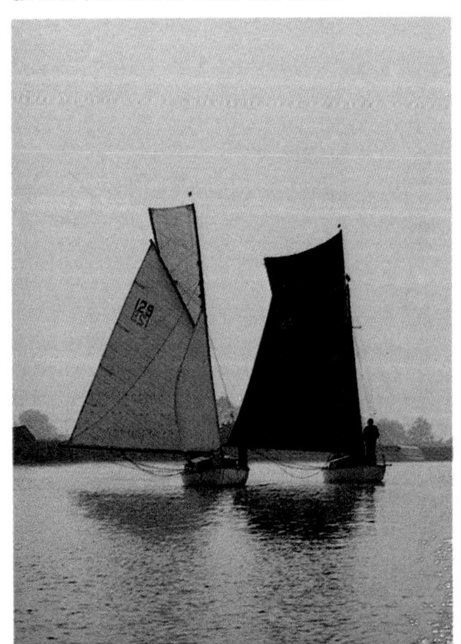

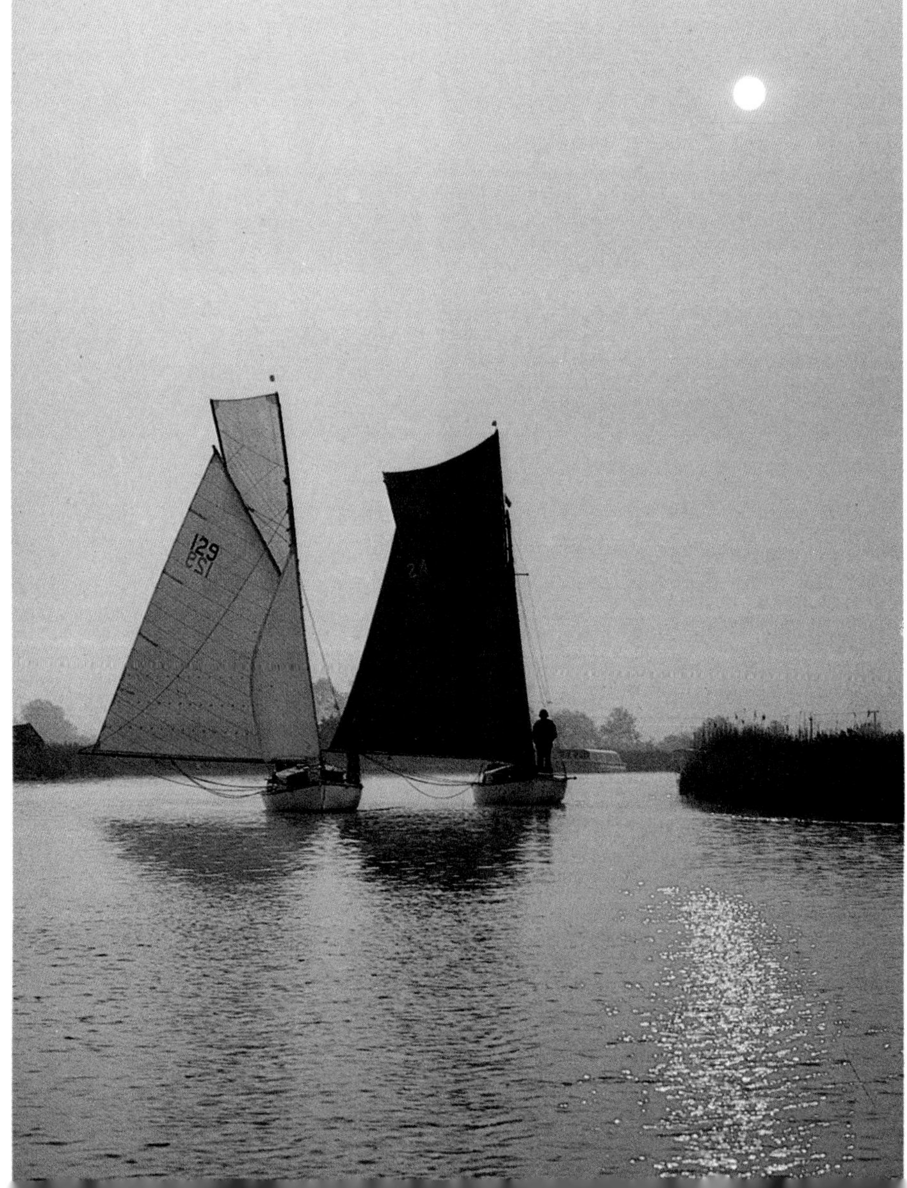

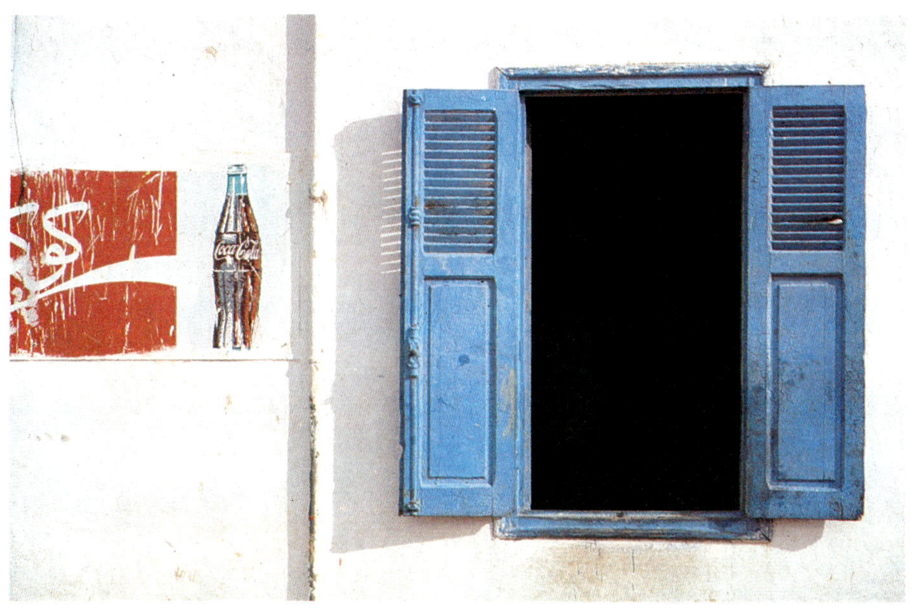

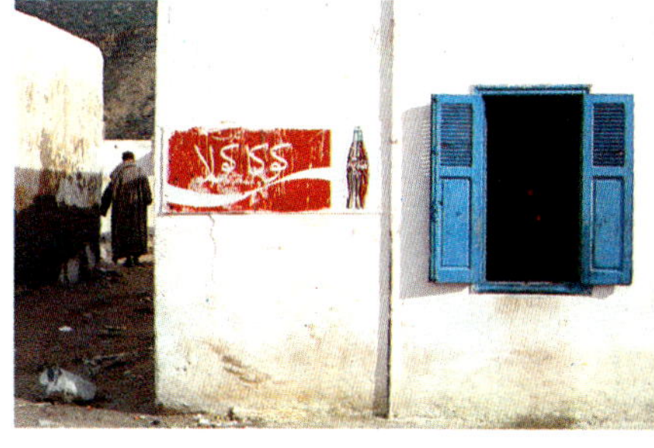

LOOK AT THE EDGES
Composition depends on what you want to emphasize. The small picture above shows a dusty street corner where the viewer hardly knows whether to focus on the poster, the window or the figure around the corner. At left, photographer Michael Busselle decided to leave out the figure and emphasize the pattern, color and "East-meets-West" theme.

EMPHASIS IN PRINTING

It takes practice, luck, experience, intuition or all of these to master the many possibilities of composition for a particular photograph. But if you get it wrong in the camera, you can sometimes adjust the balance or emphasis of a photograph during the enlarging process. Some photographers prefer not to alter the image at this stage, feeling that the way it was seen at the moment it was taken is all important. But for most of us, it is a good opportunity to vary the balance of a composition. This can be done before making the print by changing the framing of the image on the enlarger baseboard for the desired effect.

CROPPING THE FINISHED PRINT

Alternatively, the finished picture can be cropped by trimming. For example, an image of a long, thin subject benefits by being trimmed to this shape. Look at finished prints and see how you can improve them with more imaginative cropping—often by simply removing a disturbing background. A photograph does not have to fit the exact size of the paper any more than the subject must appear in the middle of the frame for good composition.

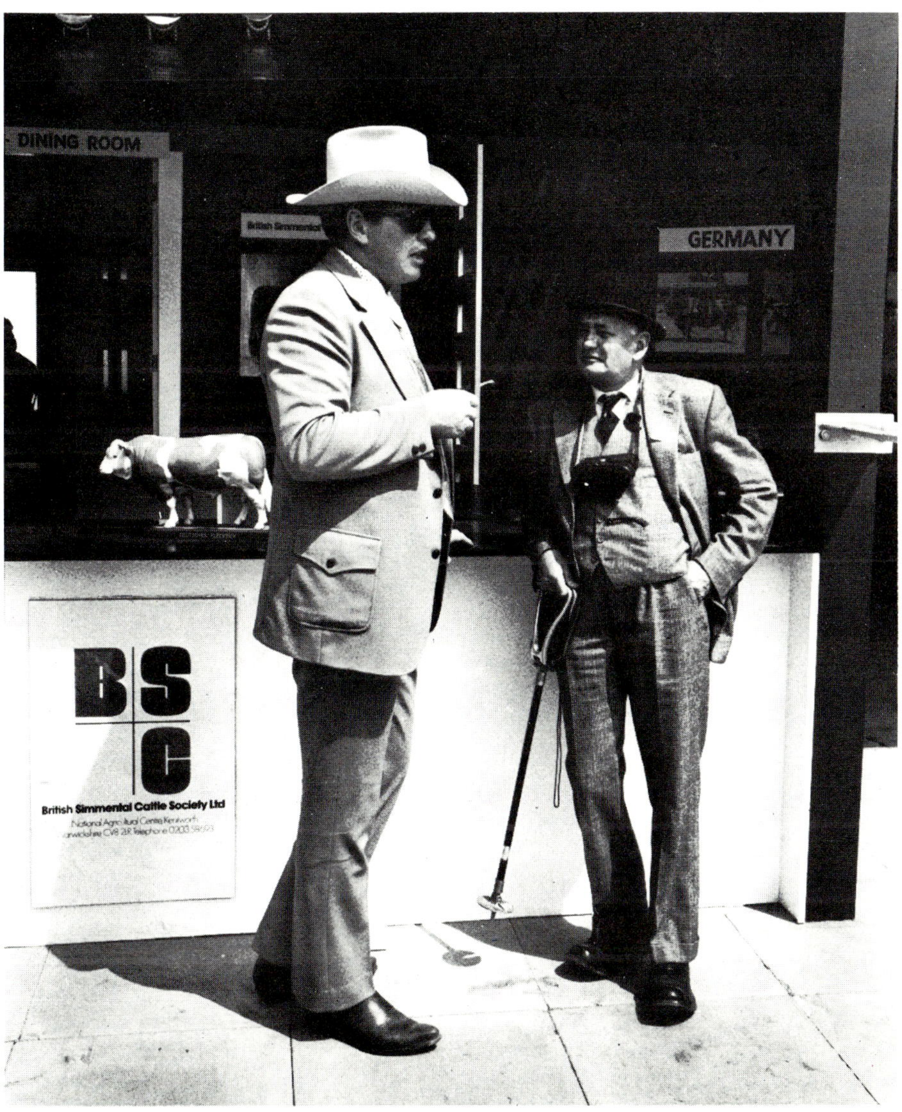

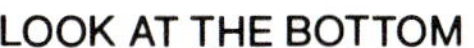

LOOK AT THE BOTTOM
Take a sheet of paper and move it around on this photograph of the two men. How do the figures look if they are cropped at the knees or if the poster is cropped out?

Choosing Your Viewpoint

Choice of viewpoint, or camera position, is very important to a picture, yet many people hardly give it a thought. Viewpoint has the greatest single influence on a photograph. If you are going to hang a photograph on a wall, you examine the room carefully, looking for the position that is best for both the room and the picture. The same amount of consideration should be given to taking a photograph. The best viewpoint is unlikely to be the first place from which you saw the subject.

EXPLORE THE SUBJECT

Occasionally the immediately obvious viewpoint is the best possible place to take a picture. Usually this is not the case. The first thing you should do after deciding to take a photograph is to walk around the subject. See how it looks from the left and right, farther away and closer, higher and lower. Explore the subject to "see" the full range of picture possibilities.

It is a useful exercise to photograph a subject from every conceivable viewpoint. You'll be surprised at how much variety of composition and emphasis you can obtain from even the simplest situation or subject.

LIGHTING

Study the effect of light on your subject and see how it can be changed simply by moving the camera. Compare the difference between photographing a subject against the light as opposed to conventional "over your shoulder" lighting. Sometimes you may need to move the camera

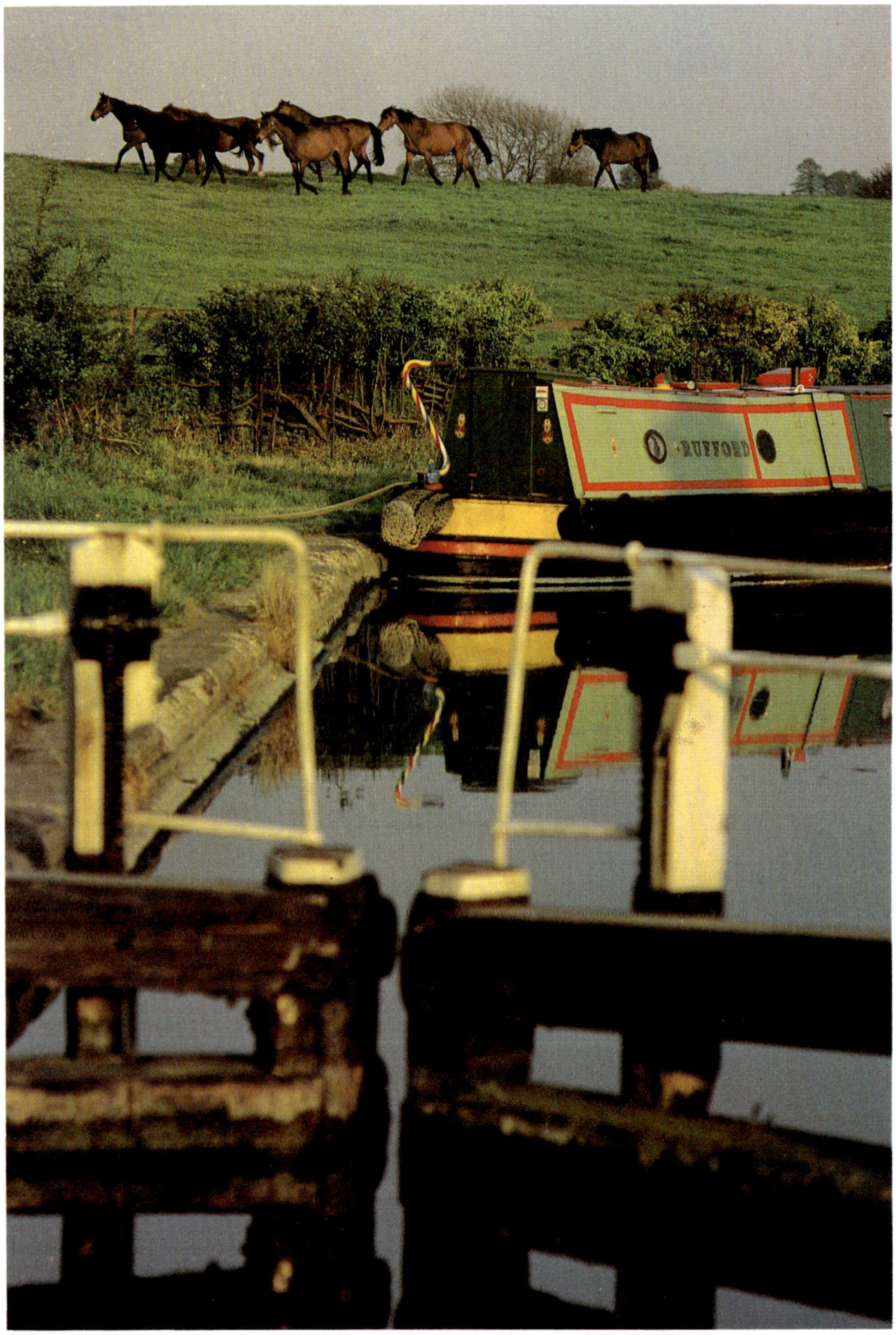

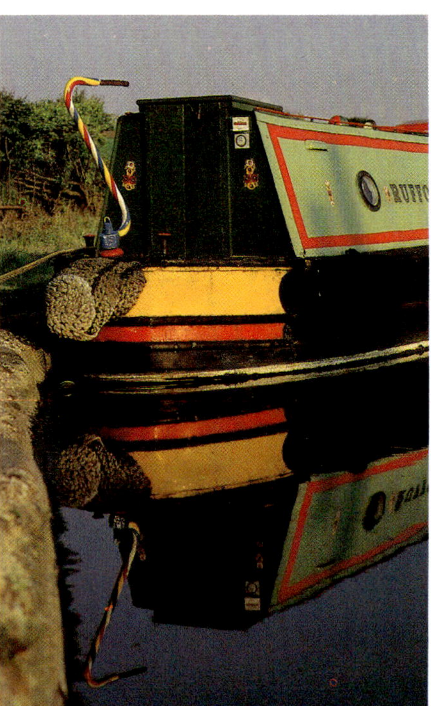

▲ The advantage of a close view is that the composition can be reduced to essentials, usually resulting in a simple, effective design. Because the design is simple, however, the smallest detail plays an important part in the photograph and must be carefully considered. For this image, Patrick Thurston positioned himself carefully so the tiller appears in the sky area, just above the bank, while the reflection just missed being cut into by the edge of the canal.

◀ Quite a different photograph is created by moving back to include more of the scene. You see the barge in its setting, with other points of interest. Camera height is important here because it controls the overlap between the foreground, subject and background. If it were any lower, the gates, barge and field would have been confusing.

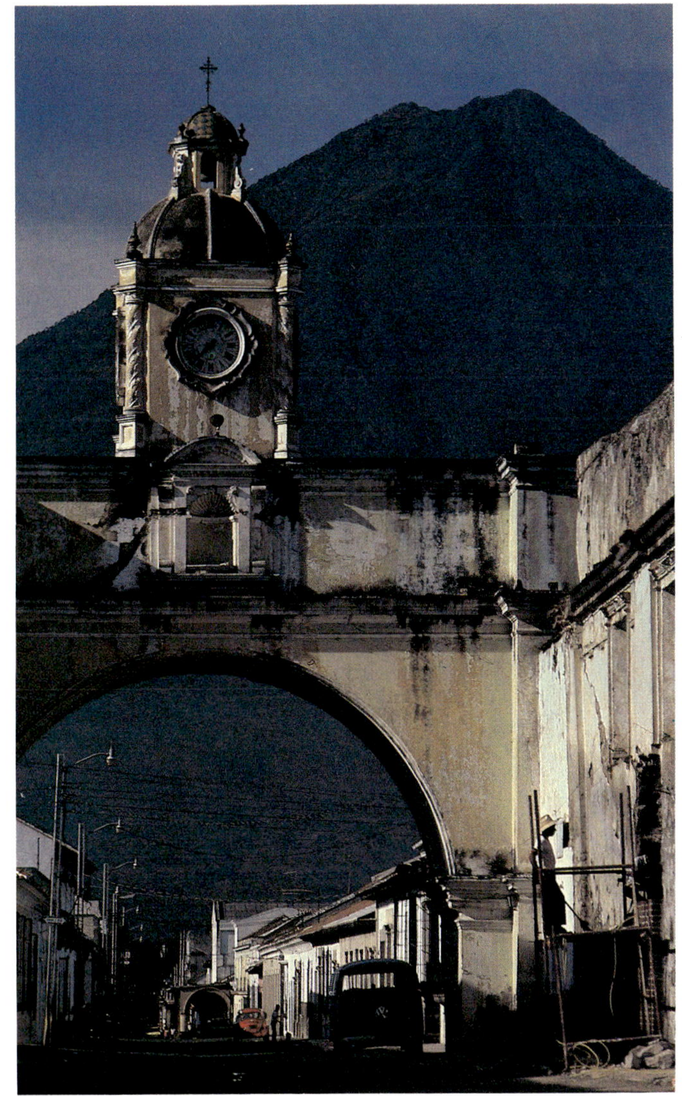

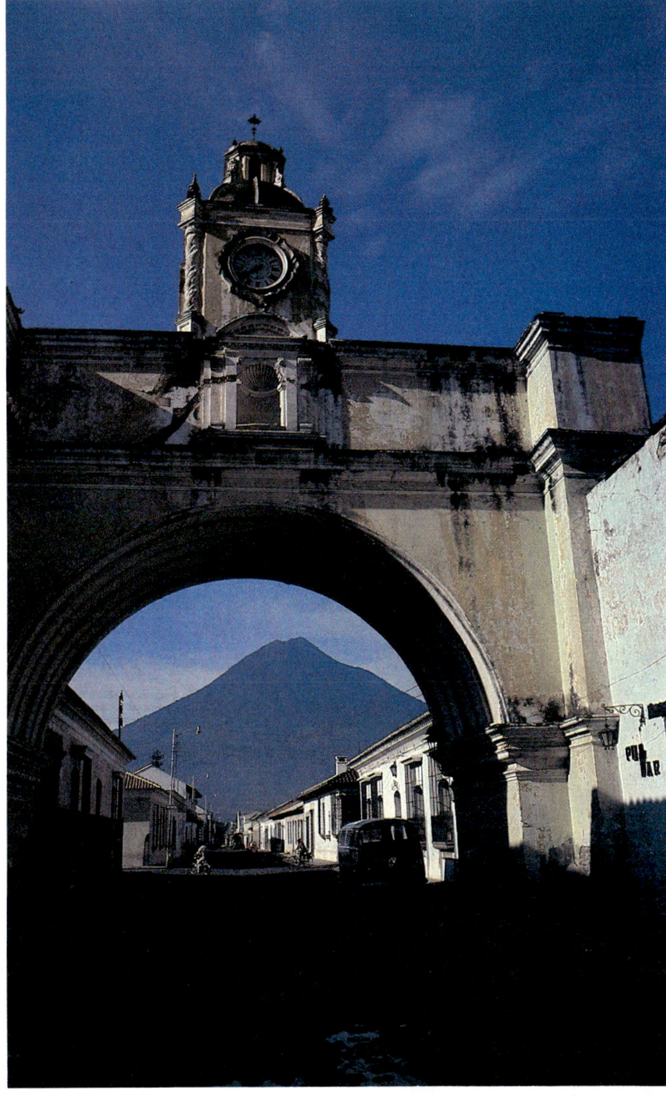

so part of the subject hides the sun to prevent flare.

Where the texture of a subject is important in a picture, the direction of the light is crucial. A head-on shot of the subject will rarely show the texture. Shooting into the light will destroy detail completely. It is important, therefore, to consider the effect of lighting when choosing your viewpoint.

PERSPECTIVE

Another aspect of photography that depends totally on viewpoint is perspective. By changing viewpoint you change the relationship between the size and proportion of objects in the picture area.

You can learn a great deal about perspective simply by observing what happens to the apparent sizes of objects as you move closer or farther away from the subject. For example, from a distance, a person standing in front of a building is overshadowed by the prominence of the building. As you move closer, however, the figure becomes proportionately more dominant and the prominence of the building is diminished.

CHANGING LENSES

Having lenses with different focal lengths is a considerable advantage when choosing your viewpoint. In fact, lens interchangeability will often encourage you to change your viewpoint. For example, a longer lens enables you to use a more distant camera position but still obtain an image of adequate size. For a portrait, the perspective effect on a face is unflattering when a standard 50mm lens is used closer than about 5 feet (1.5m). A longer lens enables you to shoot at a greater distance and still get an image that fills the viewfinder, but without the apparent distortion.

▲ A new viewpoint combined with a change of lens can make a spectacular difference in perspective and scale. For the picture on the left, Anne Conway used a 135mm lens. Moving 100 feet closer and using a 28mm lens, the archway seems to grow and now dominates the volcano.

A wide-angle lens enables you to include more of a scene without having to move farther away. This is a particular advantage when taking pictures in a confined space, and it also allows objects quite close to the camera to be included in the foreground. This can be useful in landscape photography to produce an impression of depth and distance.

Changing lenses and viewpoints gives you the opportunity to make very dramatic changes in the appearance of a scene, as you can see in the accompanying photographs.

FRAMING

Having decided on a general position for your camera, you should consider *slight* changes of viewpoint. Perhaps one step to the left to exclude an intrusive color, or a fraction lower so you include an interesting piece of foreground will make a great difference in the final result.

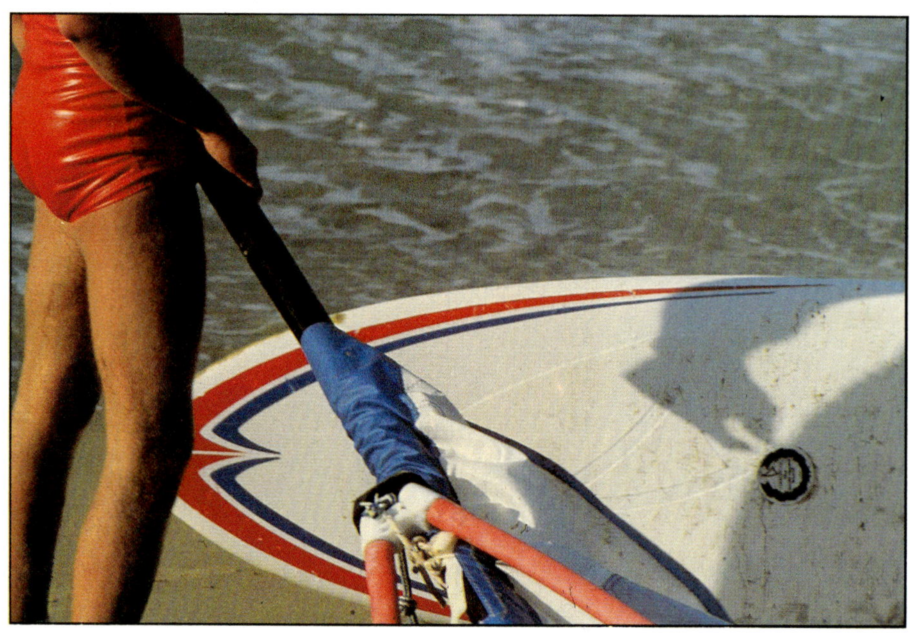

▲ Tessa Harris used a very close viewpoint to emphasize the graphic quality of the strong colors and shapes of this windsurfer as he dismantled his craft on the beach.

▼ When the figure moved, the shapes became much simpler, so Tessa lowered her viewpoint slightly to include waves rolling onto the beach. This created a more interesting background.

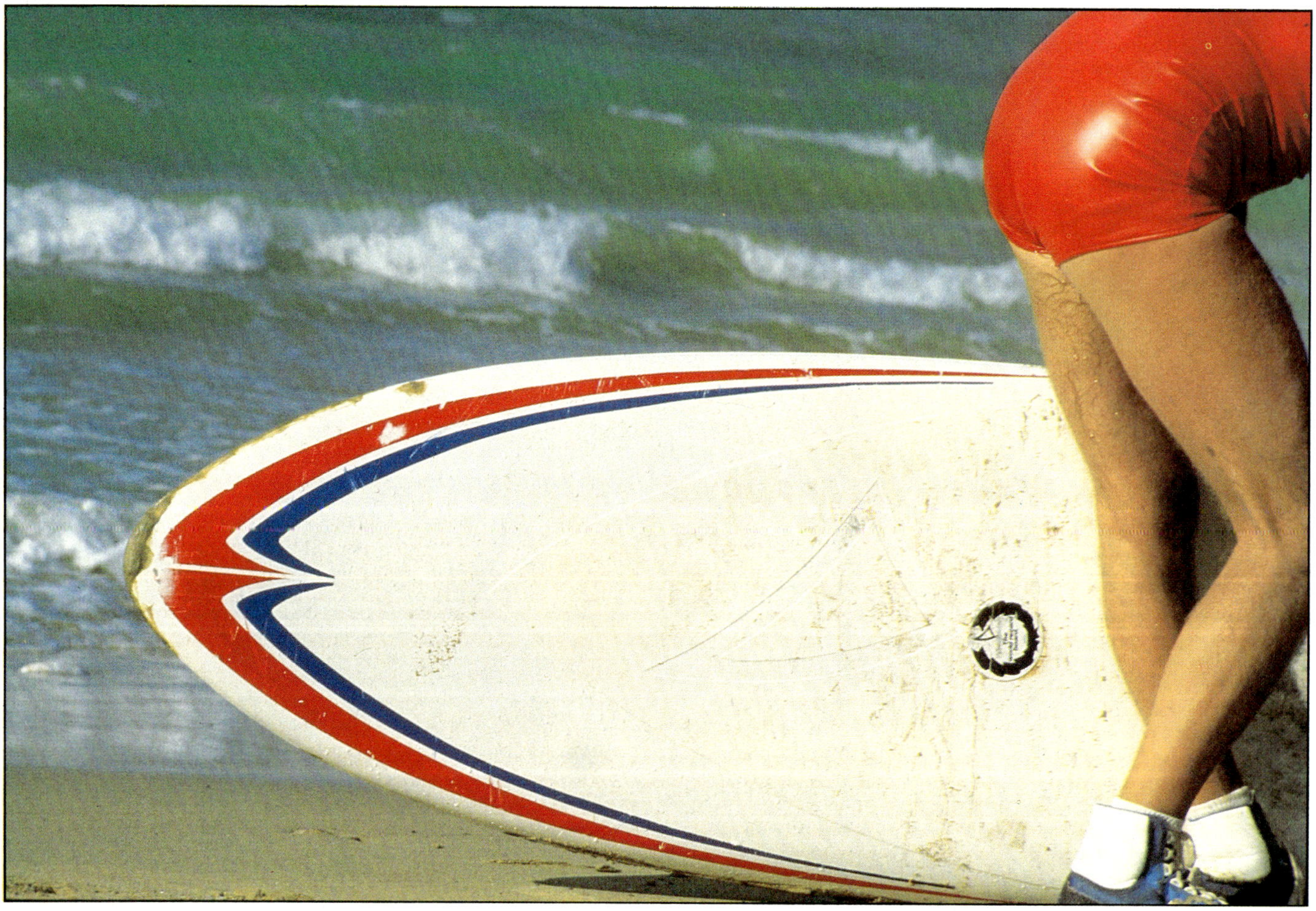

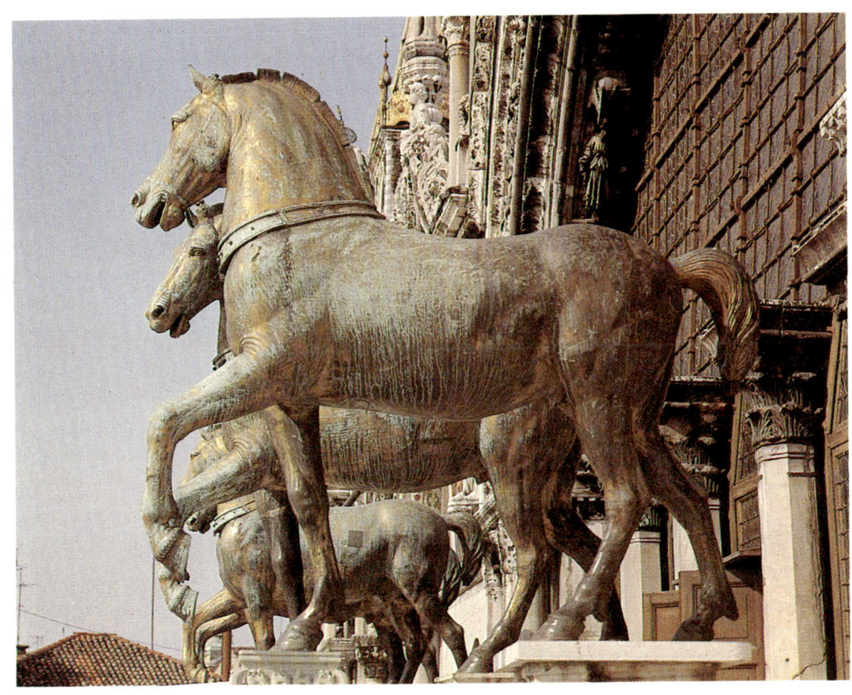

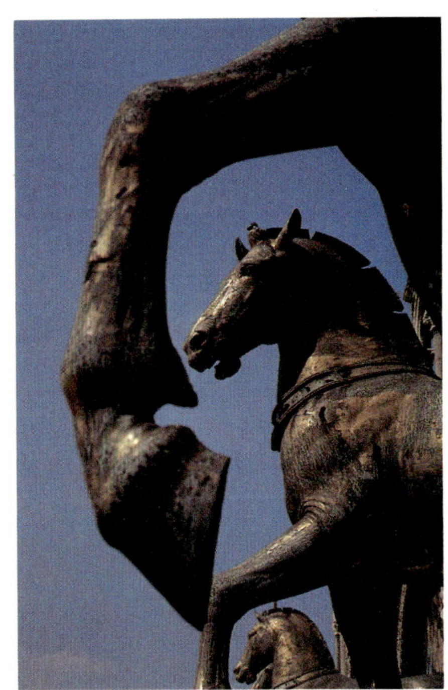

MAKE A CHECKLIST

Ask yourself these questions: When was the last time you took a picture from ground level? From the top of a building? From a chair? When was the last time you focused your camera at less than 10 feet (3m)? It's surprising how easily you can lapse into a routine without exploring the full possibilities of a subject.

Consider making a checklist of possible viewpoints and trying them next time:

- From left and right.
- From behind.
- From a high viewpoint.
- From close up.
- From far away.
- Including foreground interest.
- Using a foreground object to frame the subject.
- Directly into the light.
- Lying on the ground.
- Directly above the subject.

These pictures were taken from the balcony of St. Mark's Basilica in Venice. They show how, by careful choice of viewpoint, you can control exactly what is in the picture to make a personal interpretation. For the picture above, Van Phillips chose a viewpoint that accurately reflects what the horses look like. In the other four shots, Malcolm Crowthers was trying to dramatize a quotation from Petrarch, for whom these horses seemed "to neigh and paw the ground with their hooves." Lower left: Crowthers lay on his back, hanging over the balcony slightly, to "capture" the descending hoof. The impression is helped by the viewpoint.

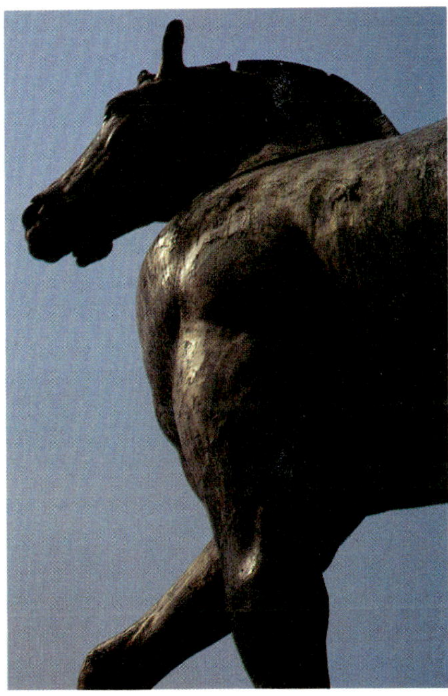

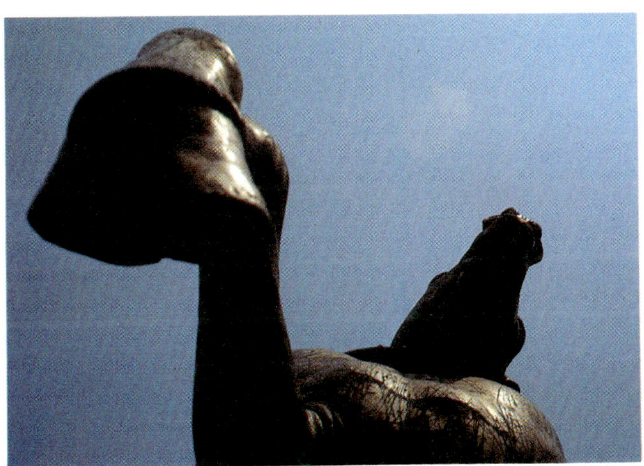

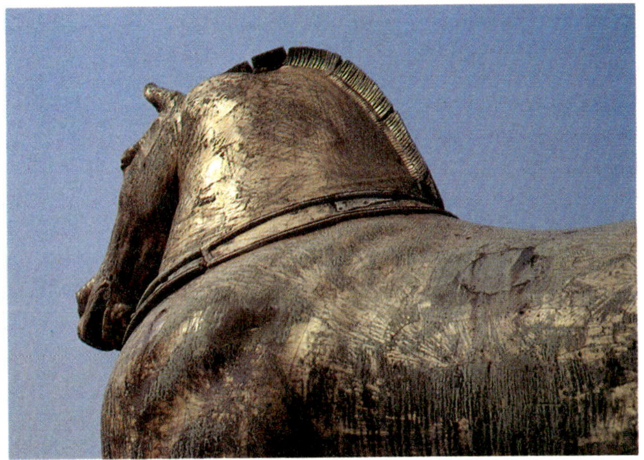

The Right Moment

Sometimes, the moment you release the shutter is of vital importance. The split-second decision a photographer makes when he presses the shutter release is the crucial factor in the majority of great pictures. Henri Cartier-Bresson has described it as "the decisive moment," and it can occur as dramatically in a landscape or portrait as in a sports photograph.

REACTING QUICKLY

Judging the right moment to take a photograph is important. For photos of people, it is often obvious. For example, in a sports shot, the best time will usually be at the peak of the action or when the subject reacts with a spontaneous expression.

Other subjects are more difficult. A landscape may appear static, but if you look carefully, you will see that it is constantly changing. The position of the clouds may change, and this will affect the quality of the light. The time of day will also affect the color and strength of the light, and the time of year will alter the basic appearance of the landscape. At one moment it may be possible to include a bird in your composition or a passing car or person. Or, the wind may shift direction and change the shape of the trees.

Taking the photograph at the correct moment is not always easy, but it can make an important difference in your pictures. Watch carefully and take advantage of opportunities as they appear. You may never get a second chance.

Photography has one unique advantage over other visual arts: It can record an occasion or event at the instant it takes place. You will not be able to capture every moment of an action, nor is that action likely to occur in precisely the same way again.

▶ One of the many interesting aspects of this photograph is the incongruity of the scene—monks playing in the snow. Mario Giacomelli caught the peak moment of the action precisely, captured in the strong graphic shapes of the whirling cloaks. In rapidly changing situations such as this, it is best to make several exposures and choose the best composition later.

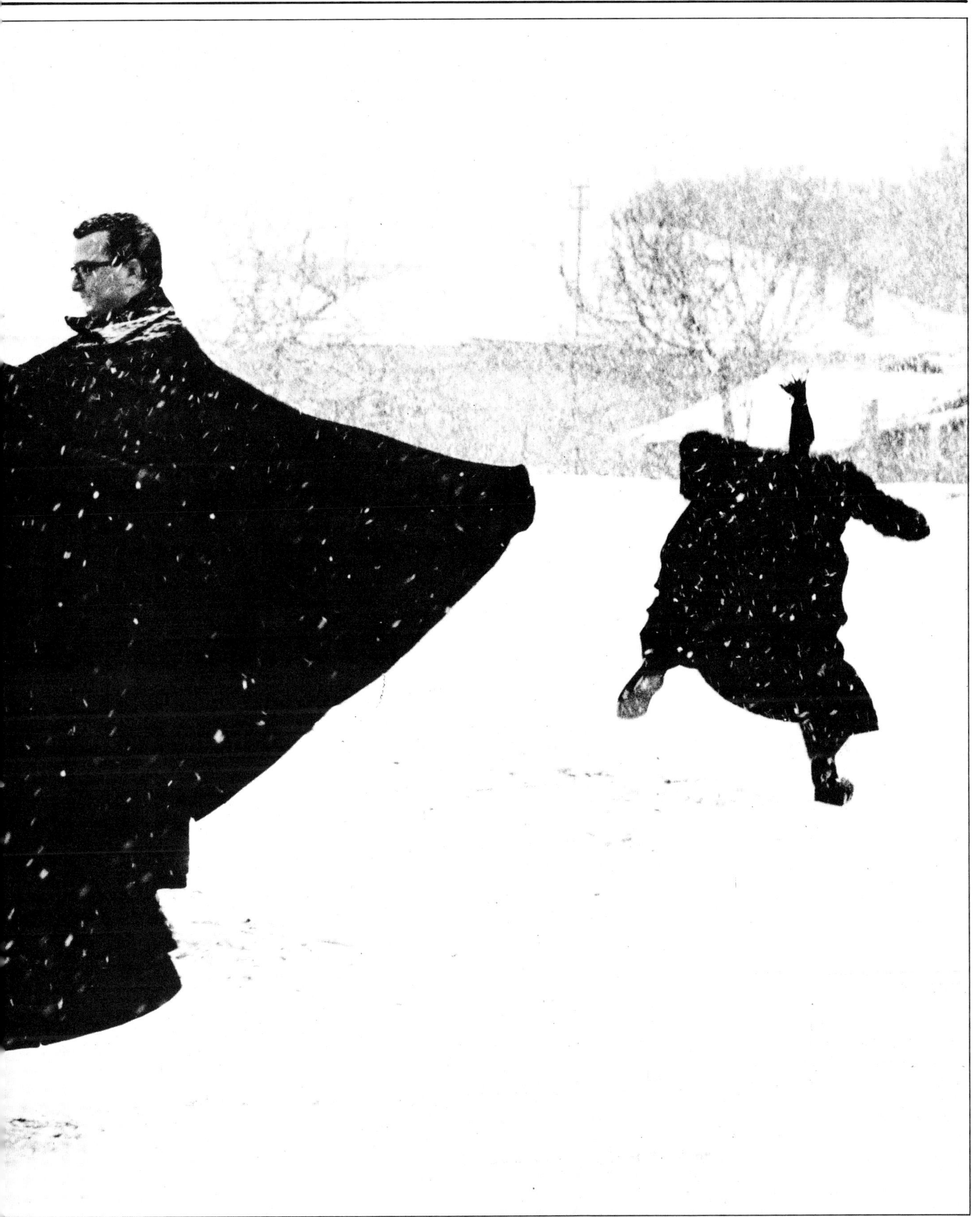

ANTICIPATION

The perfect composition rarely presents itself immediately. Usually a situation has the potential for a good photograph, but the elements have not quite come together or something is lacking. This is the time to wait and see what develops, rather than make a hasty, not quite perfect picture.

A sunset, for example, is often most spectacular a few seconds before the sun disappears below the horizon. It's worth waiting for this moment—then be prepared to take a few shots quickly.

Alternatively, the composition could perhaps be improved by including a person to give the rest of the scene a sense of scale. In that case, wait for a passerby. Don't take the picture the instant the individual appears. While waiting, you will have had time to figure out the best position for the individual. Wait until he gets there, and then take the photograph. Or, you can ask a friend to pose for you.

Once you see picture elements "coming together," you begin to anticipate a good picture. Sometimes you may even have the feeling that you are controlling things like clouds and distant people—willing them to do what you want.

SPORTS AND ACTION PHOTOS

Anticipation is a key factor in precise timing of exposures for sports and action photography. People in motion often pause at dramatic moments. This gives you the opportunity to capture the action without image blur. A basketball player at the top of his leap, a golfer at the end of his swing, or a baseball pitcher as he releases the ball are examples.

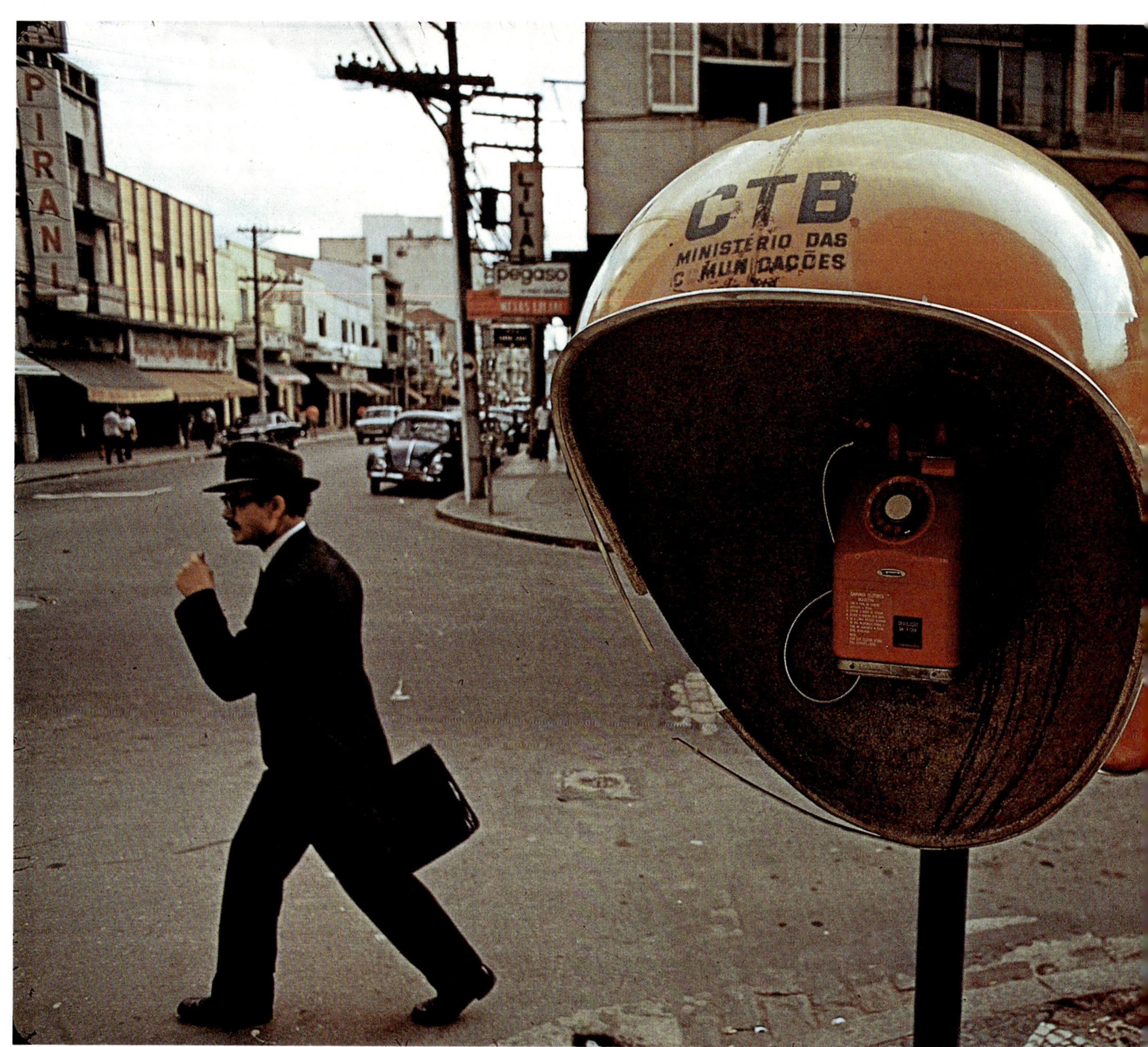

▶ Quick reactions helped David Hurn get this image of an unexpected moment of levity at a formal dinner.

▼ Often, a good photograph has to be anticipated. Bruno Barbey first composed this picture leaving a space for a person to walk into. Then he waited. When the right kind of person came along, he made the exposure.

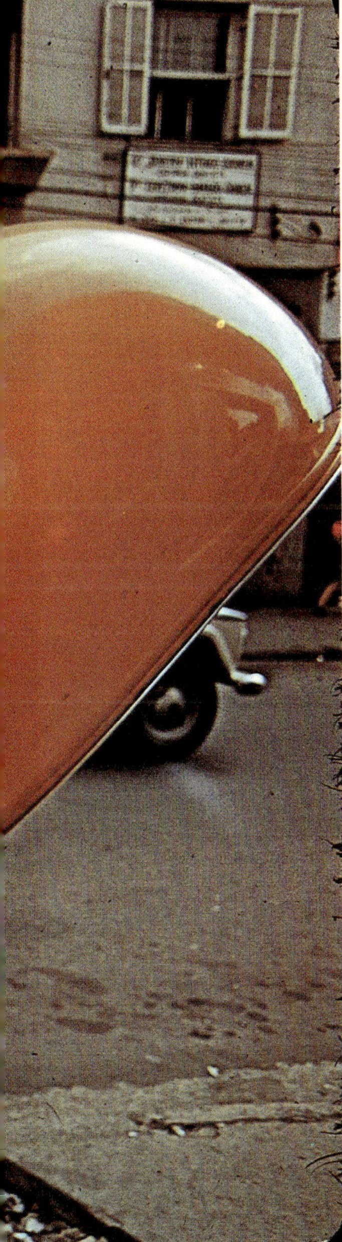

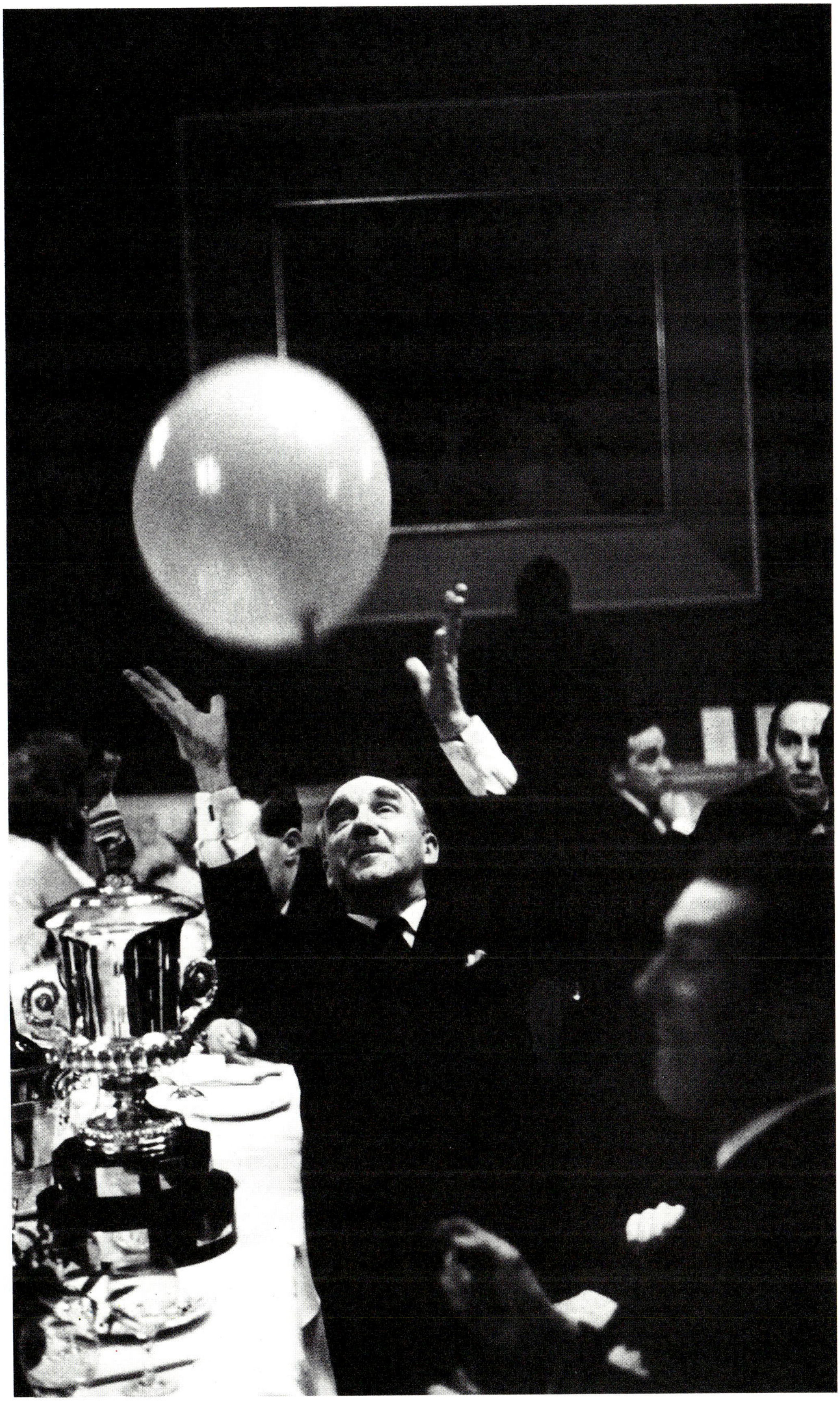

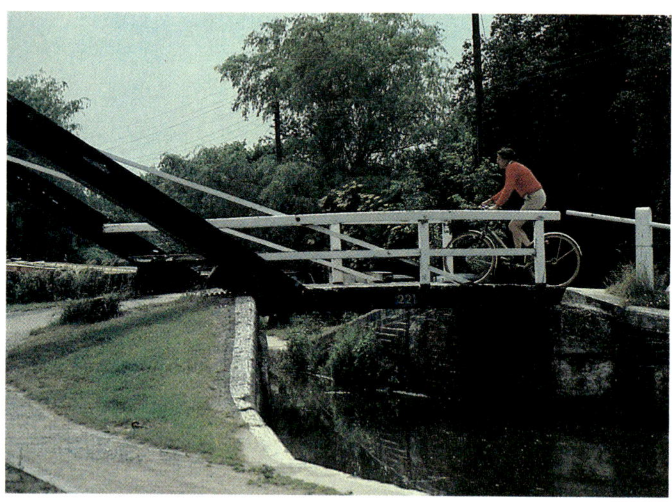

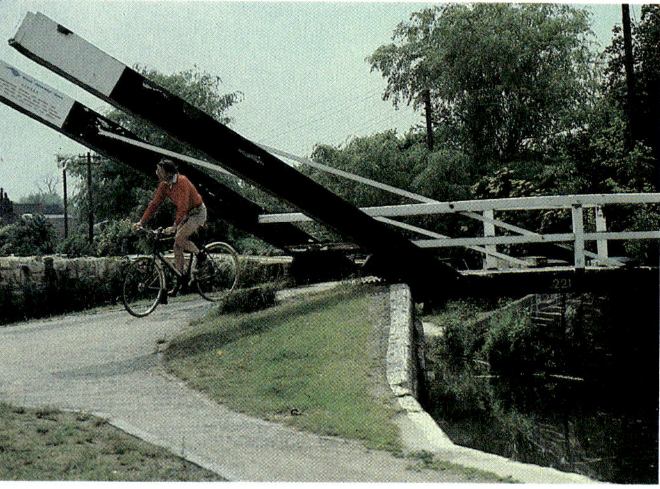

▲ When a composition includes a moving subject like this man on his bicycle, it can look unbalanced if the movement leads the eye out of the picture, rather than into it. A little forethought about basic composition can help you decide when to make the exposure. Photo by Michael Busselle.

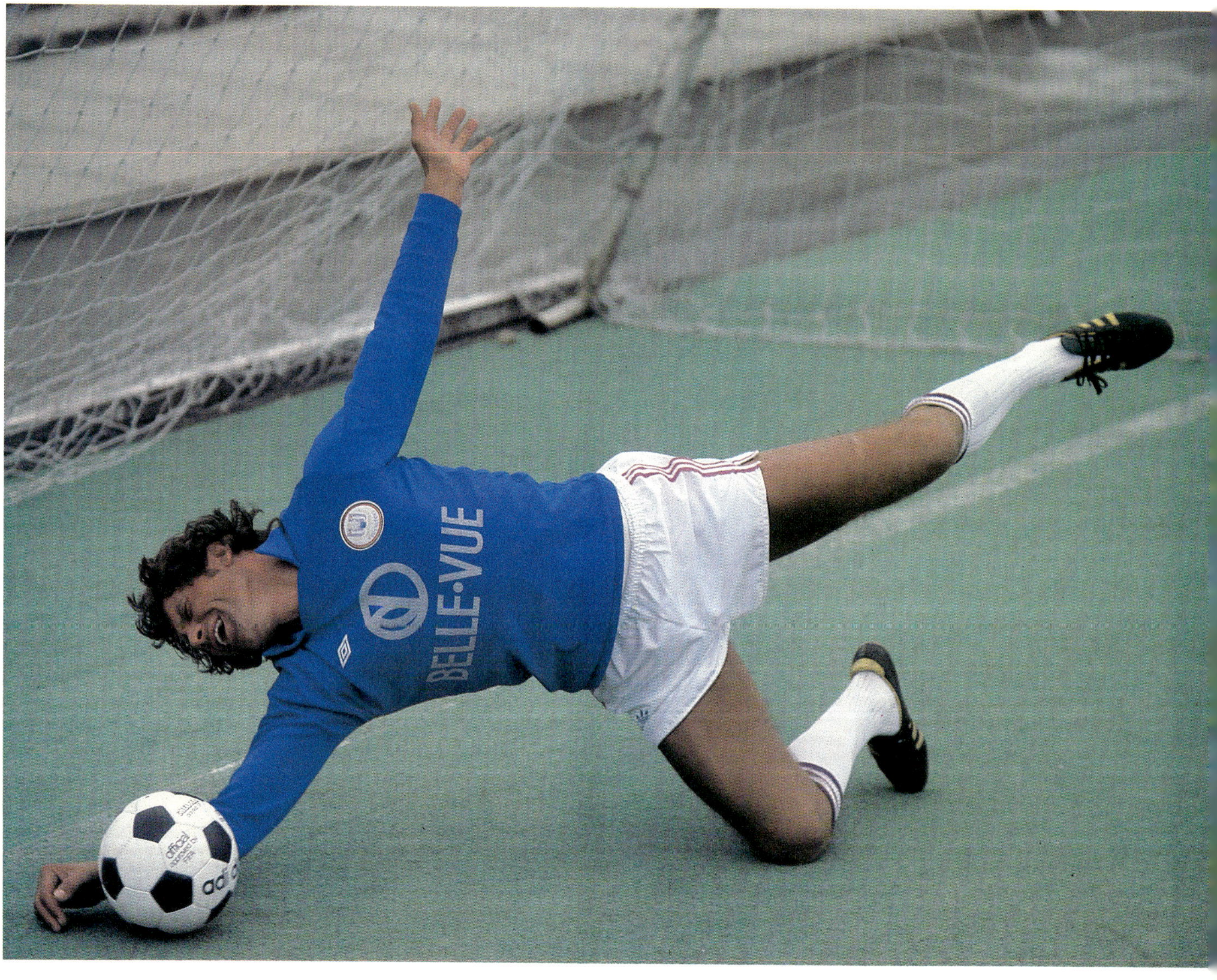

You would need almost superhuman reactions to capture the peak moment of a sports action without having followed the sequence of movements preceding it. By watching carefully, you should be able to anticipate when the action will reach its climax. Even a motor-driven camera at five frames per second can miss this crucial moment. But the photographer who pays close attention and knows his equipment should be able to get what he wants almost every time.

TAKING MORE THAN ONE FRAME

Professional photographers often shoot many rolls of film of one subject. Some amateurs believe this is to get at least one good frame. There may be a grain of truth in this, but the practice is based on more practical reasons.

To earn his living, the professional has to be sure of getting the best. Even with perfect anticipation at a particular moment, he can't guarantee that something unexpected won't happen a little later. So he continues shooting. Although you may not be able to afford the same amount of film, you can still apply this principle. Don't put your camera away after just one exposure—be ready for the unexpected. Shoot as much film as you can afford, and pick the best shot later.

CONTROLLING THE CAMERA

There is nothing more frustrating than to see the perfect picture and then find that by the time you have advanced the film, focused and set the camera controls, the scene has changed and the opportunity is gone.

Skill at handling camera controls is another vital factor when shooting action. Practice without film in your camera until handling the camera becomes instinctive. Then, when the right moment comes, you'll be ready.

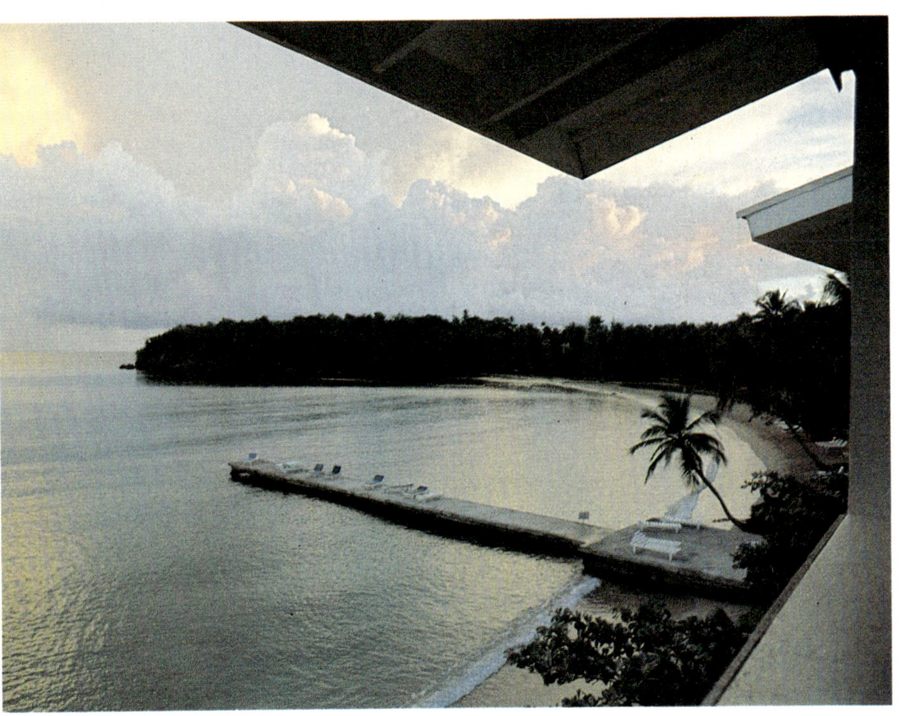

To make a good landscape or seascape photograph, timing is not critical in terms of seconds or minutes—but the time of day will certainly be important. These two photographs were taken from a hotel balcony in Jamaica. The one above was made at about 5 a.m., and the one below 6 hours later. Although the basic features remain the same, the picture is changed by the different light. In the early morning, the weak light produced a pale, moody photograph. Around midday, the colors became deeper, making the image much stronger. To experience the effects of the light at different times of day, try shooting the same scene every two hours. Photos by Gordon Ferguson.

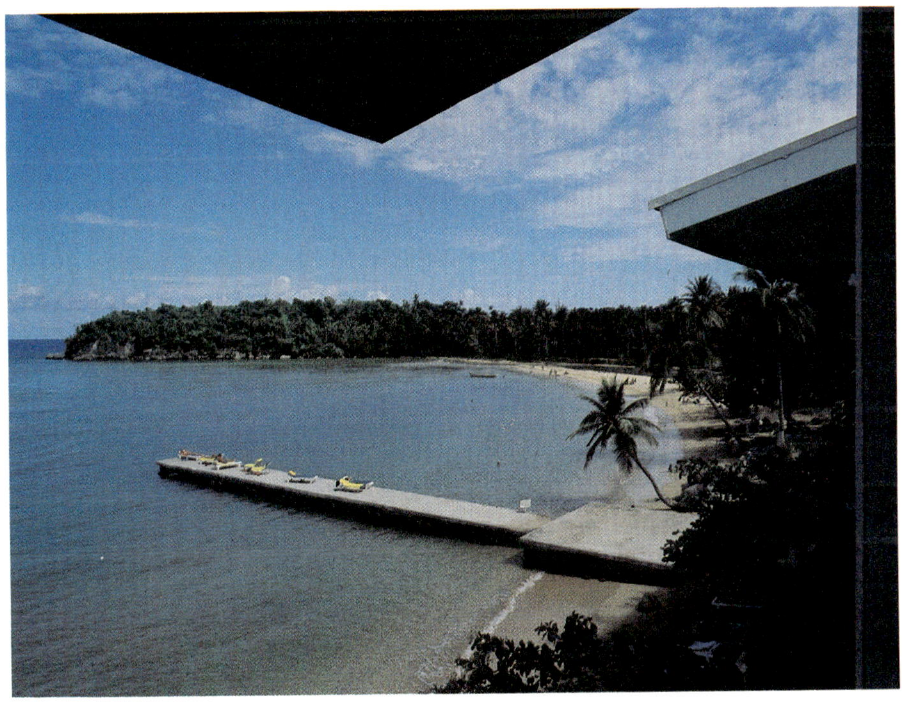

◀ Capturing the climax of an action in sports photography depends on anticipation and following each sequence of events carefully. But ability to use the camera controls well and quickly is equally important. Fast focusing is essential. A picture like this one by Tony Duffy would be useless if the player were out of focus.

Creating Silhouettes

A silhouette is the most elementary form an image can take. It is simply a dark shape on a light background. It is as interesting as the shape itself, yet silhouettes can tell a story in which the viewer mentally fills in the details. For example, the cut-out profiles of people often convey a strong likeness of the subject and reveal more than a little character.

Looking for silhouetted images is a good way to learn the basics of composition because the simple outlines show clearly how shapes within a frame relate to each other.

Shape alone is enough to identify some things, while others need more elements to be recognizable; the silhouette of a banana, for example, is enough to identify the subject, while the rounded outline of an orange is less easy to recognize.

HOW TO USE SILHOUETTES

A complete silhouette is rarely used in photography. A suggestion of color or tone, form or texture, or some background detail is usually included in the image. The purpose of such an image is to concentrate the viewer's attention on the shape or outline of the subject. A silhouette showing subdued details, rather than one with the details completely blacked out, is an effective way of doing this. By using semi-silhouettes, something is left to the imagination, and this in itself can suggest mystery.

HOW TO CREATE SILHOUETTES

Silhouettes can be produced several ways: You can use natural or artificial light,

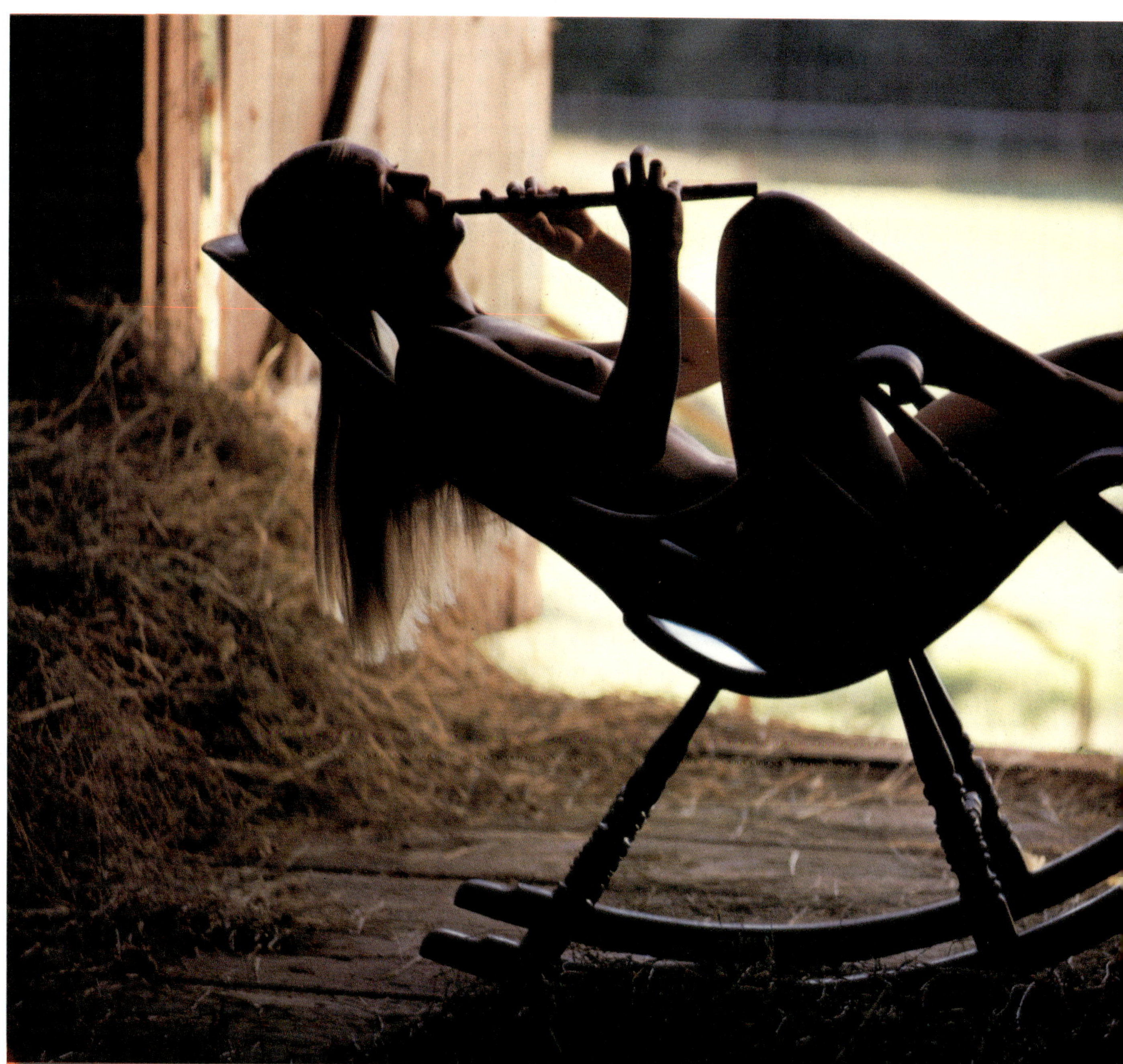

shoot into the sun, or take advantage of foggy or misty conditions.

Natural Lighting—To create a silhouette, use a background that is brighter than the subject. A simple way to do this in natural light is to place the subject in front of a window or open doorway, with the light behind the subject. Outdoors, simply photograph the subject against the sky. Base exposure on the brightness of the background and the subject will appear in silhouette.

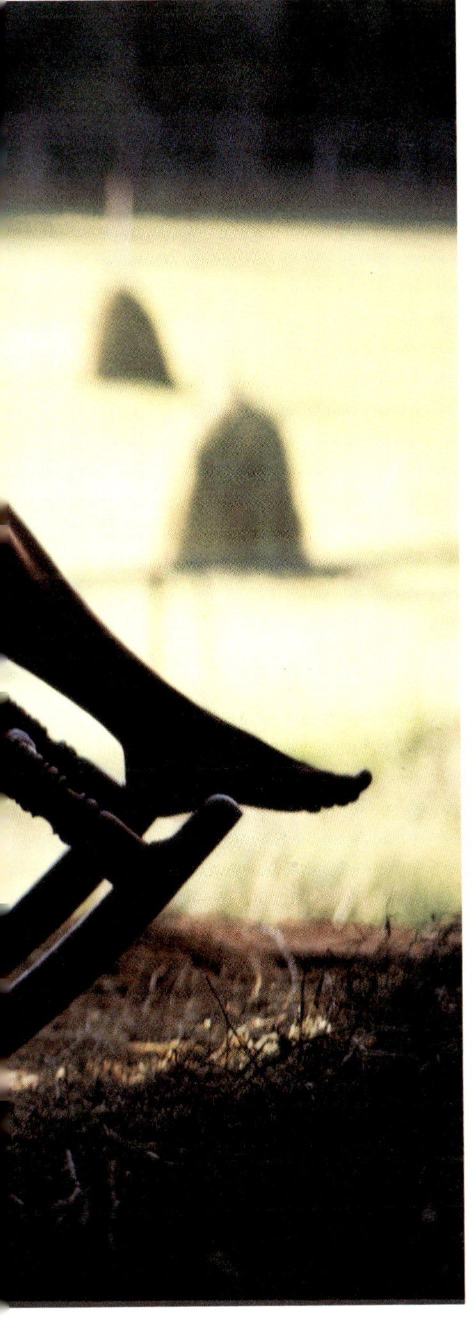

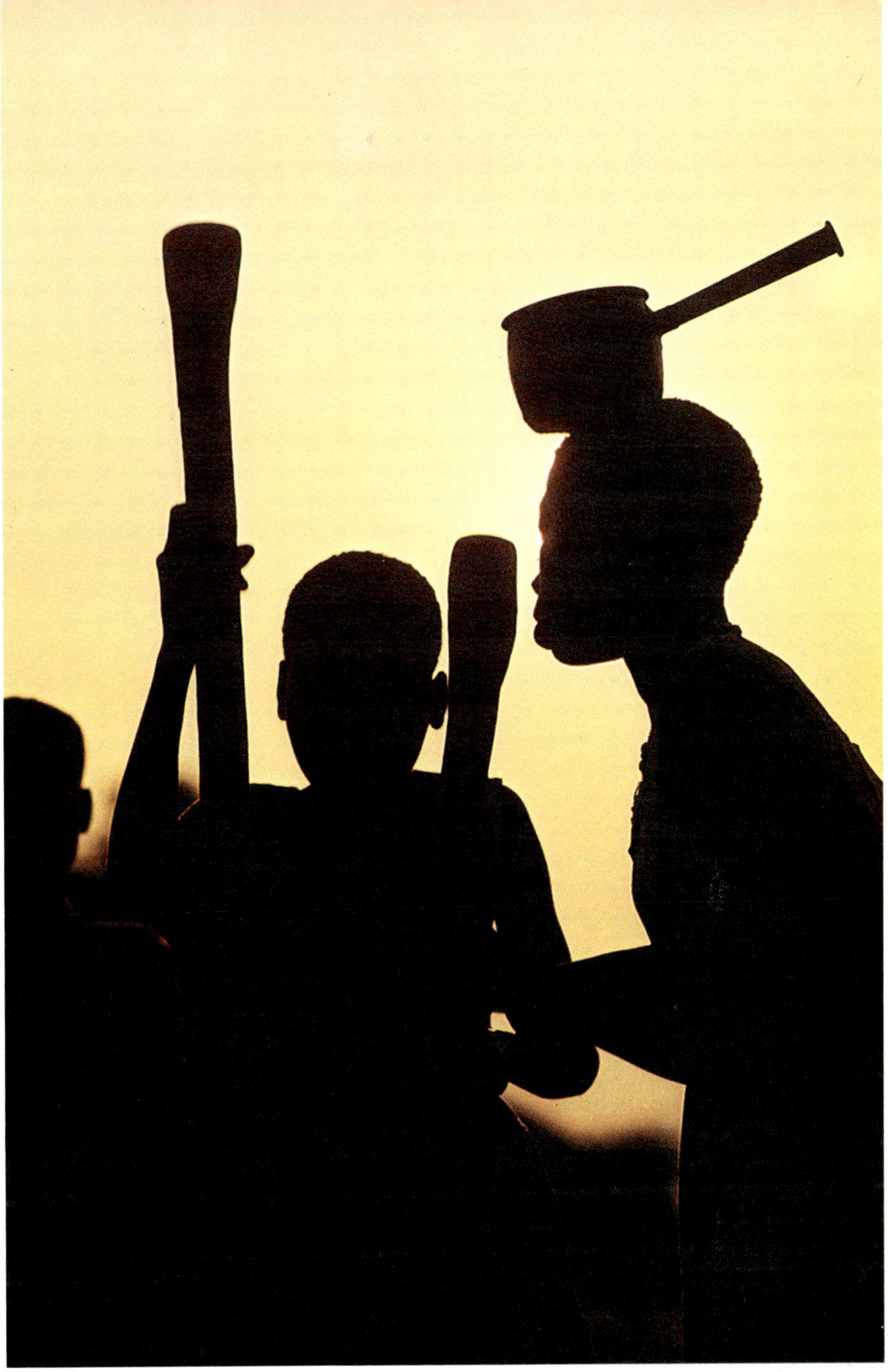

▲ This silhouette was created by shooting toward the sun. John Bulmer positioned himself so the sun was behind the figures. He determined exposure from the sky to underexpose foreground detail.

▶ Silhouettes can frame a photograph too, providing foreground emphasis without competing with the main subject.

◀ The girl is carefully positioned in a doorway so both she and the rocking chair present a clear, explicit outline. Photo by Michael Boys.

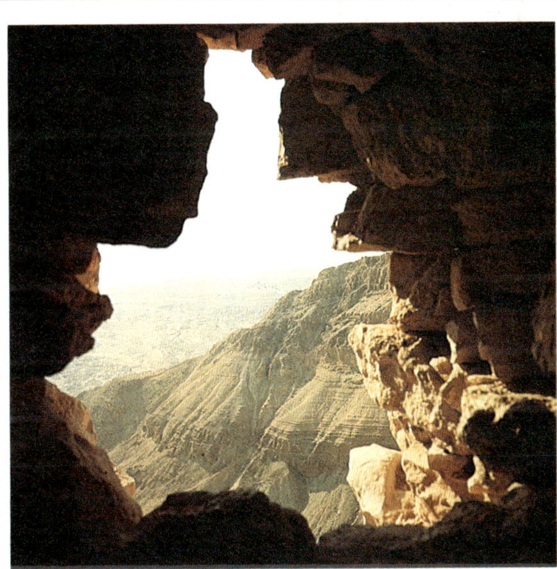

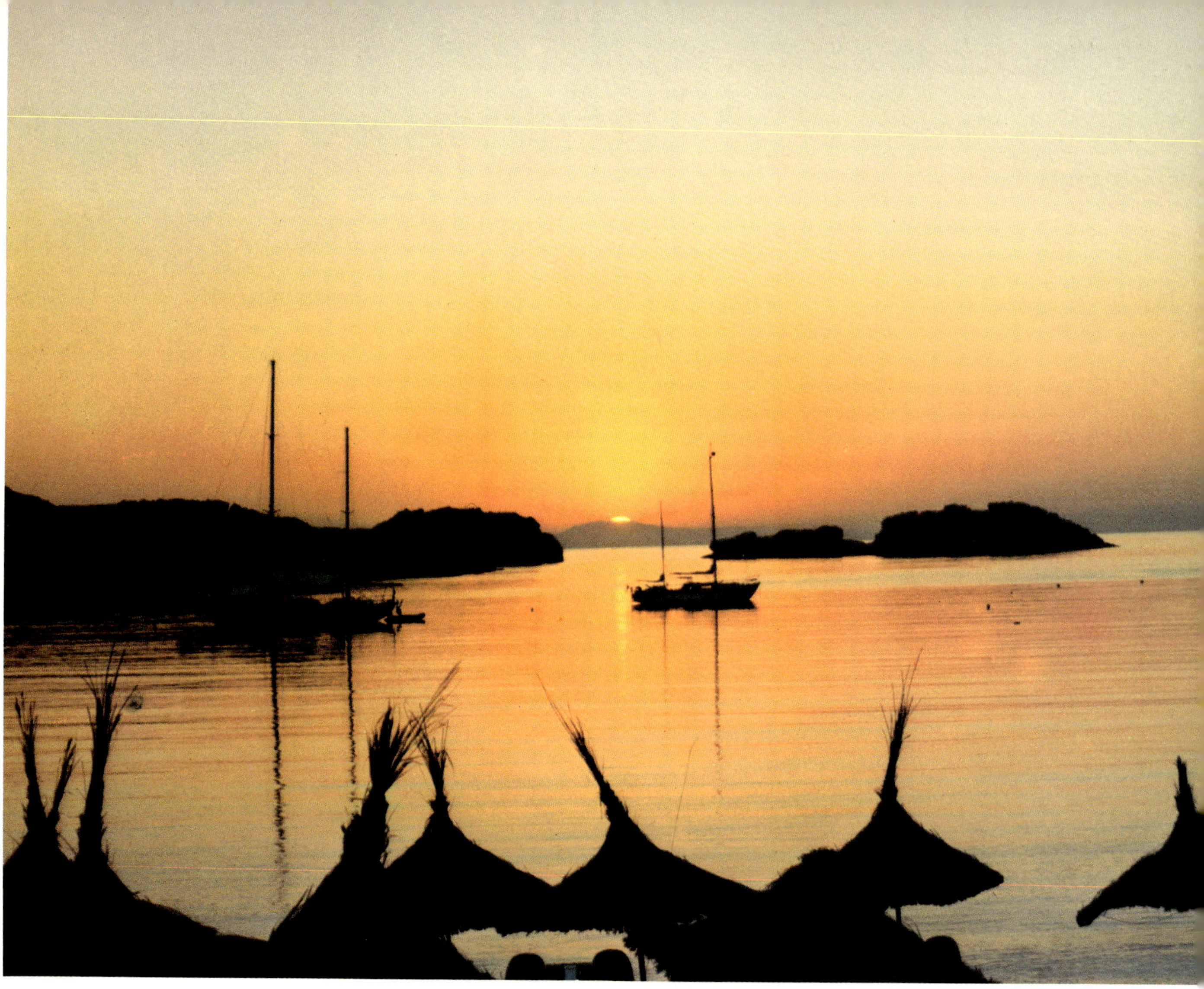

Studio Lighting—With studio lighting it is possible to control the light more precisely than with natural lighting. Limit the light falling on the subject and be sure it illuminates only the background.

In all cases, it is important that exposure readings be taken only from lit background areas to be sure that the subject itself remains as an underexposed dark tone.

The Sun—Shooting toward the sun is a convenient way of producing a silhouette, especially if the background has a light tone, such as water, sand or sky. Again, expose for the highlight areas. Shield the lens from direct sunlight because this can cause flare and lower image contrast which reduces the effect of the silhouette. Even a lens hood is not always adequate protection when pointing the camera toward the sun. A useful trick is to throw a shadow over the lens by holding your hand or an 18 to 20 inch (0.5m) piece of cardboard in front of the lens—out of the field of view of the lens, of course. Never look directly at the sun through the viewfinder or any other optical instrument.

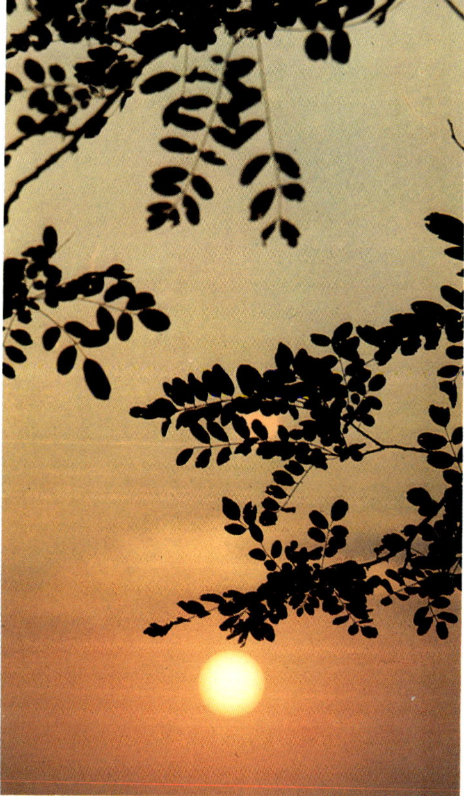

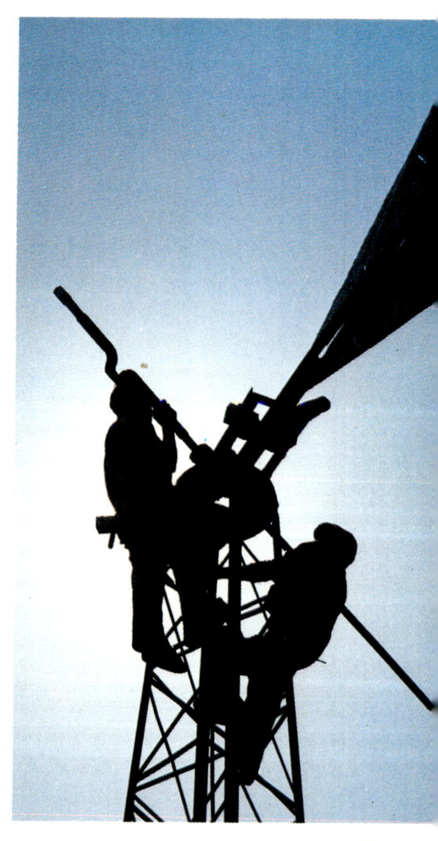

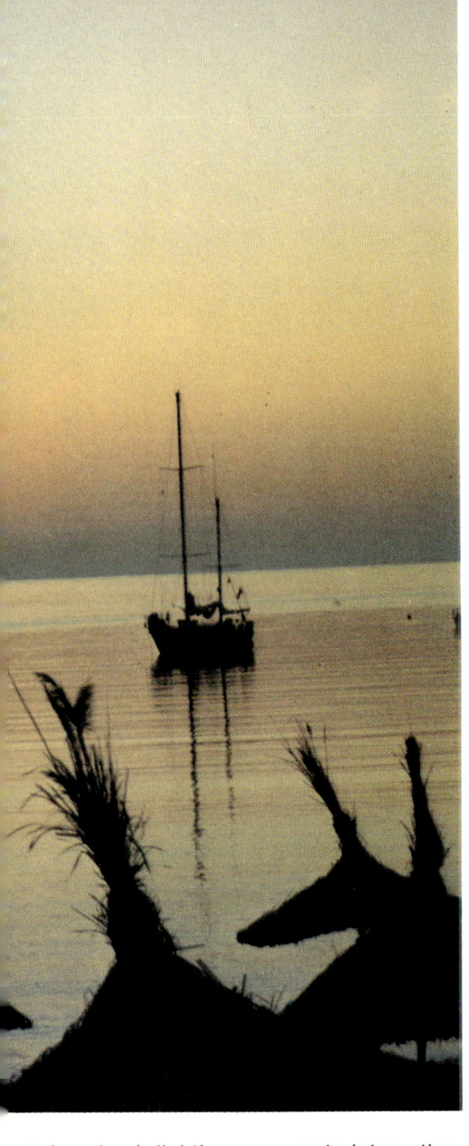

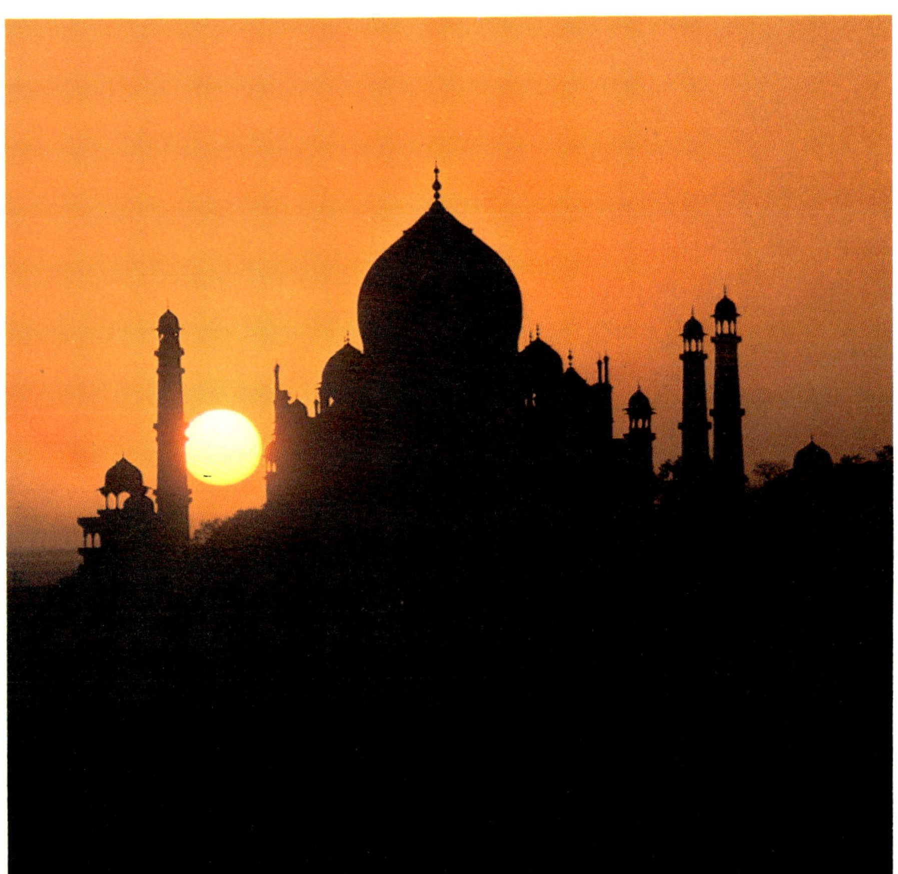

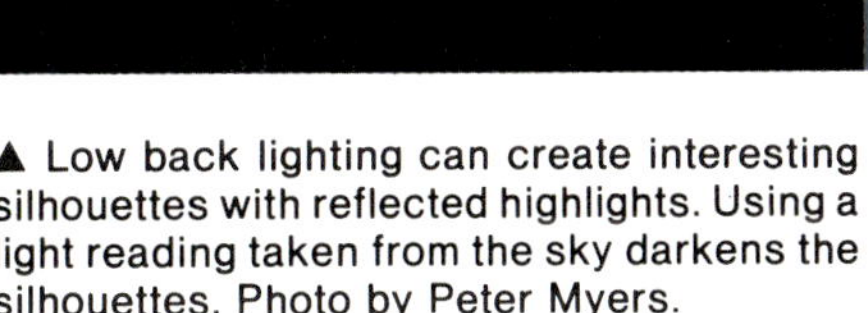

▲ Low back lighting can create interesting silhouettes with reflected highlights. Using a light reading taken from the sky darkens the silhouettes. Photo by Peter Myers.

▶ Top right, right: When shooting toward the sun, consider how important its placement is. With the sun rising, the light is strong, resulting in high contrast and a black silhouette. Before dawn, the softer light reflected from the sky creates less contrast. The top picture was exposed for sky. The lower one was exposed for the building. Photos by George Rodger.

◀ Far left: You can find good silhouette subjects almost anywhere. A sunset framed by a pattern of leaves is more interesting than a sunset alone. Photo by George Rodger.

◀ Left: Look for unusual shapes. The dramatic diagonal was created by shooting from a low position, looking up. Placing the sun behind the subject increased contrast. Photo by Spike Powell.

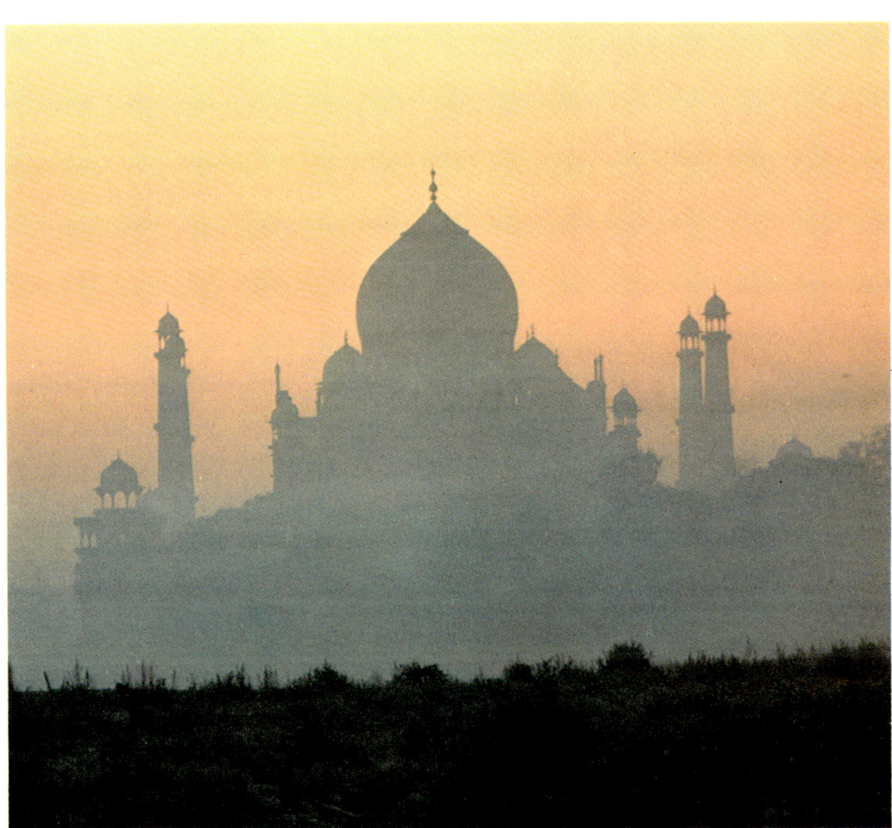

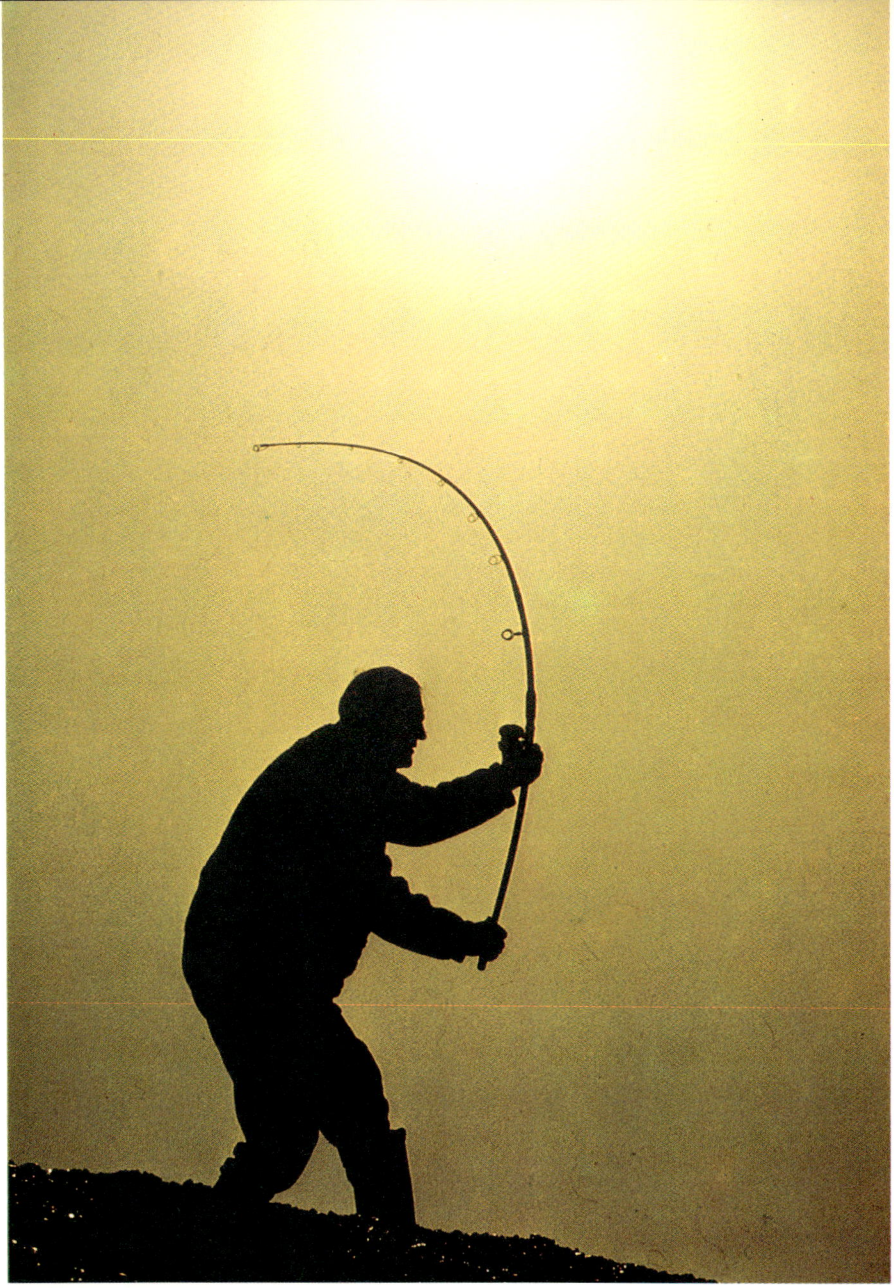

◀ A background of mist, and a low camera position created this bold image. The mist stops flare from the sun by veiling it. Note how the silhouette emphasizes the tension of the fishing rod.

Below left: For this photograph, Chris Smith aimed into the sun, which is masked by one of the figures. He used a low camera position to be sure the cyclists made clean, clear shapes against the sky.

▼ Camera position here is important. Michael Busselle moved in slowly until the moment the deer were clearly on the horizon.

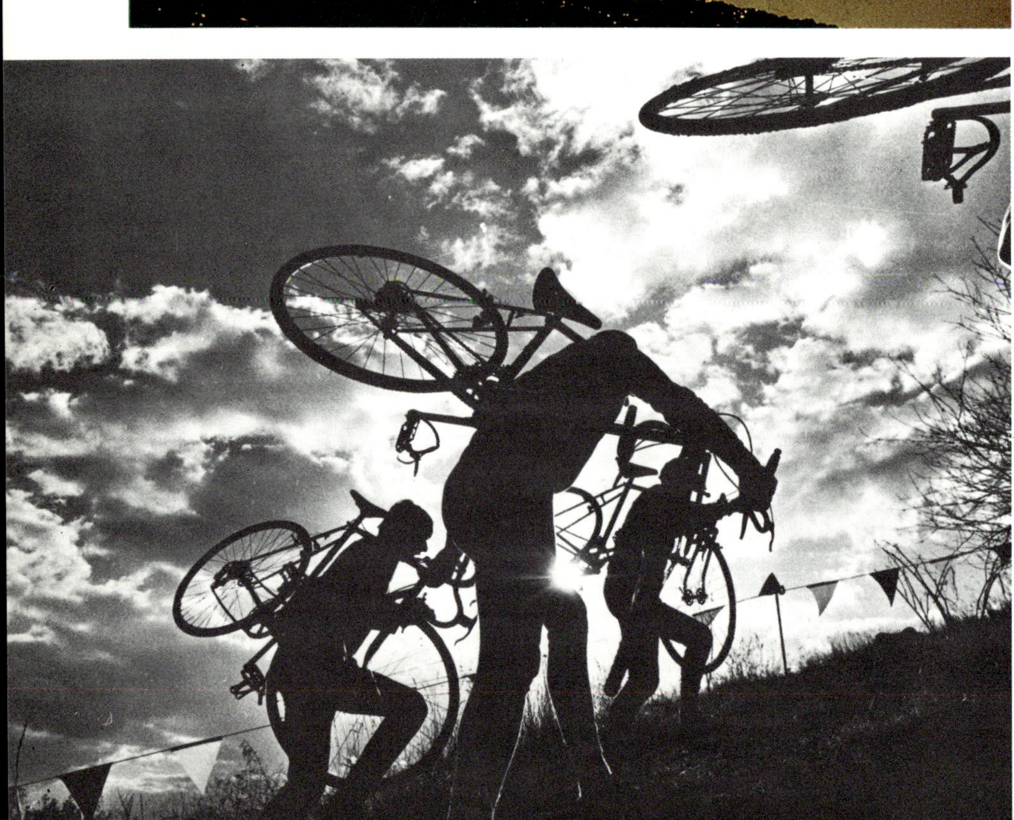

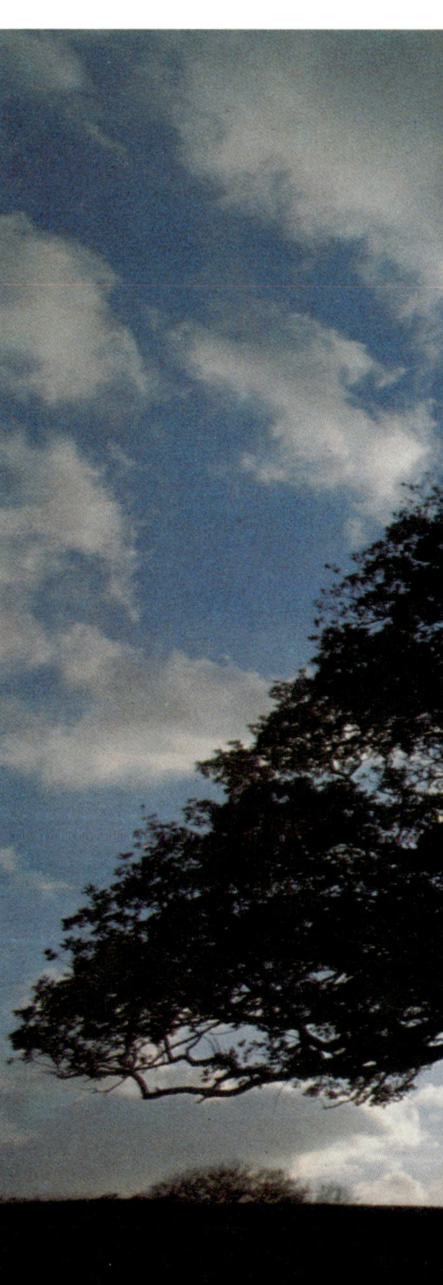

Fog and Night Lights—Fog or mist subdues background details so only the objects in the immediate foreground are seen clearly, another way of creating silhouetted images. A complex subject like a woodland scene can be reduced to an image of stark simplicity in mist or fog, especially when combined with back lighting. Street scenes at night can also result in bold silhouetted pictures under these conditions. Exposure for subjects like these is fairly critical. Too little will produce muddy tones in the background and too much will weaken the silhouette effect. A useful method is to take an average from both the darker foreground and the brightest highlight in the background.

SILHOUETTE AND VIEWPOINT

Viewpoint is always one of the most vital decisions a photographer has to make. By finding a position that gives a silhouette effect to your subject, you achieve one of the main aims of good composition—separating the center of interest from the background. Of course there are other ways of doing this, such as using selective focus or color variation, but a viewpoint that results in a bold tonal contrast between the subject and its background is basic and often the most effective.

You may need to move to the right or left to place a highlight tone in the background behind the subject. For a portrait, you can move the subject as well.

A low viewpoint allows the subject to be silhouetted against the sky. You can shoot from ground level to increase this effect. In addition to the silhouetting effect, a low viewpoint invariably adds impact to a picture. Conversely, a higher than normal viewpoint often removes unwanted background tone and detail—as little as 1 foot (30cm) can make a big difference. This is why many professional photographers prefer rigid camera cases they can stand on to give them a slightly higher viewpoint when nothing else is available.

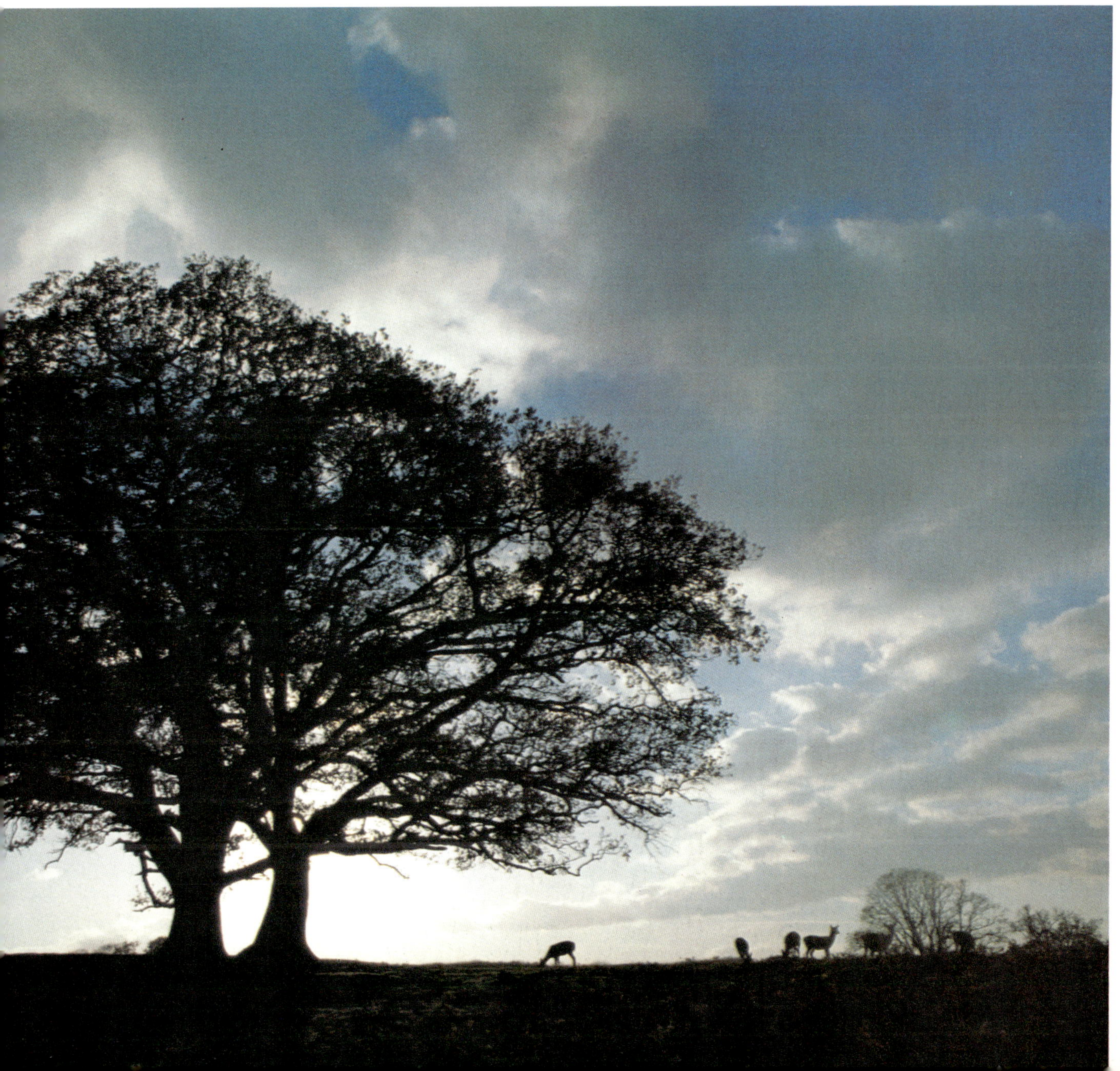

Line and Shape

If you trace the main outlines of successful photographs, you will find that the resulting tracings have a pleasing and balanced quality. This is because these lines represent the basic framework of the picture. Without a sound basis it is unlikely that a satisfying photograph will be produced.

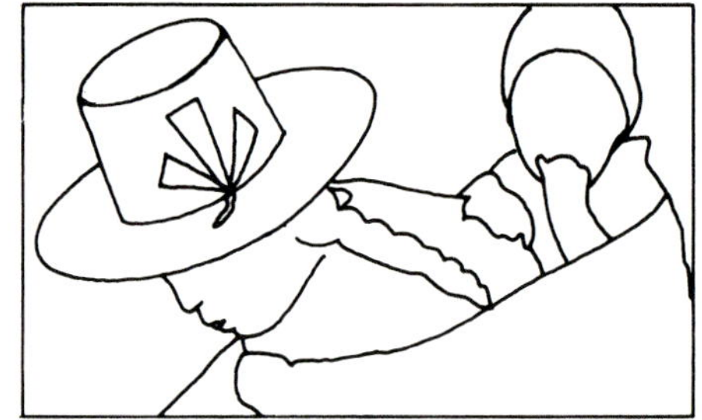

◀ Tracing the main lines and shapes of the photograph below gives a well-balanced and recognizable image. The tracing makes it easier to see the picture's basic composition—a series of circles with a strong, carefully placed, diagonal that breaks the harmony of the circles.

▼ Bottom: When a subject is in partial silhouette, the image has to rely on the subject's shape for impact. Although simple, a photograph like this requires careful composition. The tower was silhouetted and placed in the frame to add interest and balance the composition.

MAKING TRACINGS

In some photographs the main outlines are very clear, but in others, the main shapes and lines may not be obvious. To discover which elements make up the basic framework of a picture, trace the

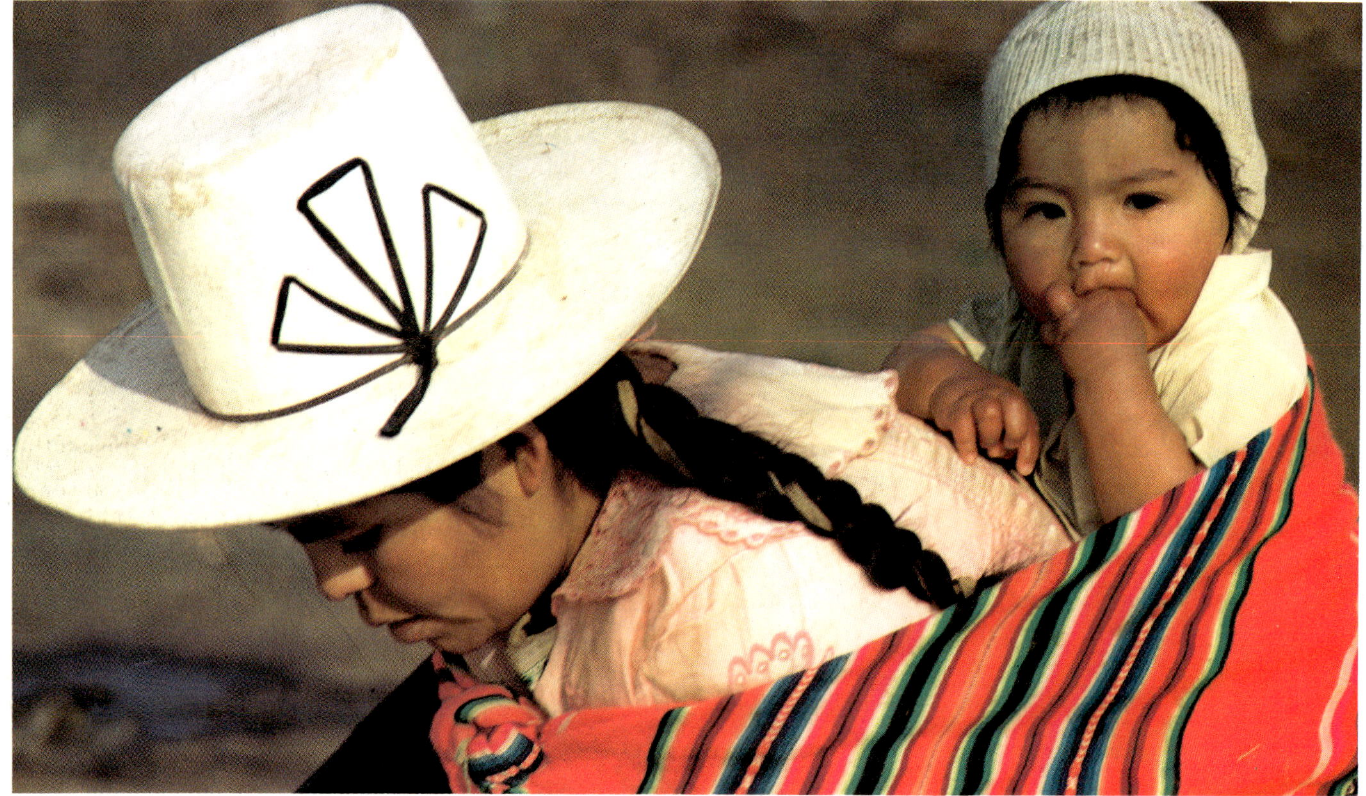

dominant lines and shapes of photographs you like and one in which you find the composition disappointing. Then compare the results. It should be easy to see why one fails and others are successful, and which elements influence the overall structure.

DOMINANT LINES AND SHAPES

Lines and shapes are created by a variety of things:

1) The outline of the main subject.

2) When a picture includes a horizon or other equally strong division, the line it creates is usually dominant and its position strongly influences the overall balance.

3) Boundaries between contrasting areas of tone or color can be important elements in the composition.

4) Lines created by the effect of perspective can add to or detract from overall balance.

The effect of shape is most easily seen in photographs in which the main subject is either silhouetted or boldly contrasted against the background.

Shapes created by lighting that causes strong highlights or shadows can be equally dominant. In hard directional light—midday sunlight, for example—background shapes and shadows can become more powerful than the subject. Once you start to look for them, these elements become easy to recognize.

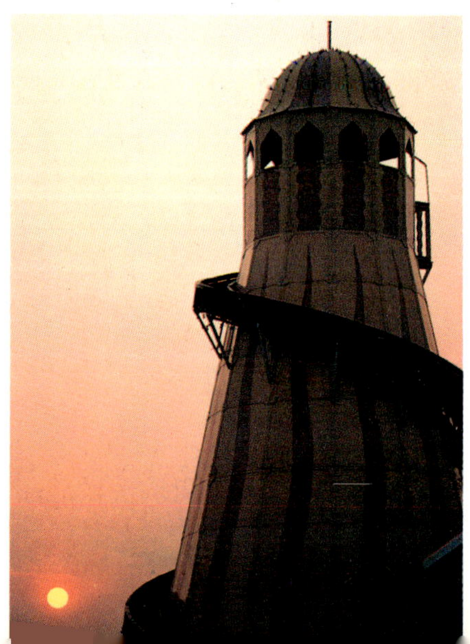

Visualizing a rough sketch of the subject is the first important step in the process of composing a picture. Train yourself to notice these lines and shapes in the viewfinder long before you consider taking the picture. Without this awareness, creating well-composed pictures is often a happy accident.

▶ Usually it is not advisable to divide a photograph down the middle. In this case, however, the dominant shapes are completely symmetrical and the strong central division enhances the effect.

▼ Horizontal lines emphasized by bands of color produce a restful image. Here, the photographer has taken particular care to position himself so the trees are seen clearly in silhouette.

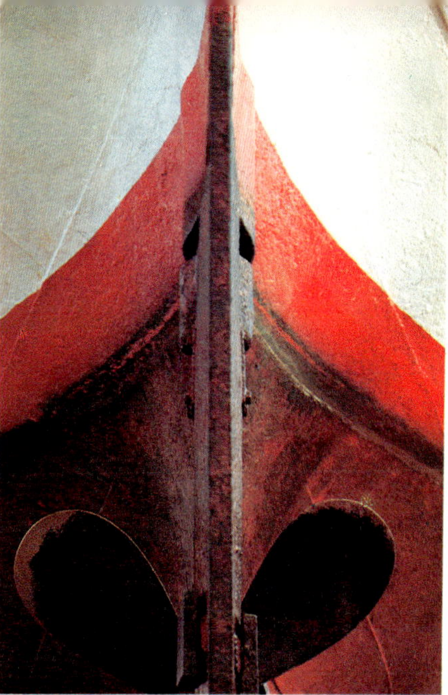

CONTRAST

Shapes and the way they react with each other is also important. Contrast is one way to make sure the subject draws the attention of the viewer. An effective way of achieving this is with a contrasting shape or line.

In a portrait, for example, you can enhance the roundness of face and eyes by using the model's arms and shoulders to create an angular contrast. You can also achieve contrast with even a small vertical line such as a human figure or a tree on an otherwise uncluttered horizon.

Contrast in shape alone is not always enough to achieve the desired impact; sometimes contrasting tone or color is needed. For instance, a red triangular sail on a blue sea is much more striking than a blue sail.

ALTERING THE MOOD

Lines and shape can have a strong effect on the mood of a picture. Where horizontal lines predominate, as in many landscapes, a relaxed and passive quality is created. A strong diagonal line is much more vigorous and assertive. When several similar shapes exist in the image—curves in a still life of a bowl of fruit, for example—the effect is usually restful and harmonious. Contrasting shapes or lines at different angles create a busy and a more exciting impression.

CONTROLLING LINE AND SHAPE

With many subjects you have a limited degree of control over line and shape. In portraits and still lifes, you can create shapes at will—but with landscapes you can only control the viewpoint and the way the picture is framed. It is often possible to minimize the effect of undesirable lines in a picture by choosing a viewpoint that allows foreground details to interrupt or obscure those lines. To introduce diagonal lines, work from a different viewpoint or tilt the camera.

You can soften obtrusive shapes by hiding part of their outlines behind other details, or by cropping in the camera. A different viewpoint often alters the lighting effect and reduces the tonal contrast between a shape and the background.

When you see which of these elements contributes to the picture and which detracts, it is usually possible to find a way of stressing the former and subduing the latter. And if no solution is possible, your awareness will spare you from wasting film on a disappointing result.

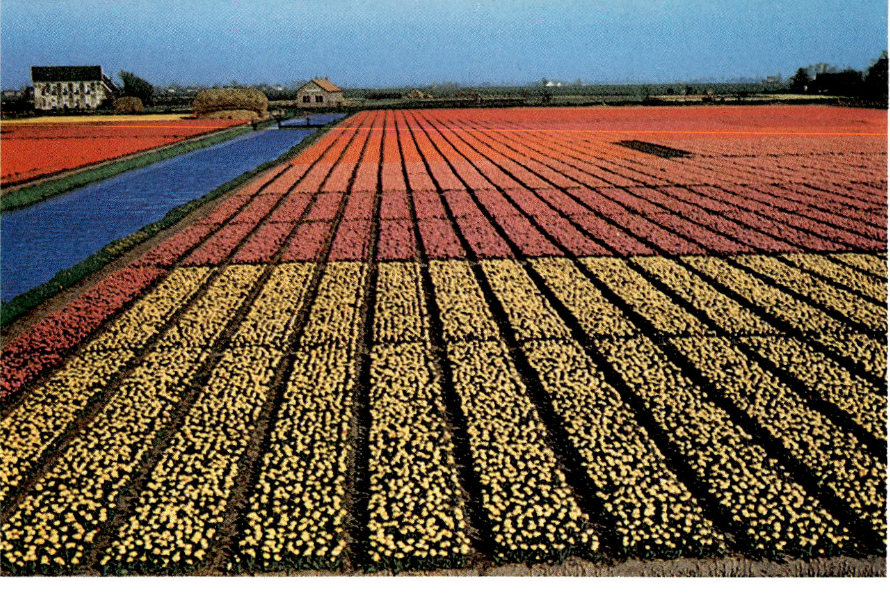

▲ George Rodger climbed on top of a shed to gain a high viewpoint for this image. This was essential to capture the interplay of the repeated straight lines in the tulip field.

▼ The rhythm of curves and lines in the Sydney Opera House produces an exhilarating, almost abstract, composition. When photographing buildings, look for repeated lines and see how they echo or conflict with the shape of the subject. Photo by Gordon Ferguson.

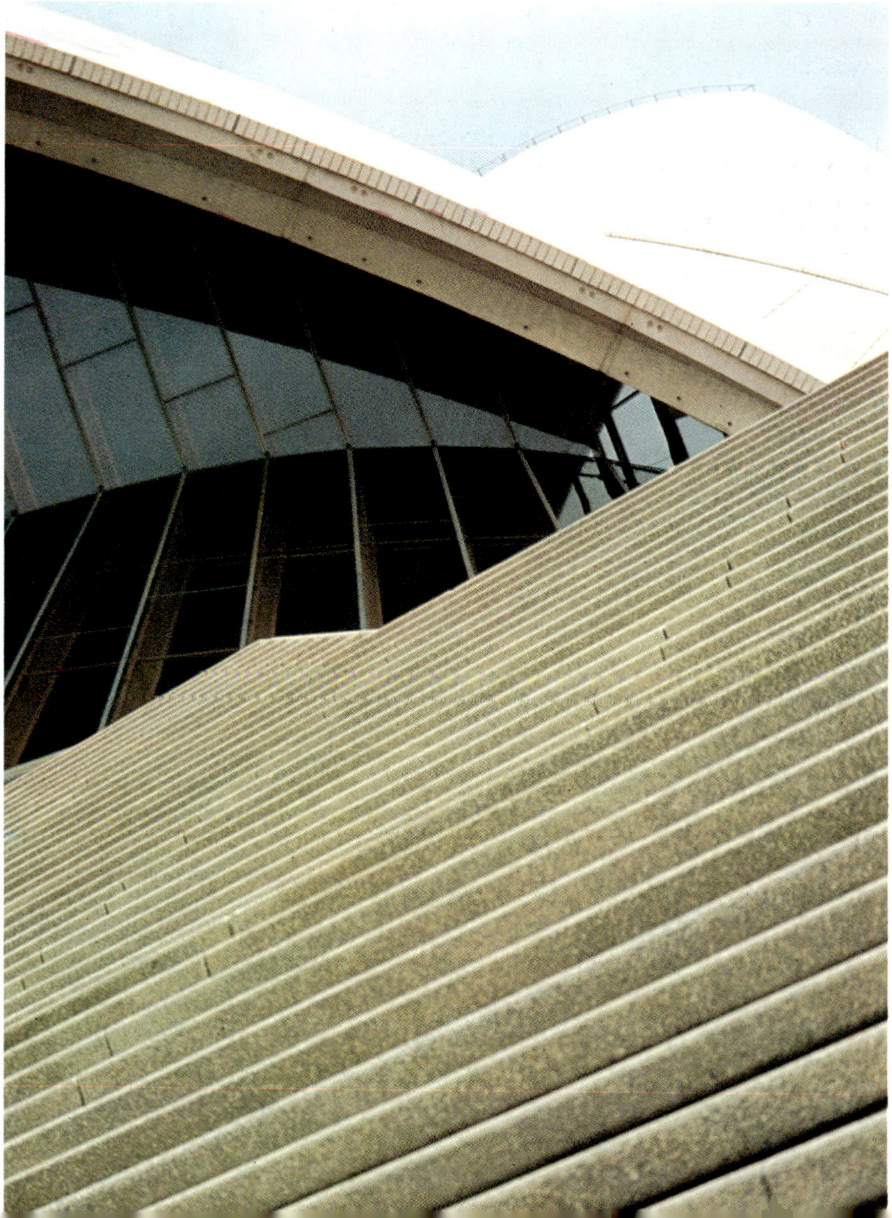

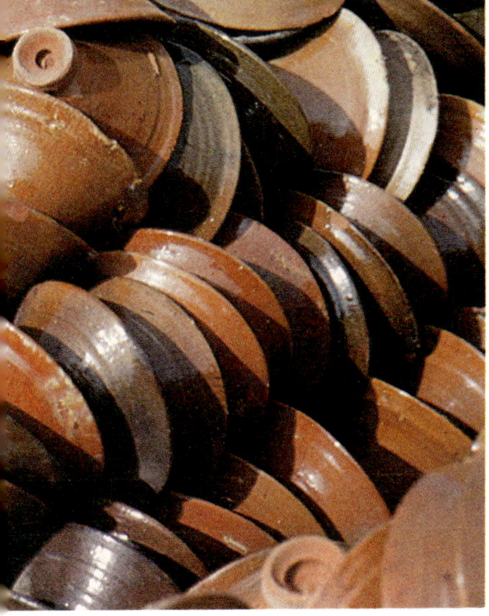

▲ Look for repeated curves or lines in haphazard arrangements.

► Contrast of color and shape prompted Michael Busselle to make this photograph. Try changing camera position to get the most effective contrast.

▼ Look at shapes from above. The strong diagonal of this pier is emphasized by bright directional sunlight and the dark shadow areas.

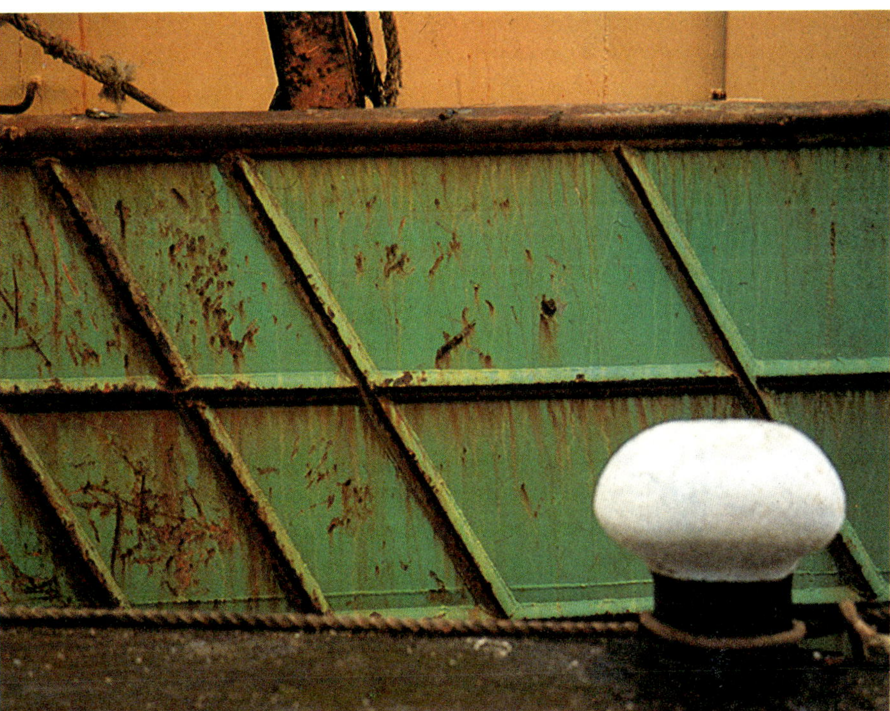

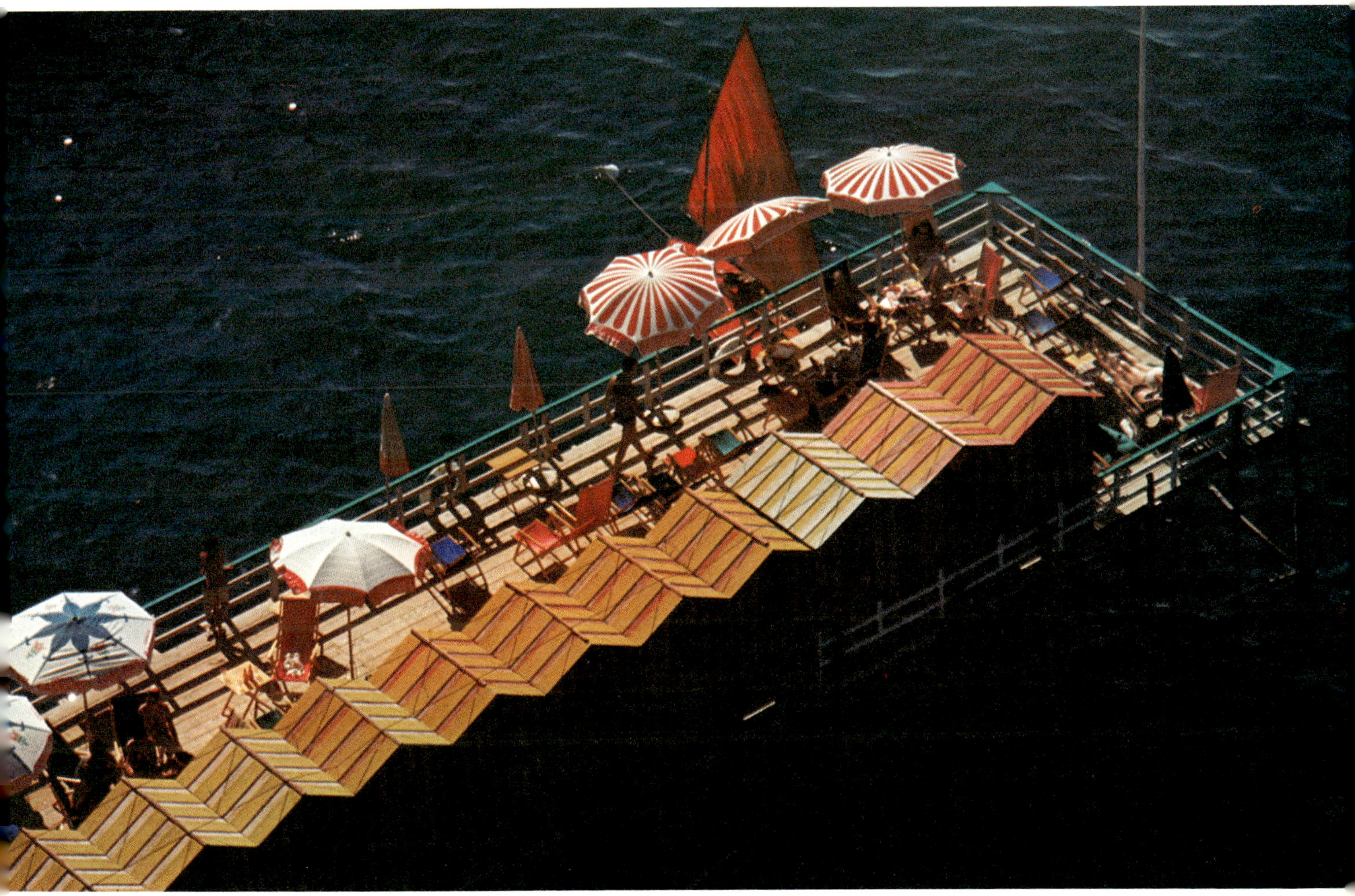

Discovering Patterns

In our lives, we are surrounded by patterns. In photography, these patterns can tease, amuse or stimulate the imagination. Skillfully used, the repetition of shapes or lines in a photograph helps create a rhythm and order that can make a particular picture memorable. The patterns the photographer uses need not always be exact geometric repetitions like the arches in a colonnade; they could be an impression of a pattern, such as expanding ripples of water, or branches traced against the sky.

WHERE TO FIND PATTERNS

Finding patterns is very much a question of being aware. To develop your "eye," look for locations with strong patterns and see how they are formed.

Patterns exist almost everywhere. Transient patterns exist only at a certain moment or from a particular viewpoint, such as faces in a crowd, a flock of flying birds or a parade of soldiers. There are also static patterns such as the windows in an office building or a row of houses, the bark of a tree or the ripples left in sand after the tide has gone out.

HOW TO USE PATTERNS

It is unlikely that a picture relying solely on patterns will have any lasting appeal, although it may have an initial impact. Therefore, patterns should be used only as a strong element of a photograph and not as the sole reason for taking it.

A strong pattern can create a reassuring, restful and ordered atmosphere in an image. But remember that patterns are usually busy and complex, so the main subject of the picture should be simple and bold, and placed in a dominating position within the frame. Otherwise, that subject may be completely overwhelmed.

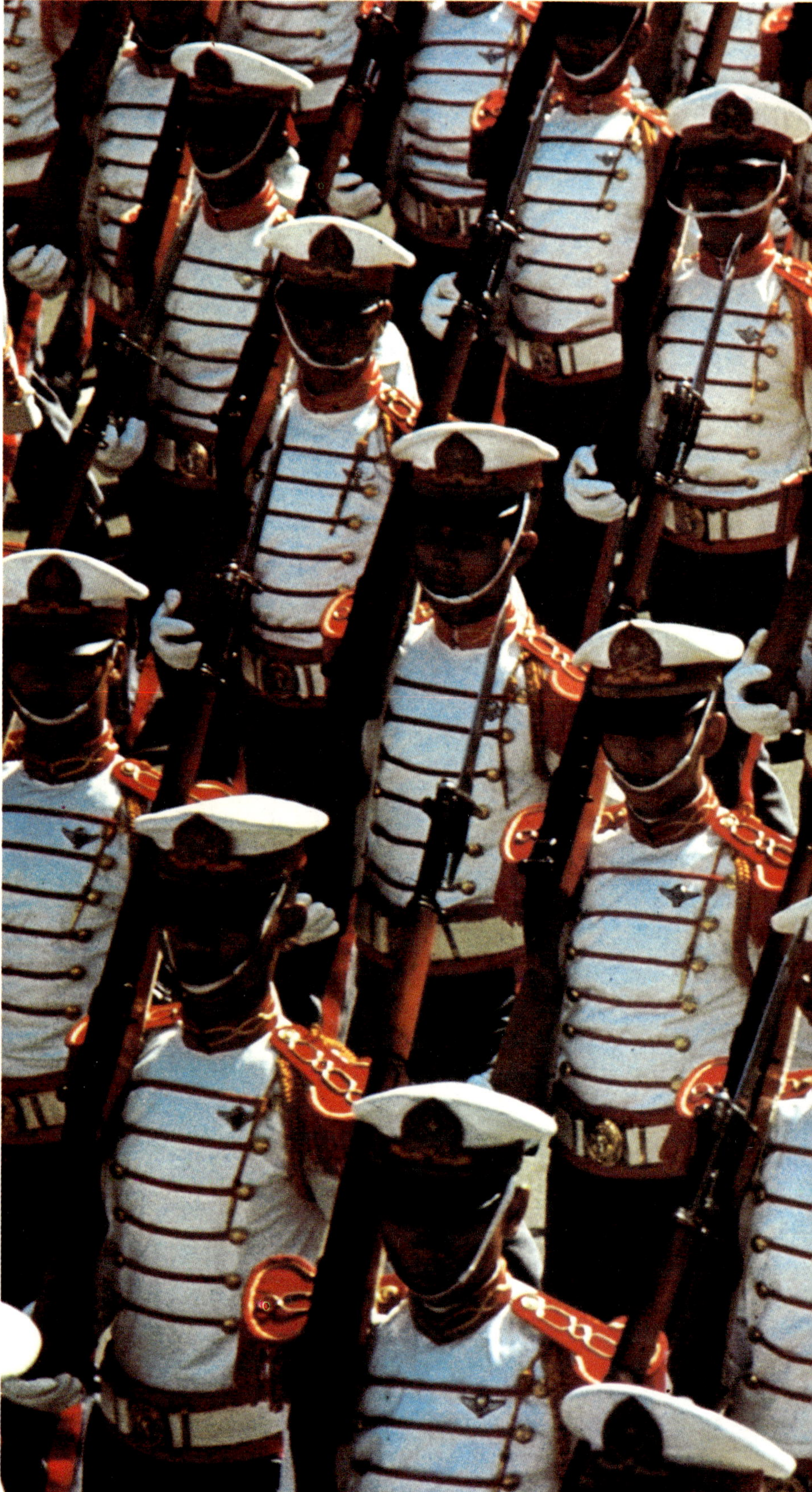

▶ REPETITION
This diagonal pattern of soldiers creates a more dynamic effect than the usual straight rows. The buildup of repeated shapes, angles and details contributes to the overall result. The high viewpoint is important—at ground level the pattern would not have emerged as clearly. Photo by Bruno Barbey.

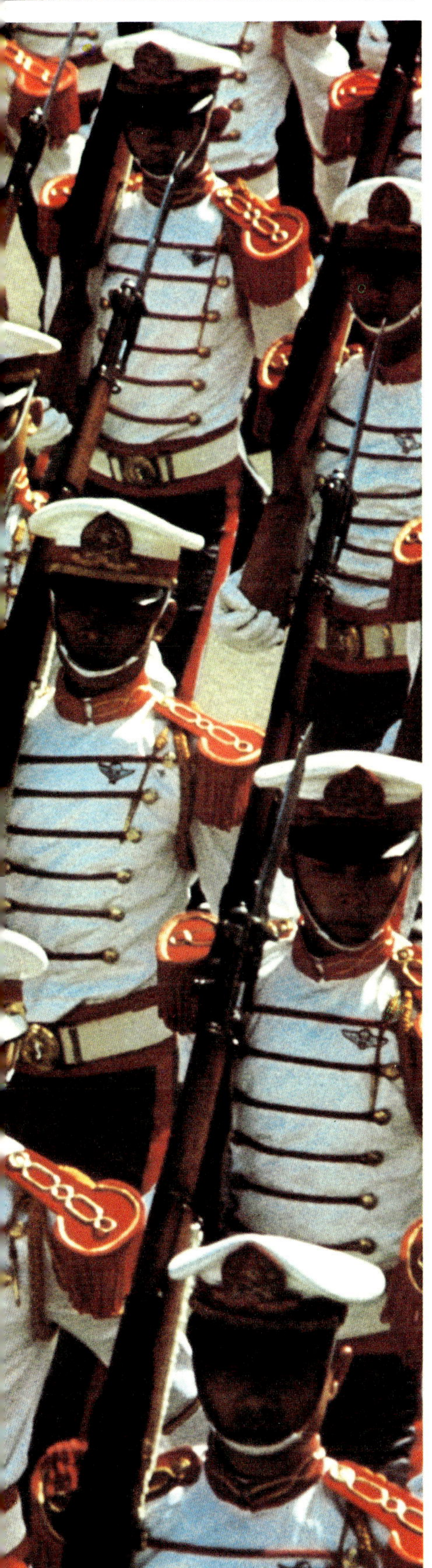

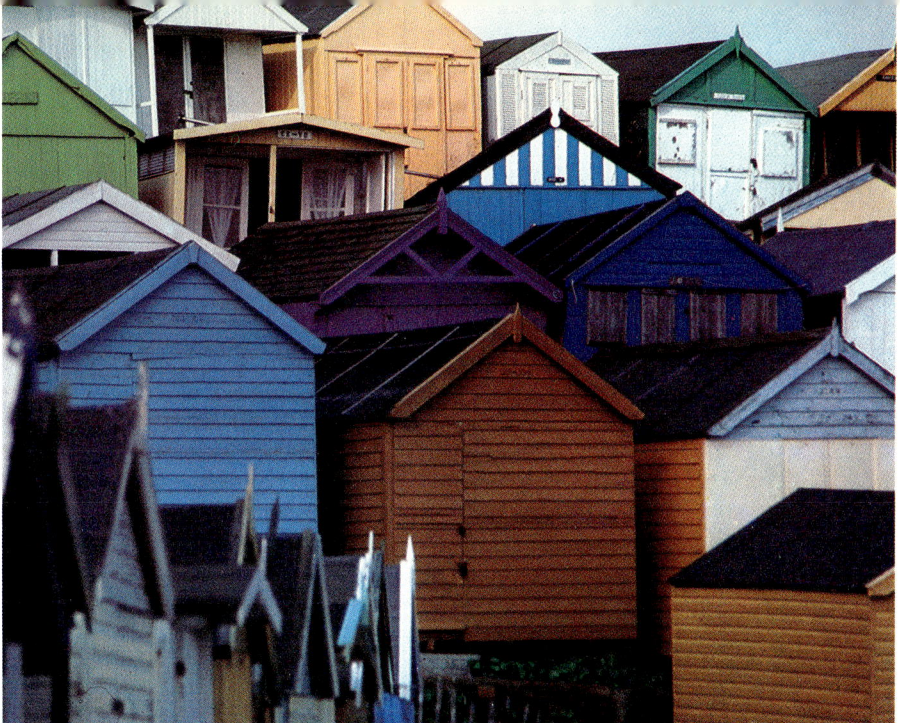

▲ This apparently disorganized mass of beach huts is visually held together by the strong repetition of the triangular roof shapes. Michael Busselle tried different viewpoints until he found the most effective combination of colors and perspective, with the interplay of light and shadow. If this photo had been composed to show the huts in straight lines, with each shape and angle identical, the image would lose the interest created by oddities in the pattern.

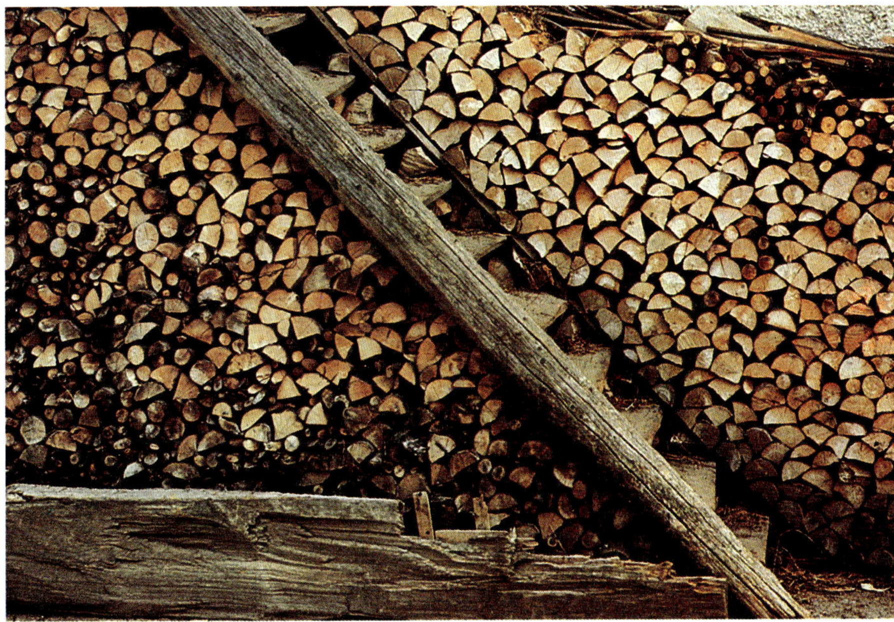

Sometimes a purely repetitious pattern can be boring—especially when the scale suppresses individual quirks and surprises, as in the photograph of a pile of logs at right. But as a background to the strongly diagonal ladder, the logs work well. They emphasize the simple structure of the ladder and do not compete with its lines. A more varied background, farm implements, for example, might have competed.

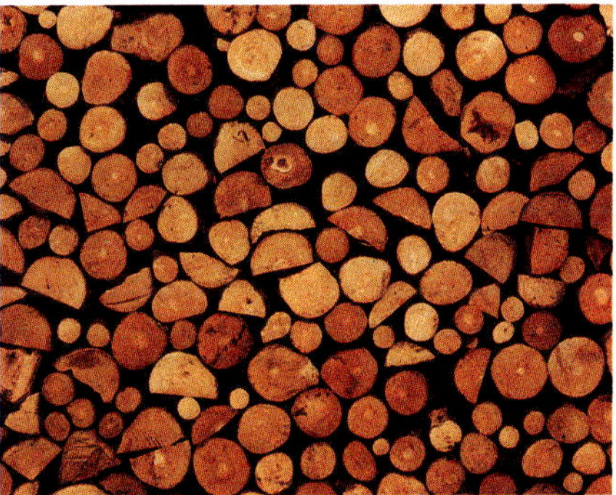

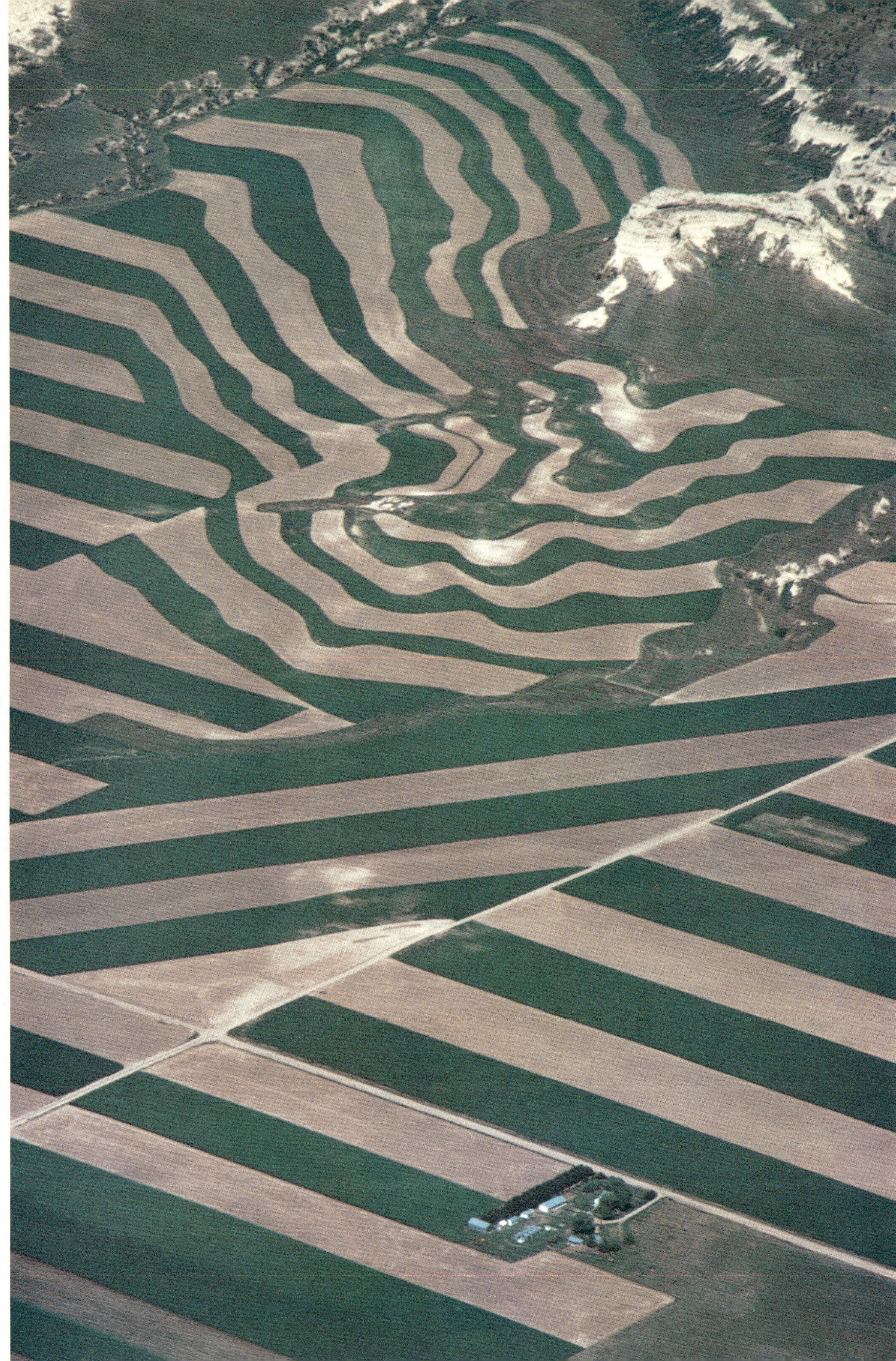

◀ When you notice the farm buildings at the bottom of this photograph, the image acquires a sense of scale. Then you no longer see the image as an abstract design. You see a pattern created by the contour of the land and plowed fields.

HOW LIGHT AFFECTS PATTERNS

A subject with inherent pattern, such as a pile of logs or a row of houses, may not be greatly affected by a change of light. But there are other images where the pattern is created or revealed by the nature of the light. A pattern of this sort may exist for only a short time. For example, consider the patterns caused by sunlight on the ripples of water. It is easy to photograph many frames on a subject like this, with each image different. In many instances, the shadows make a pattern but a slight shift in the angle of light causes the pattern to disappear.

PATTERNS AND COLOR

A pattern is made up of lines and shapes. In a b&w photograph, these are formed by highlights, shadows and contrasting shades of gray. In color photography, lines and shapes are often formed entirely of color.

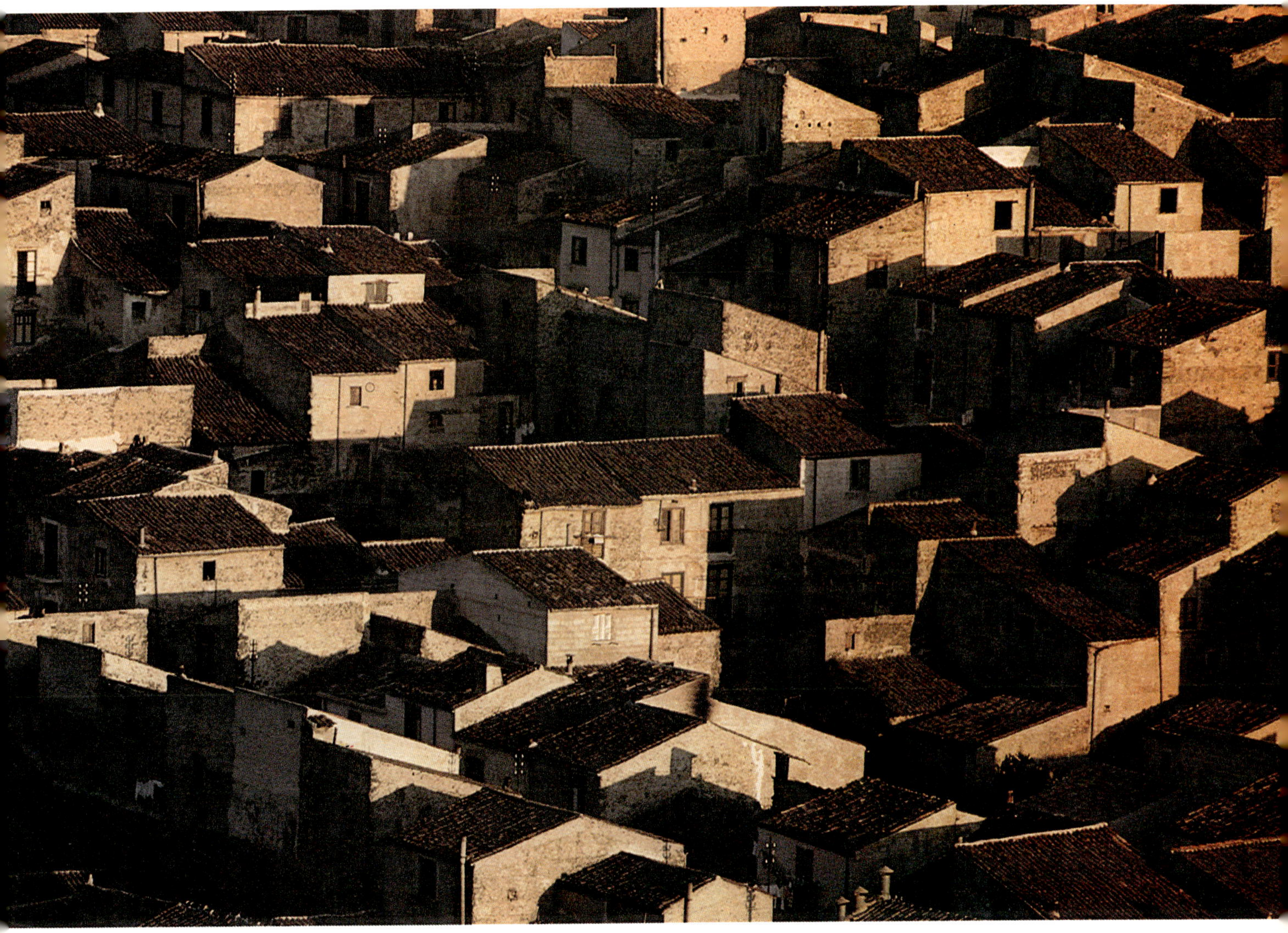

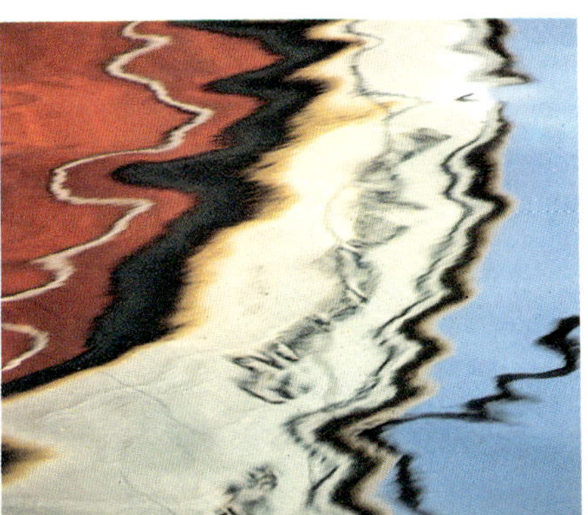

◀ This reflection of a colorful boat on rippling water creates a transient pattern that will change with the movement of the water and the position of the sun.

▲ This is a view of an Italian village, taken in late afternoon when the sun was at a low angle. Very strong light created dense shadows and strong highlights, making a pattern that would be just as obvious in b&w.

The colors of the subjects become as important as highlights and shadows. Strong colors make a pattern obvious. It is possible for a pattern to be produced by color alone. The colors in landscapes and woodland scenes can make strong patterns. Close-up photography often reveals beautiful patterns in the colors of flowers and insects, or you can find beautiful rainbow patterns in soap bubbles and oily water.

Patterns exist everywhere but you must look for them. It is really only a question of "tuning in" visual awareness to uncover a limitless source of subject matter.

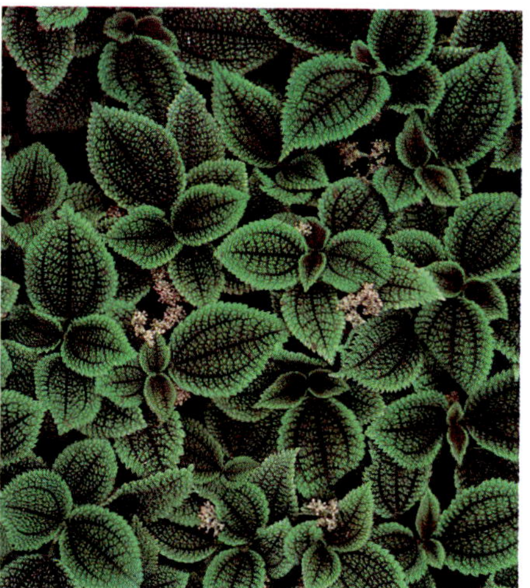

Patterns can be natural or man-made. They can be revealed by light, color or viewpoint. These pictures show strong patterns of one kind or another. Some are immediately obvious, such as the repeated shapes of the honeycomb, the sea urchins, the cars seen from above and the house fronts. Others, such as the umbrellas or the stone wall, depend on light and shadow to make the pattern obvious. Close-ups of details often show pattern more effectively than photographing the whole—such as the leaf patterns and the fir trees.

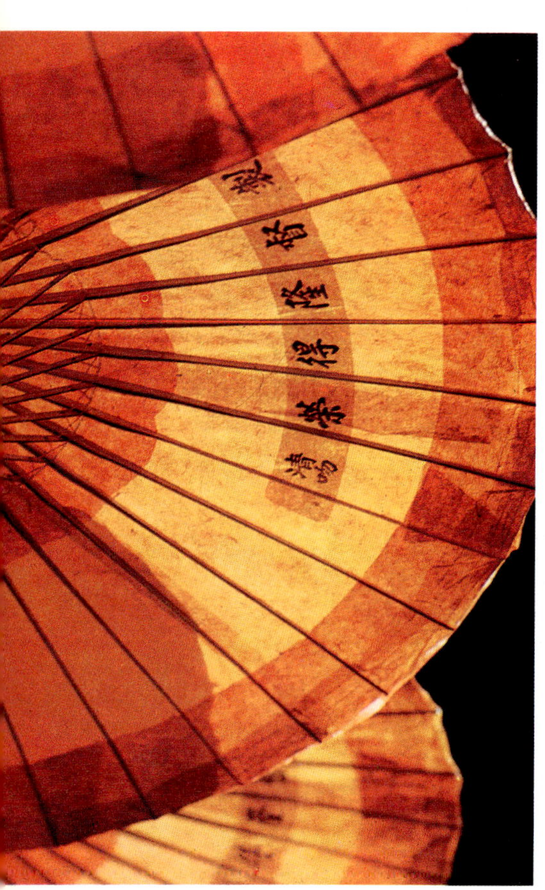

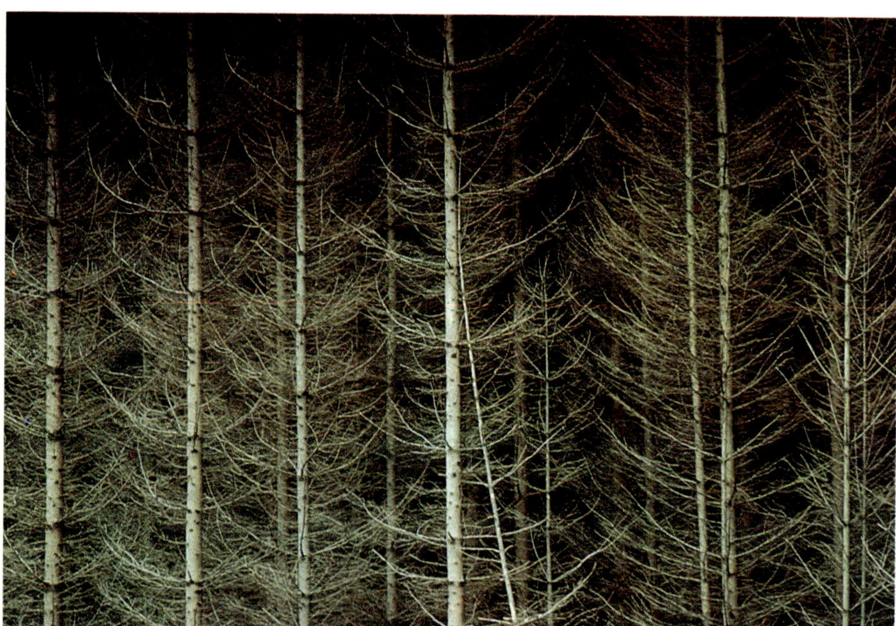

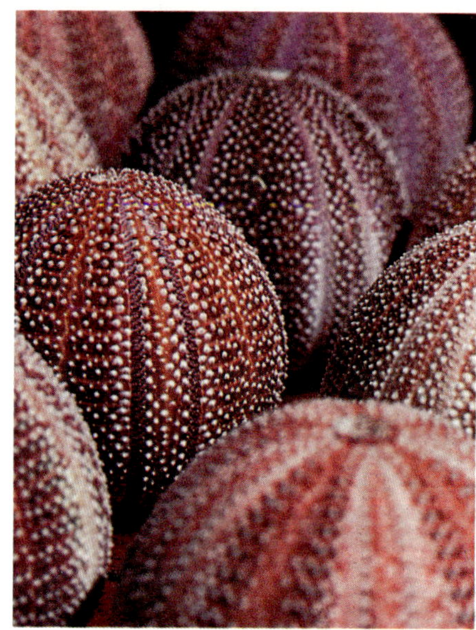

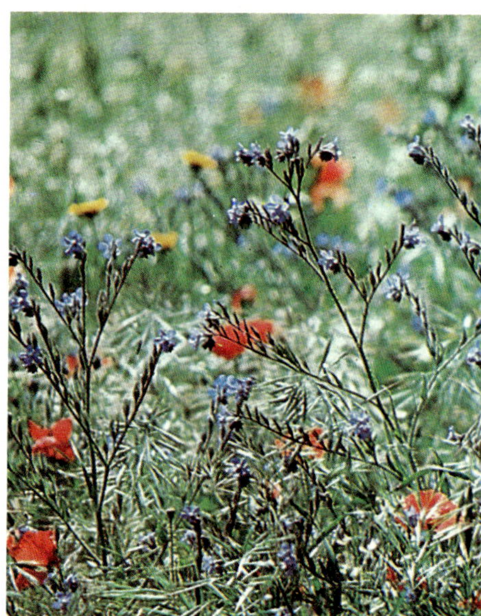

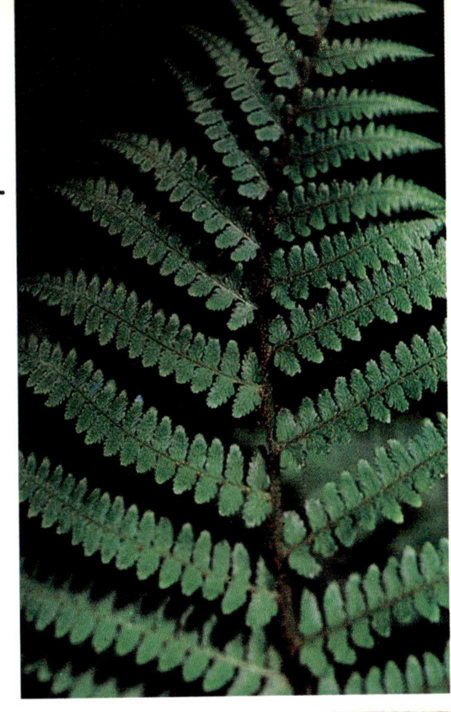

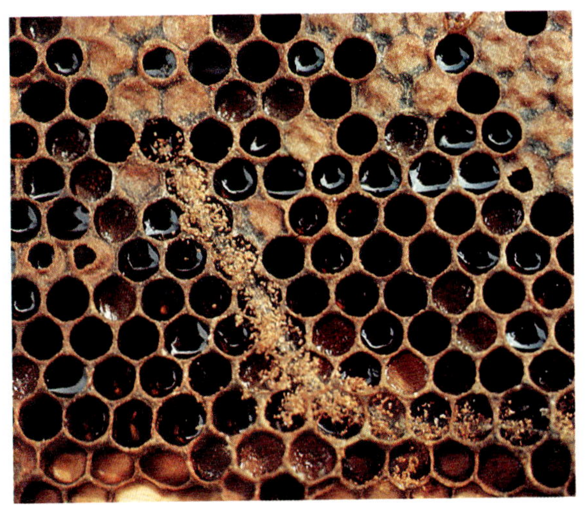

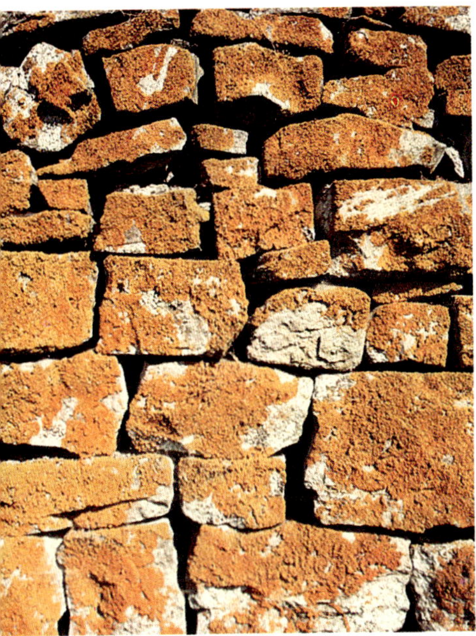

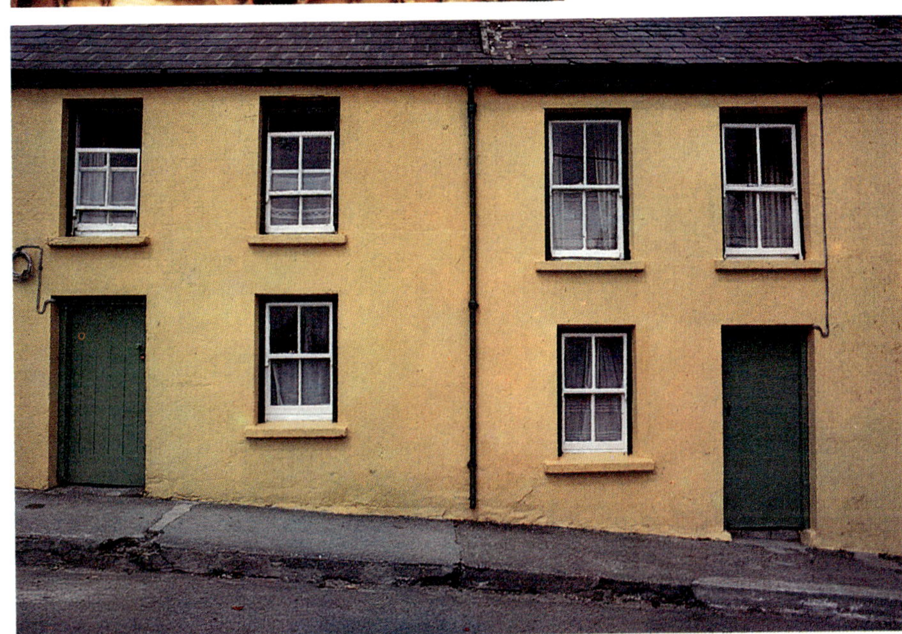

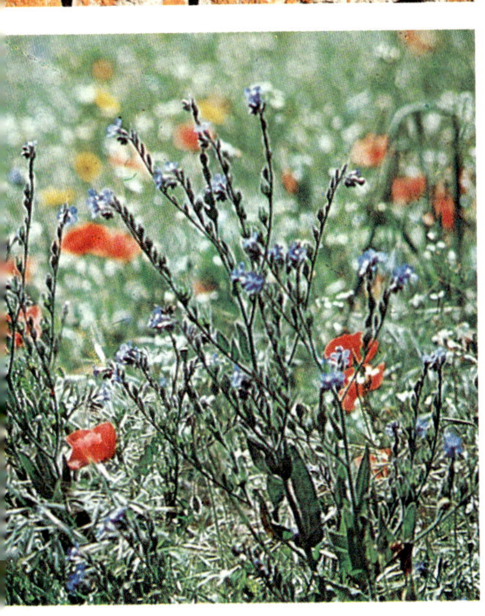

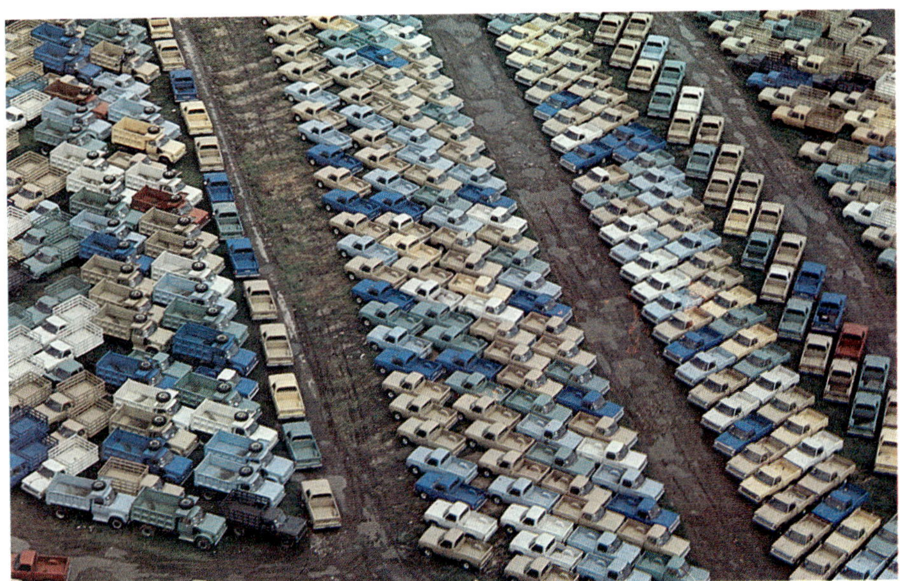

Emphasizing Texture

One of photography's special qualities is its ability to convey texture so realistically that you know what objects feel like just by looking at pictures.

The texture of a surface shows how it feels to the touch—whether it is rough or smooth, hard or soft. It is possible to take a picture of a group of objects—a piece of metal, an egg, some silk and an orange, for example—and give a really accurate impression of how each one would feel. In fact, wood grains can be printed on surfaces so convincingly that you have to touch them to tell genuine from fake.

TEXTURE FOR REALISM

The ability to convey texture is vital for photographs that are intended to look particularly realistic. You can see excellent examples in food and still-life photography, where the photograph sometimes becomes almost more real than the product. If you want an unreal quality, texture is the first thing to omit. For example, dream sequences in films are almost always shot with soft-focus attachments. To show texture, the image must be as sharp as you can get it.

Professionals specializing in still-life photographs often use large-format cameras to achieve a feeling of texture, but you can get good results with a smaller format. You must have the textured surface in precise focus, keep it very still, and set the lens aperture small enough for adequate depth of field. A fine-grain film is usually best for emphasizing texture.

▼ Michael Newton's use of soft, low-angled light works well with this range of textures, including fabric, paper and metal.

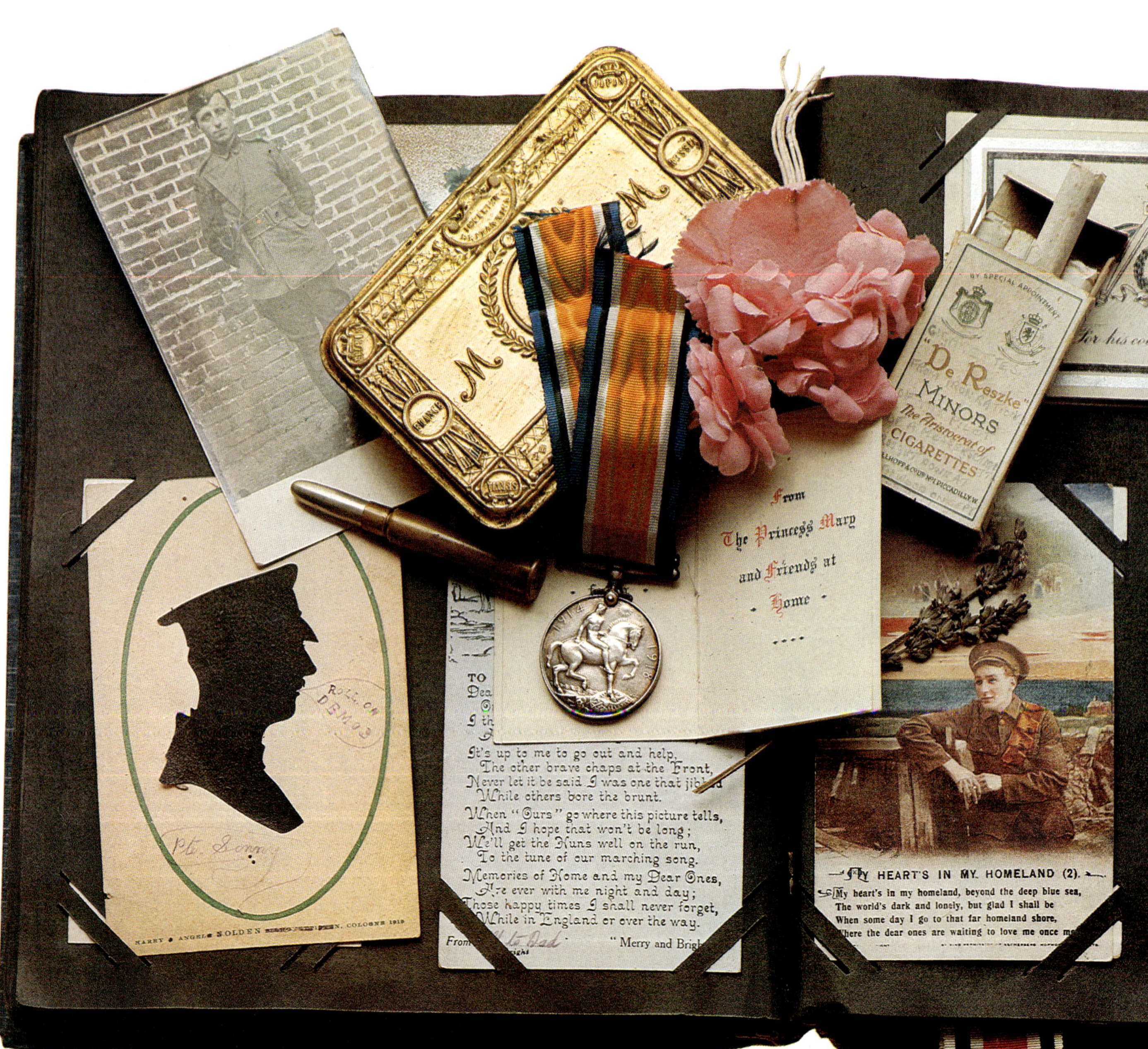

▶ Paul Forrester's skillful use of light emphasizes texture in this photograph. The combination of lighting angle and large depth of field gives good focus and defines textures very well in the foreground and middle area. Although this image was made on sheet film, similar quality is possible with 35mm color film.

Below right: Close camera position, precise focusing and shallow depth of field isolate the subject and emphasize its textural detail. Photo by Eric Crichton.

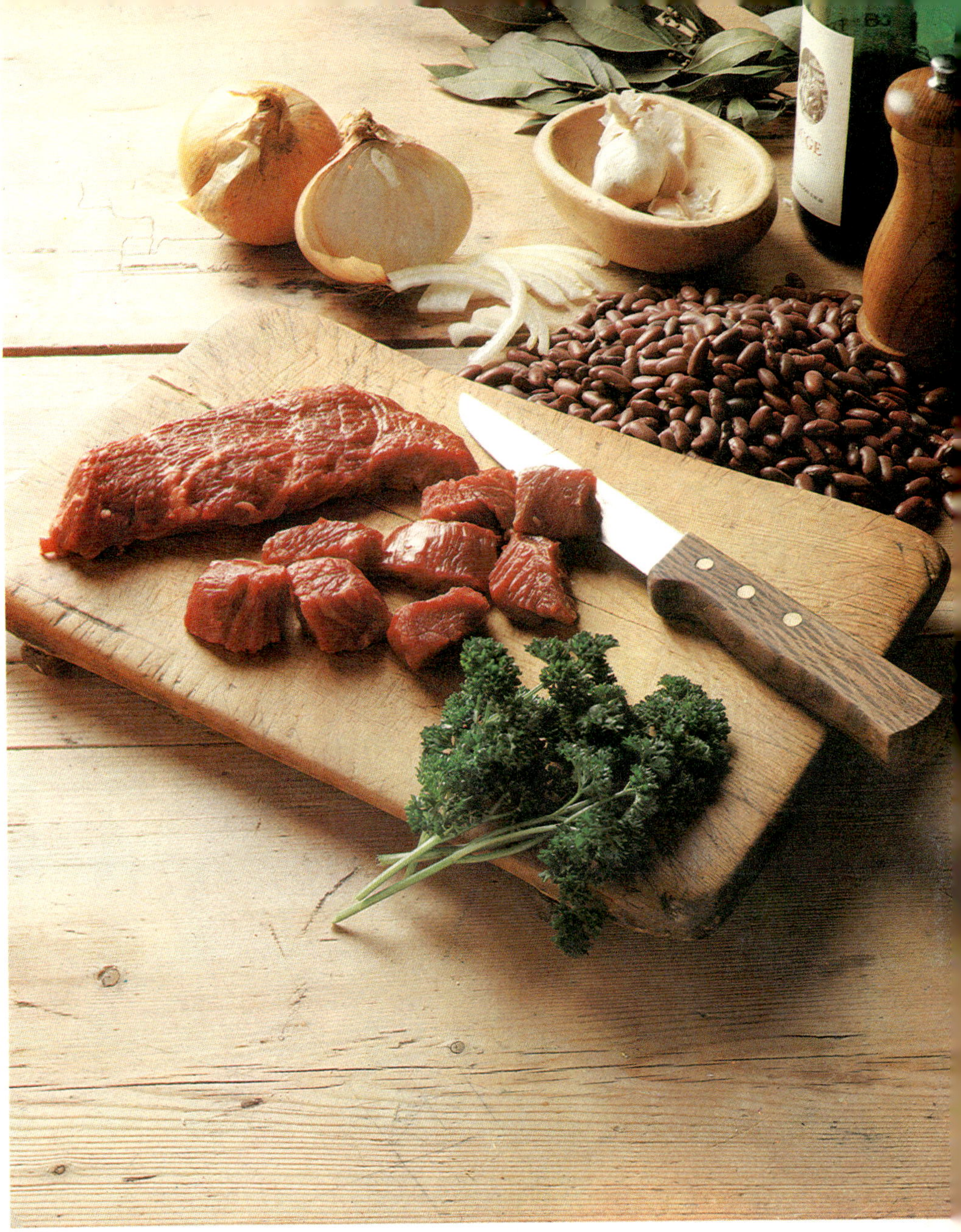

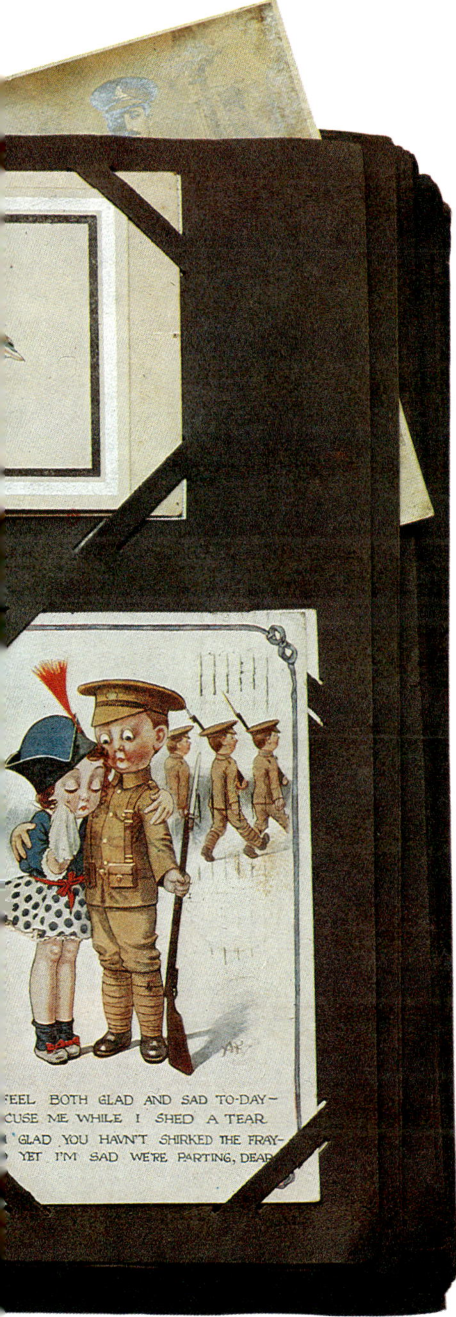

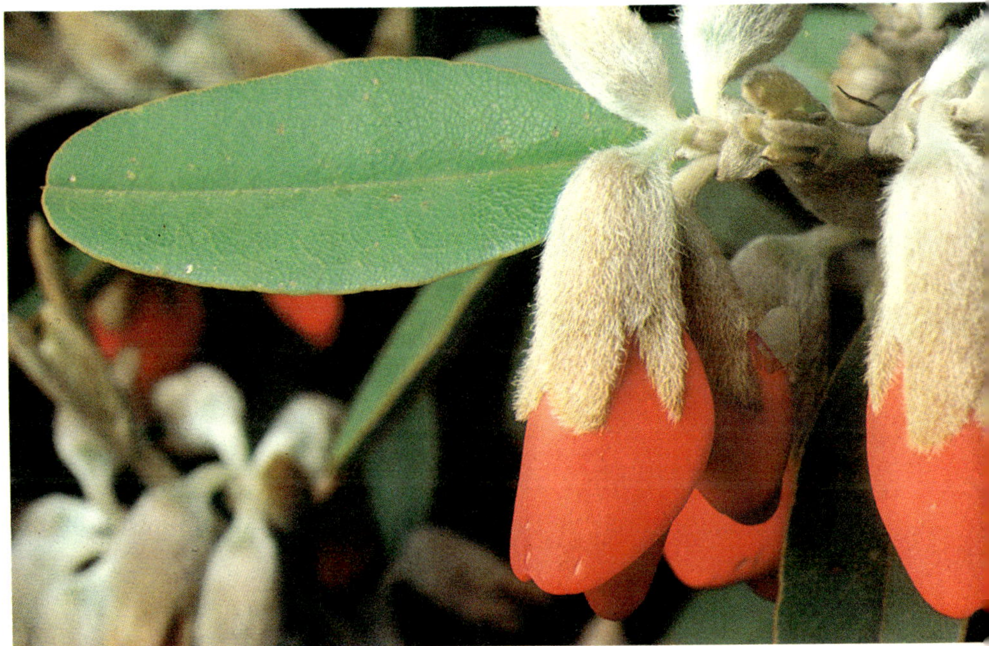

HOW LIGHT AFFECTS TEXTURE

The way you light an object to reveal texture depends on its surface. A subject with a coarse texture and wide range of tones, like the bark of a tree, can be photographed with a *large* front light. This gives *soft* light. However, a surface with a subtle texture that also has an even tone and color, such as an orange, should be lit so highlights and shadows are created within the tiny indentations of its surface. This means that the light source should be small and directed at the subject from an acute angle so the *hard* light literally skims across the surface.

With a subject with a more pronounced texture, such as a stone wall, slightly softer lighting at an acute angle is preferable. Otherwise shadows created by the indentations become too large and dense.

Shape is also important. With a flat surface such as a stone wall, light has the same effect over the whole surface, whereas the light on a rounded surface, such as an orange, varies.

As a general rule, subtle textures require harder and more directional lighting than surfaces with a more pronounced texture. But to achieve the best results, you have to be aware of the distribution of highlights and shadow tones, and the gradations between them, which the light creates on the surfaces of the subject. If you want textural quality above all else, you may find that your techniques create undesirable effects in other elements of the picture. In fashion photography, for example, the lighting used to bring out the texture of cloth may have an undesirable effect on the model's skin.

HOW TO ACCENT TEXTURE

One method of accentuating texture is to increase the contrast of the lighting, either by directing it from a sharper angle when it is controllable, like studio lighting, or by changing the camera position.

Aiming toward the sun is an effective way of doing this, especially when the sun is low in the sky. Don't point the camera directly at the sun, but position the camera so its angle to the surface being photographed is roughly equal to the angle at which the sun strikes that surface.

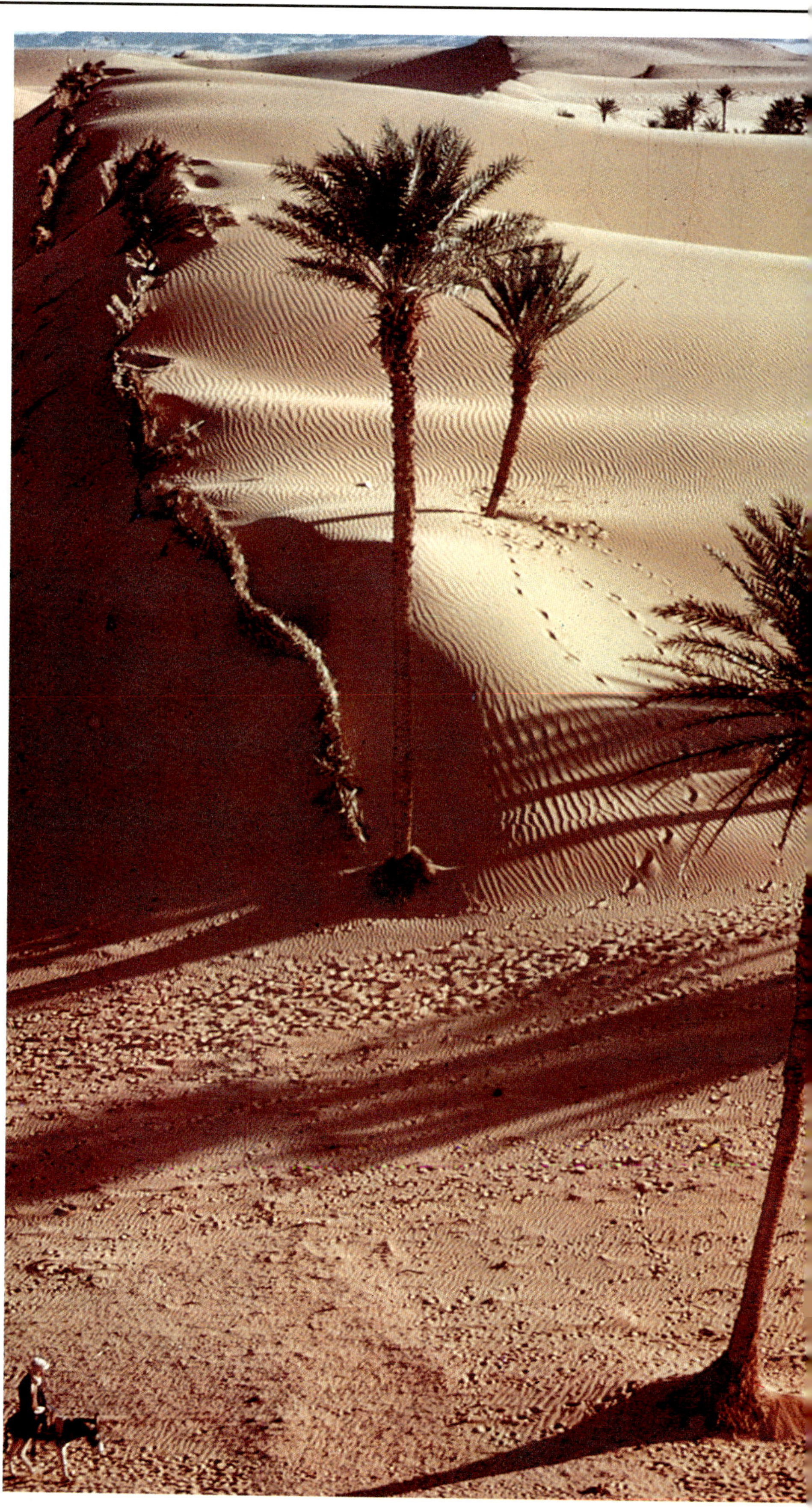

▶ A low sun will accentuate the texture of the sand, but also produces strong shadows. Bracketing exposures will result in a series of photos with the shadows lighter and darker, producing different renditions of the scene. Consider doing this when you have no control over the light. Photo by George Rodger.

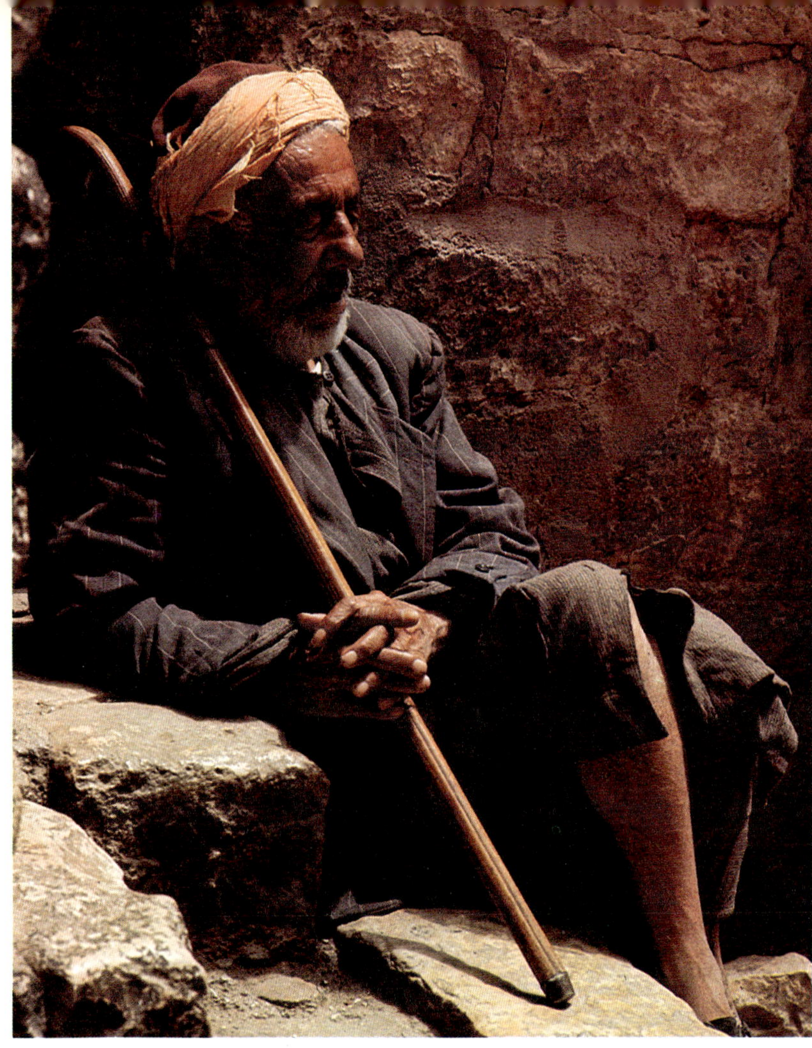

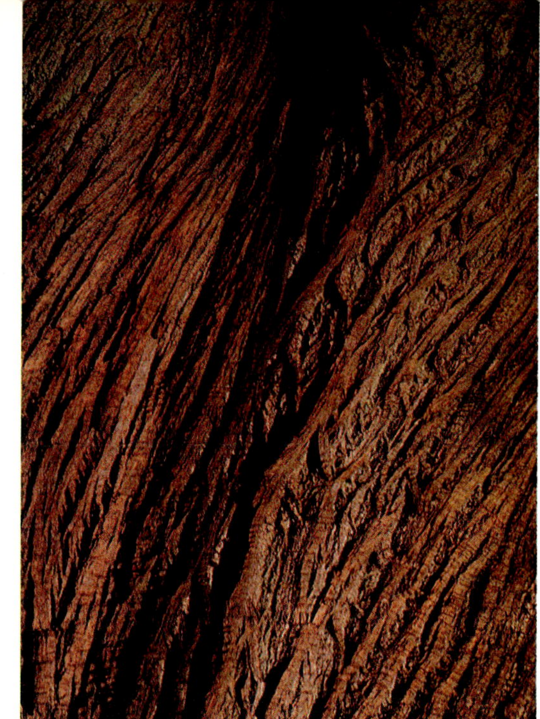

▲ Bark has a pronounced texture that is obvious in almost any light. Hard, directional light, which is good for emphasizing texture, often creates dense shadow and loss of shadow detail.

◀ Similarly, skin texture can be revealed by hard, directional light. This type of light is usually more effective on dark skin. On white skin, it tends to be unflattering. Photo by Michael Busselle.

▶ By moving in close, Eric Crichton emphasized the inherent texture of this cabbage. Here, soft light reveals delicate textures that would be lost in the shadows from a strong directional light.

Below right: Texture like this peeling paint is emphasized by strong side lighting. The shadows imply a three-dimensional effect.

▼ In Colin Barker's picture of a leaf, the texture is made obvious by the extreme close-up view.

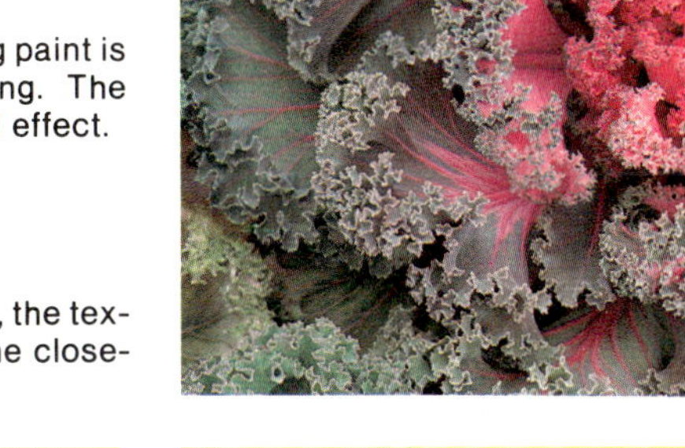

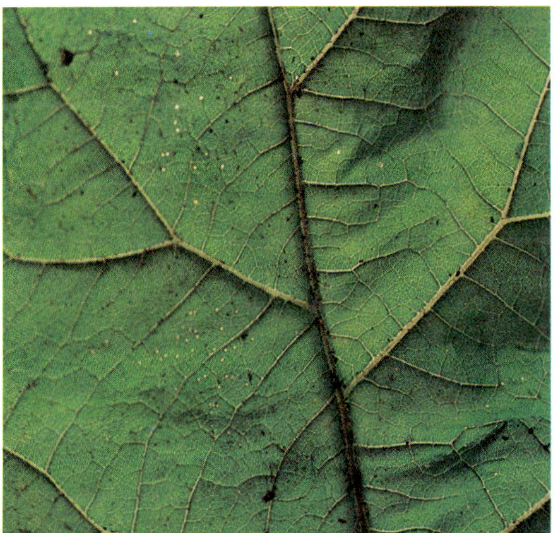

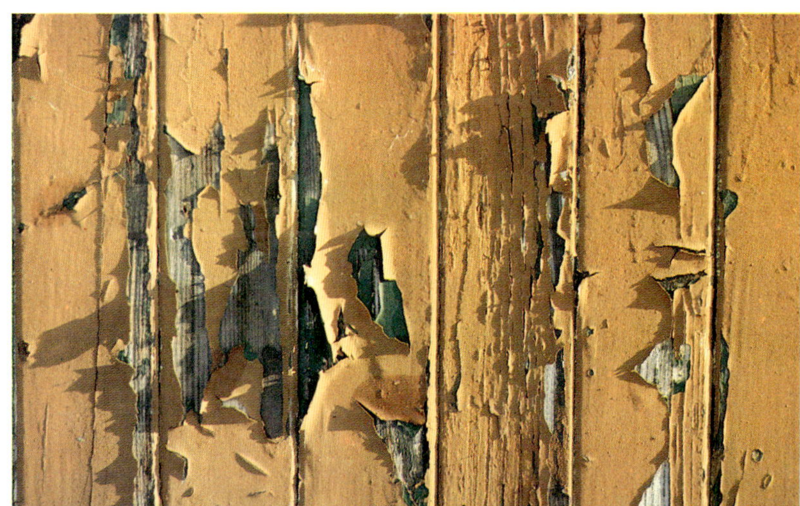

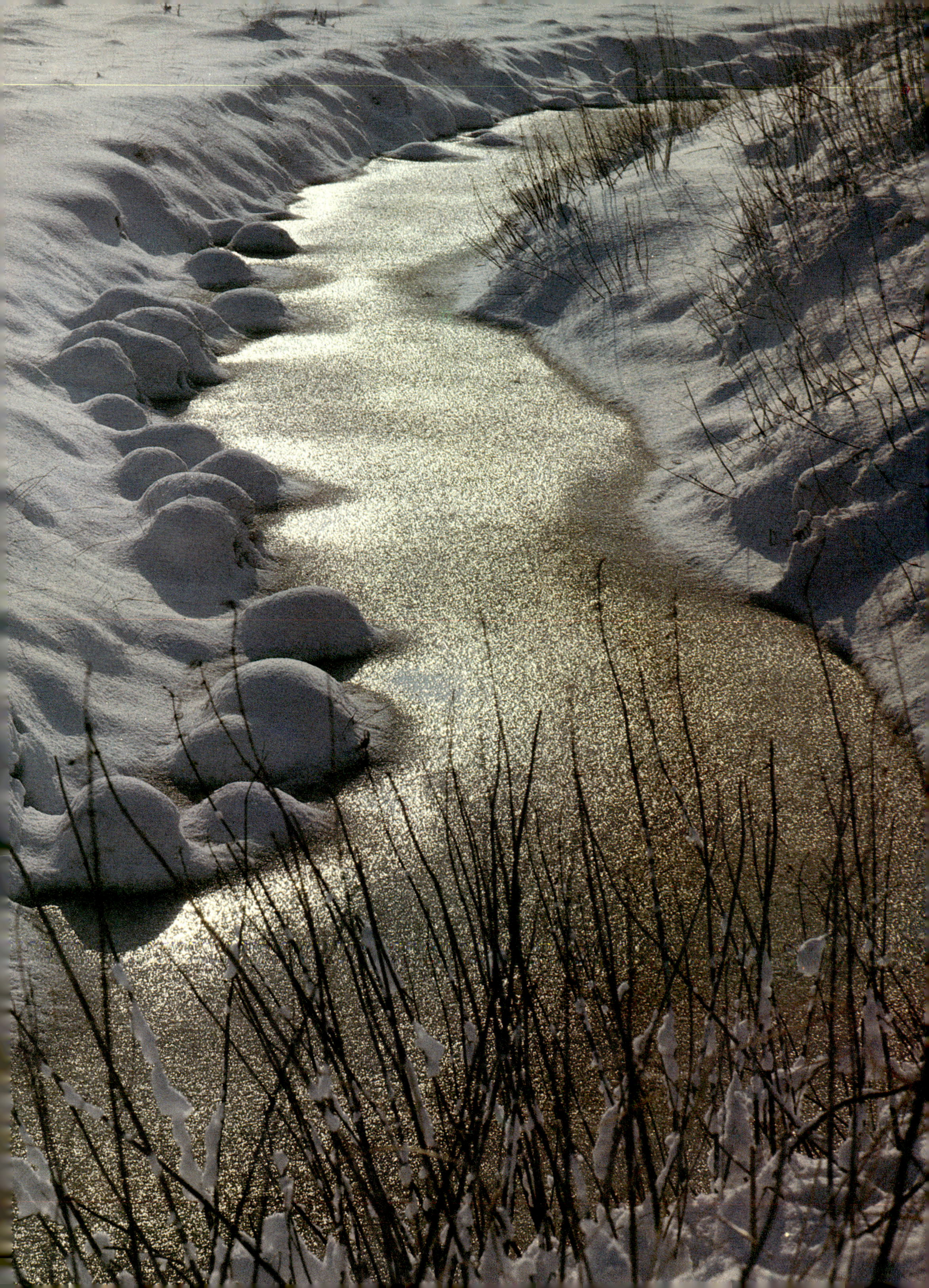

Contrast can also be increased by choice of film—the slower the film the higher the contrast. In b&w photography, and with some color films, it is possible to increase the contrast by using special processing techniques. Although it is possible to create exaggerated effects this way, it reduces subtlety, and other elements of the picture may be sacrificed.

Exposure can often be used to accentuate texture, particularly if you use lighting with reasonably high contrast. In this situation, underexposure will often increase the textural quality of the subject. Skin tones in a portrait, for example, will have a stronger texture when they appear darker than usual—portraits of men often display this technique.

The opposite technique is used to minimize skin texture, as in fashion and beauty photography, where a soft, front light creating low contrast is often combined with overexposure for a more ethereal effect.

The key to a picture showing strong texture is a really sharp image. Although light, camera angle and exposure can all contribute, success ultimately depends on a sharp picture with good definition. Make sure you focus the camera accurately. Stop down to at least *f*-8. If this requires a slow shutter speed, use a tripod.

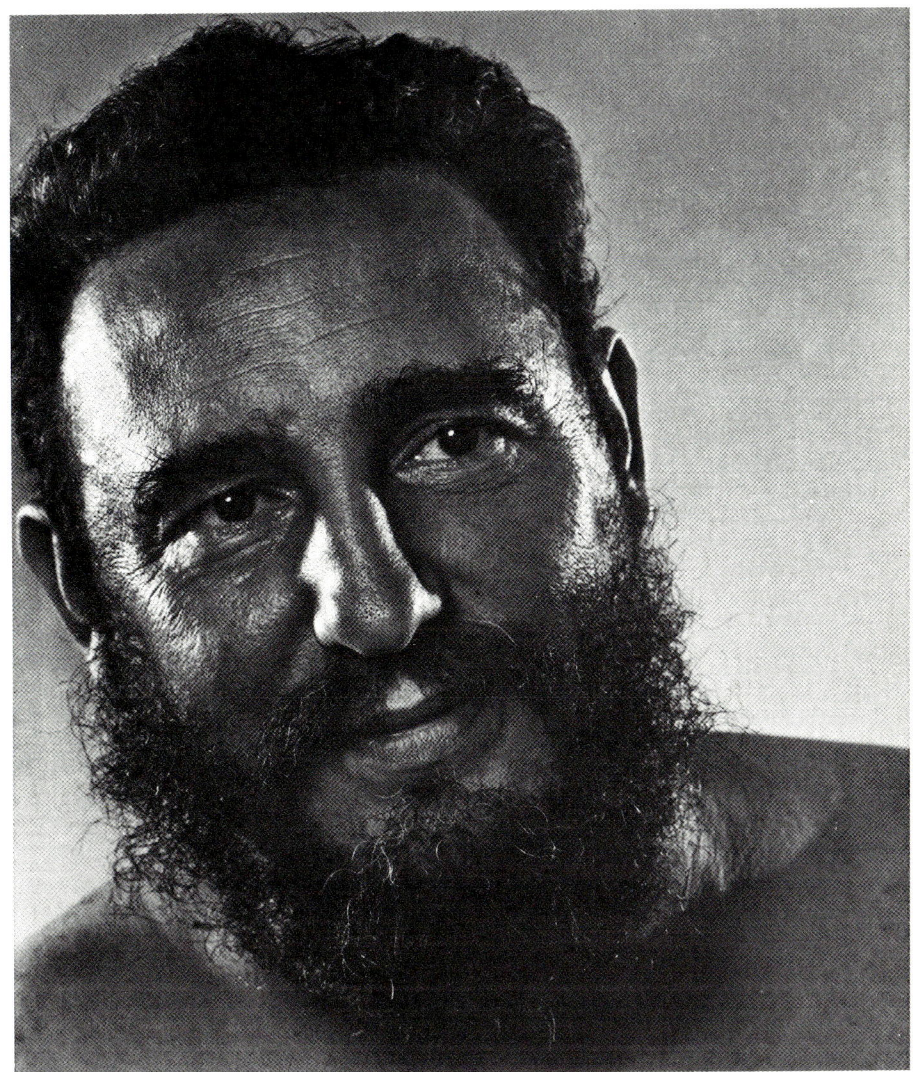

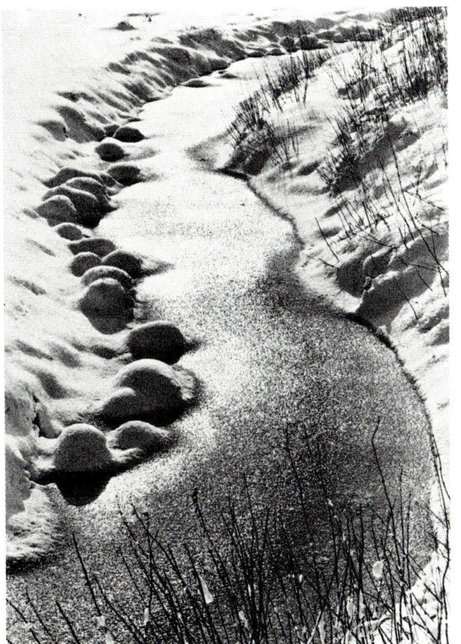

▲ Careful lighting and exposure control brings out skin texture in portraits, as in this one by Yousuf Karsh. Use this technique with care because it can also bring out unflattering blemishes.

◀ The picture at far left works as well in b&w as in color. Low back light creates strong highlights, shadow and sparkle. The strong highlights could cause a meter to suggest underexposure, so take a reading from a middle gray area or bracket exposures.

▶ Take away texture and you take away realism. Soft-focus effects result in a dreamy, romantic image.

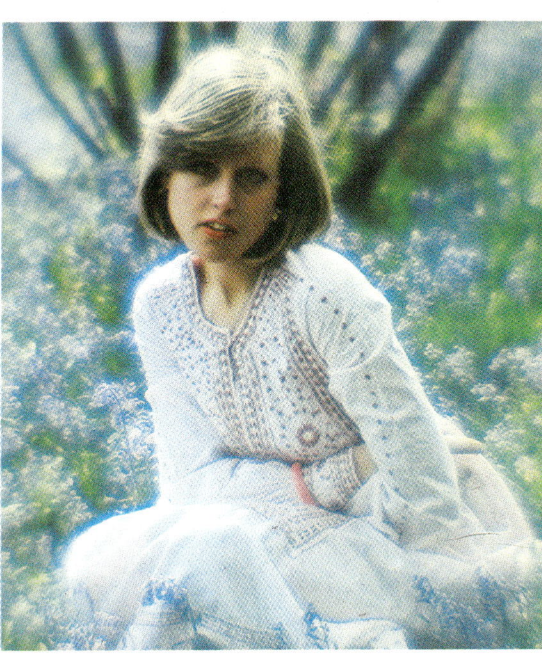

Tone and Contrast

The densities, or *tones,* in a photograph range from white to black. In between is an infinite variety of tones. It is tonal contrast, or the relationship between tones, that gives three-dimensional form and depth to a picture. The tonal contrast of an image is affected by how the subject is lit and its reflective qualities.

In color, the same principle applies, but adjacent areas may be differentiated by color rather than brightness.

TONE AND FORM

If a two-dimensional photograph is to imply a third dimension, it must include the full tonal range with subtle variations. Much of the photographer's skill lies in recognizing these tones and recording them accurately. First, you need to become aware of them in the subject, even in something white. A cloud, for example, is rarely completely white; it is usually shades of gray. It is these gradations that give the cloud form and depth.

HOW LIGHT AFFECTS TONE

If you photograph a white billiard ball along with a circular white card the same size, and light them from the front so no shadows or highlights are created, there will be no visible difference between them. If you then move the light to the side to

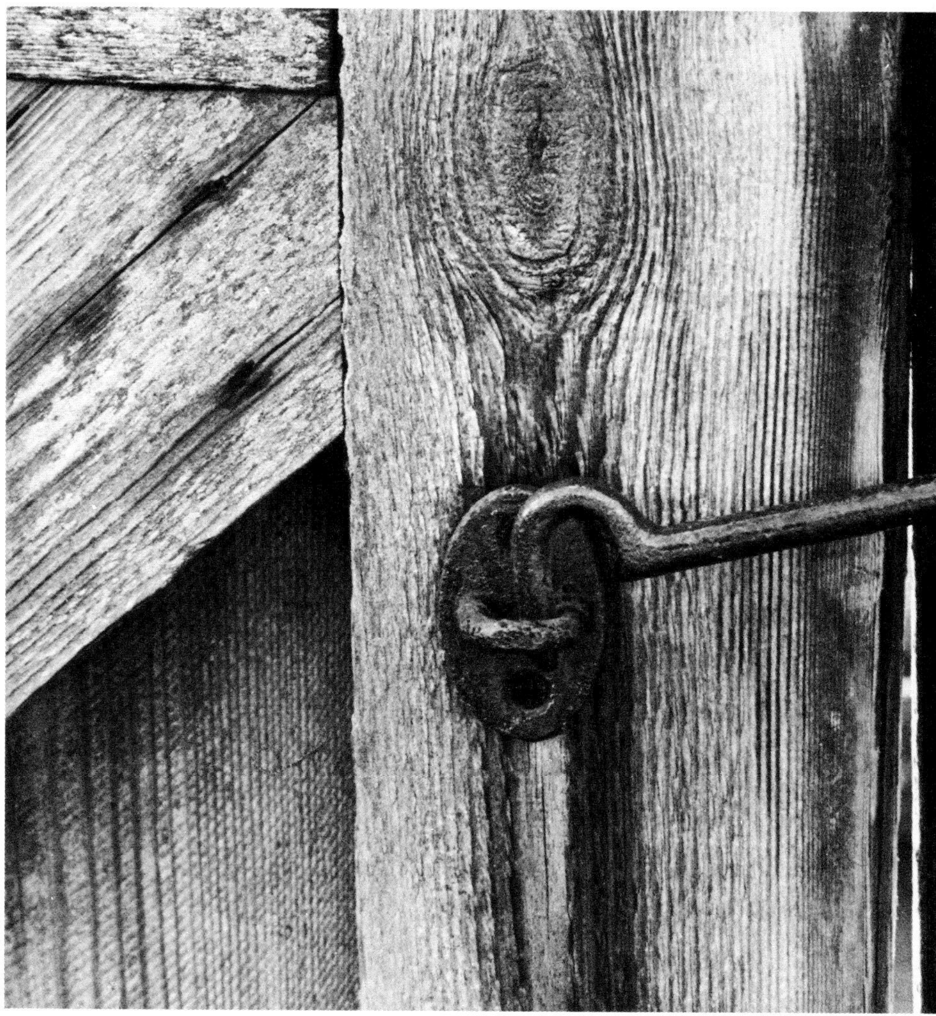

▶ To achieve a full tonal range, you must show the tonal quality of the subject with light, give precise exposure and produce correct contrast in processing and printing.

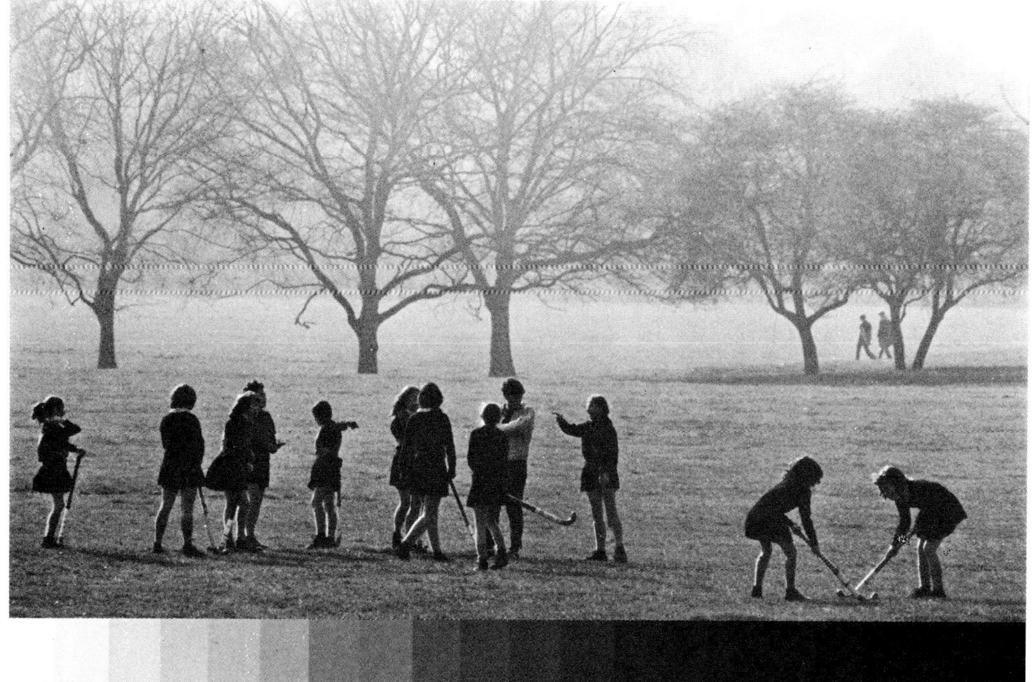

◀ Most of the tones in this photograph are only a slight variation of middle gray, as the gray scale below shows. This results from soft light accentuated by processing and printing. Higher tonal contrast could have made the overall effect less effective. Photo by Herbie Yamaguchi.

▶ Tonal difference between background and foreground add to the feeling of distance created here. Mist and early morning backlighting produce the very pale background with an almost silhouetted foreground. Photo by Herbie Yamaguchi.

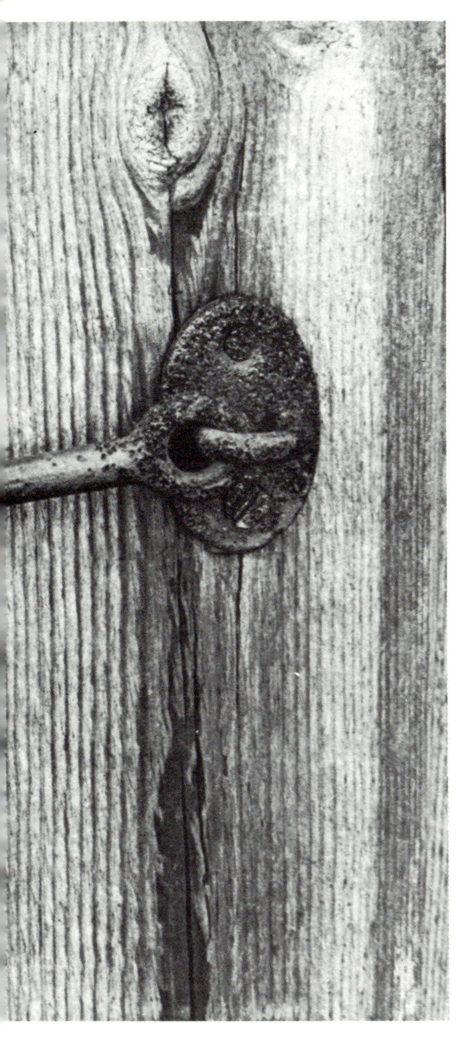

create shadows, the difference will be immediately obvious. The white ball will develop a full range of tones from white on the lit side to shades of gray to black in the deepest shadow, and so becomes three-dimensional.

Light that creates shadows creates tone. You can see the relationship virtually anywhere between light and the tones and shadows it creates—window light on a passenger's face in a bus or sunlight on the landscape outside the bus. A hard source of light, such as direct sun, creates solid tones with clearly defined steps, whereas the soft light of a cloudy day produces gently changing tones and shadows with imperceptible edges.

HOW TONE AFFECTS MOOD

There is a strong connection between the tonal range of a photograph and the mood it conveys. A picture that consists primarily of dark tones gives a somber and serious atmosphere, whereas a picture with a full range of tones, bright highlights and crisp shadows creates a lively and cheerful impression. A photograph made up of light tones has a delicate and often romantic quality.

The tonal quality of the picture should illustrate the mood you want to convey—a dark-toned, or *low key,* picture of children playing on the beach would be as inappropriate as a delicate light-toned, or *high key,* portrait to show the character of Count Dracula.

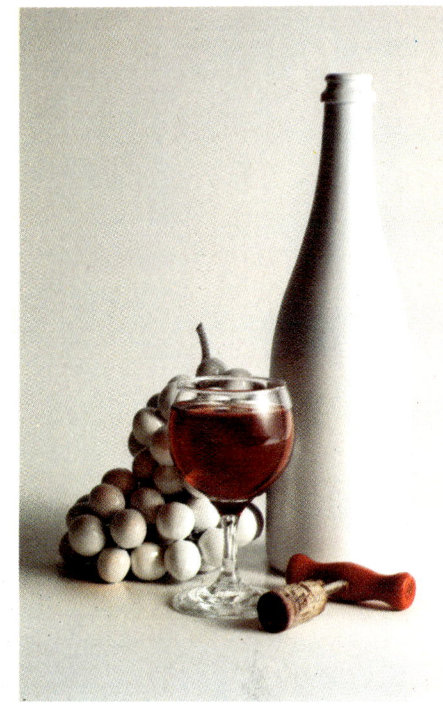

These two pictures of a white bottle show how light affects tone and how a large tonal range brings out form and distance. The same soft light was used for both, but below, front light produced an almost shadowless image. This makes the image look flat. Above, side light gives strong, well-placed shadows, adding form and depth. Photos by Michael Busselle.

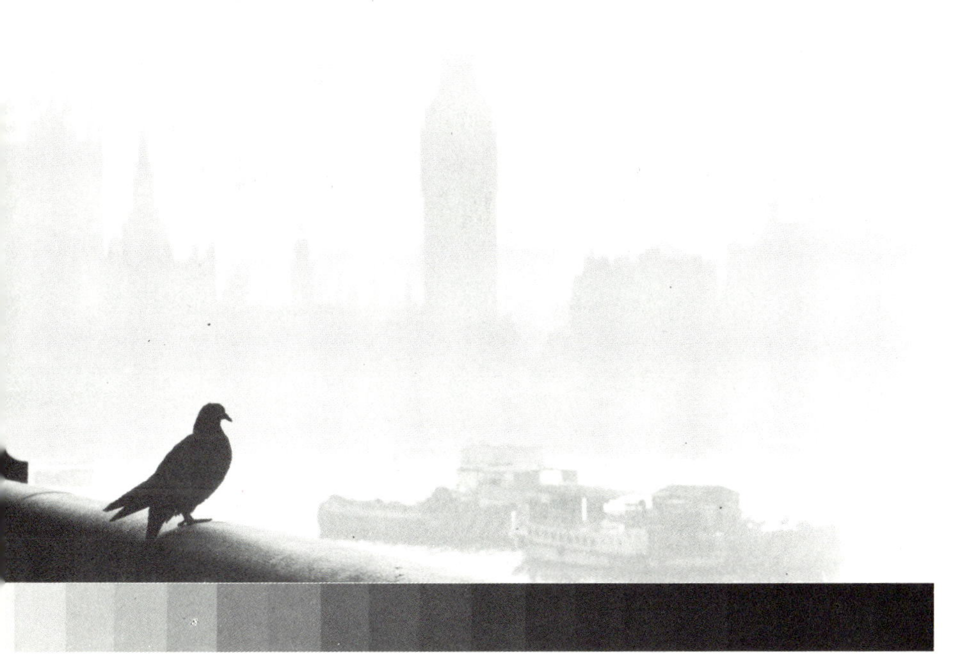

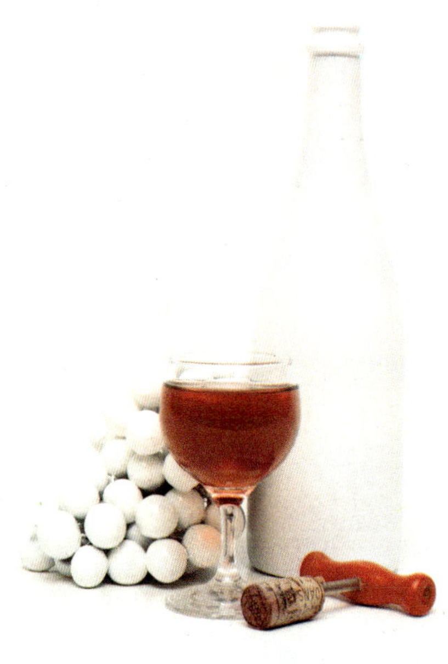

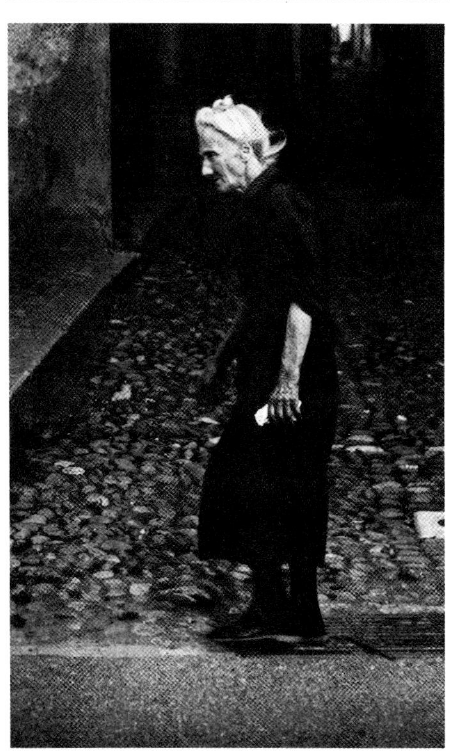

▲ Low-key pictures are usually found, not created. The somber, serious mood is helped by slight underexposure. Photo by Michael Busselle.

▼ A high-key picture has light tones with little contrast, but there are usually some areas of fine, bold detail in a darker tone, almost like a pencil sketch. Photo by Robin Laurance.

TONE AND CONTRAST

Contrast is the relationship between the darkest and lightest tones. A photograph that has a full range of tones with detail in all but the brightest highlight is considered to be of normal contrast. One dominated by very light and very dark tones, with little tonal variation between them, is described as high contrast. When there is only a small difference between the brightest and darkest tones, you have a low-contrast image.

Contrast is partly controlled by lighting. A hard, directional light such as bright sunlight tends to create a high-contrast image. Very soft light—a heavily overcast day, for example—creates a low-contrast image.

COLOR AND CONTRAST

Light and dark colors within the subject give it contrast independent of that created by light. For example, a bride in a white wedding dress standing against a dark church door is a high-contrast subject, whereas the same bride standing against a white wall is a low-contrast subject. You can also control the contrast in photographs by the way you handle the lighting.

DEVELOPING AND PRINTING

In b&w photography, and to a lesser extent with some color films, it is possible to control contrast by varying development times; the longer the time, the greater the contrast. Conversely, less development means less contrast. Your choice of printing papers can also affect the contrast. A good book to get you started in the darkroom is HPBooks' *Do It in the Dark* by Tom Burk.

For a wide range of tones:

- Wait for—or create—softer, diffused lighting.
- Measure exposure carefully. If in doubt, bracket exposures.
- Develop and print according to manufacturer's instructions.

To increase contrast:

- Use harsh, direct light.
- Underexpose by about 1 step.
- Increase development and/or use a more contrasty printing paper.

To decrease contrast:

- Use soft, diffused light.
- Use soft-focus filters or accessories.
- Decrease development and/or use a less contrasty printing paper.

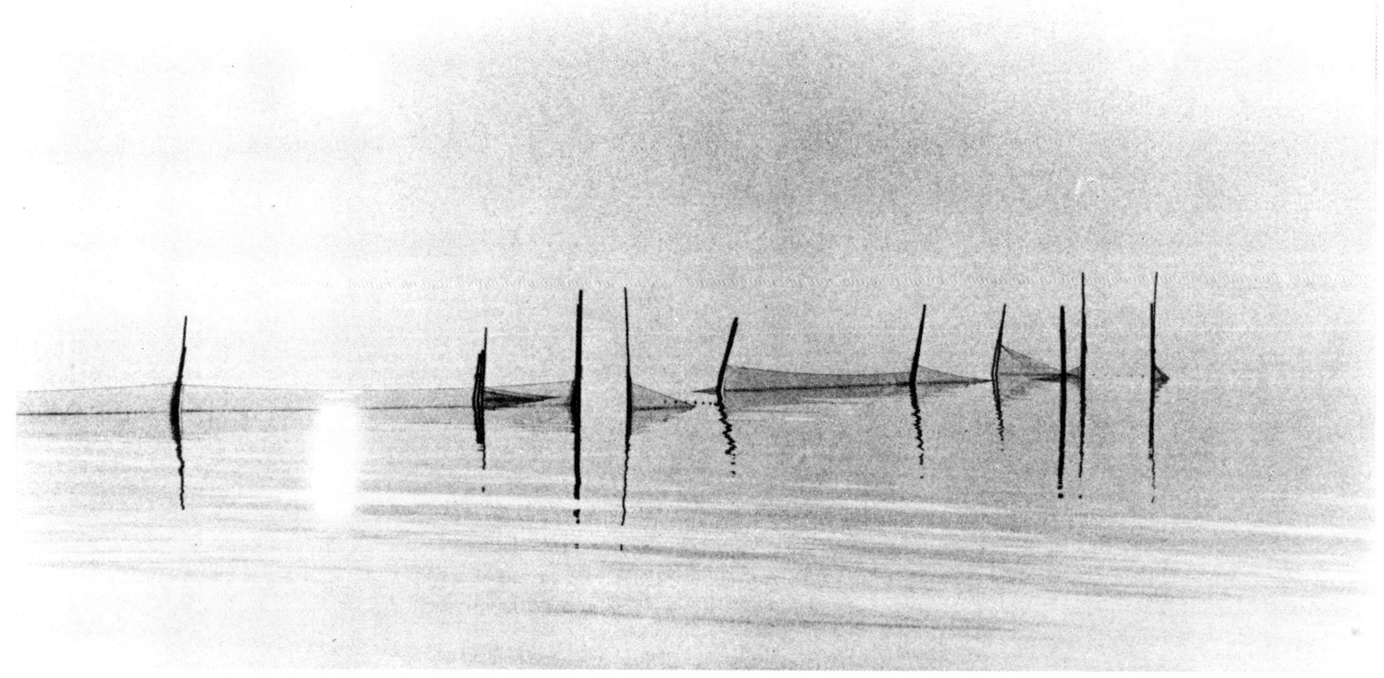

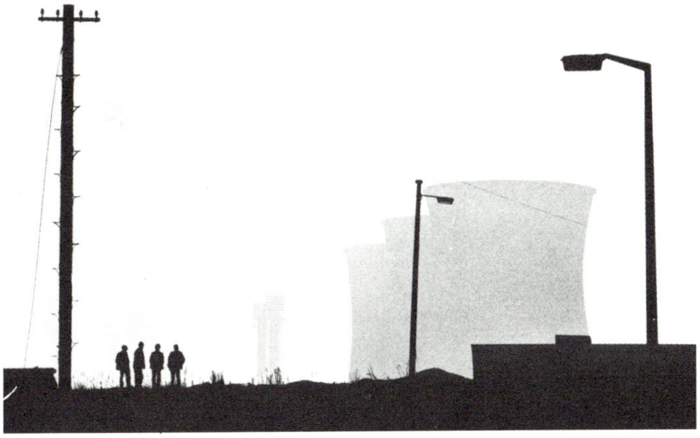

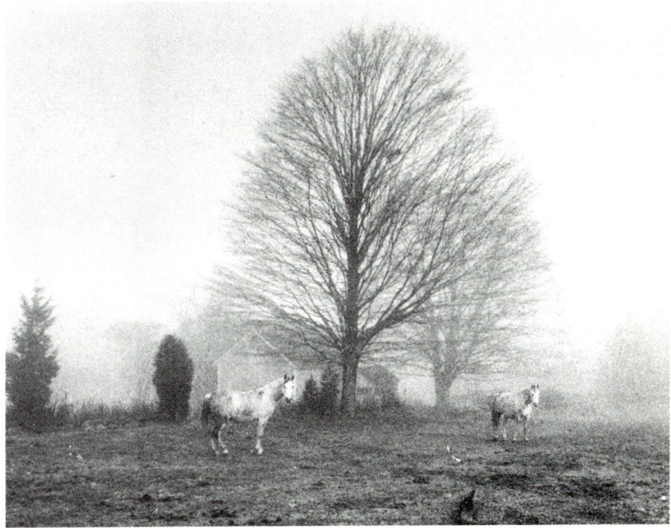

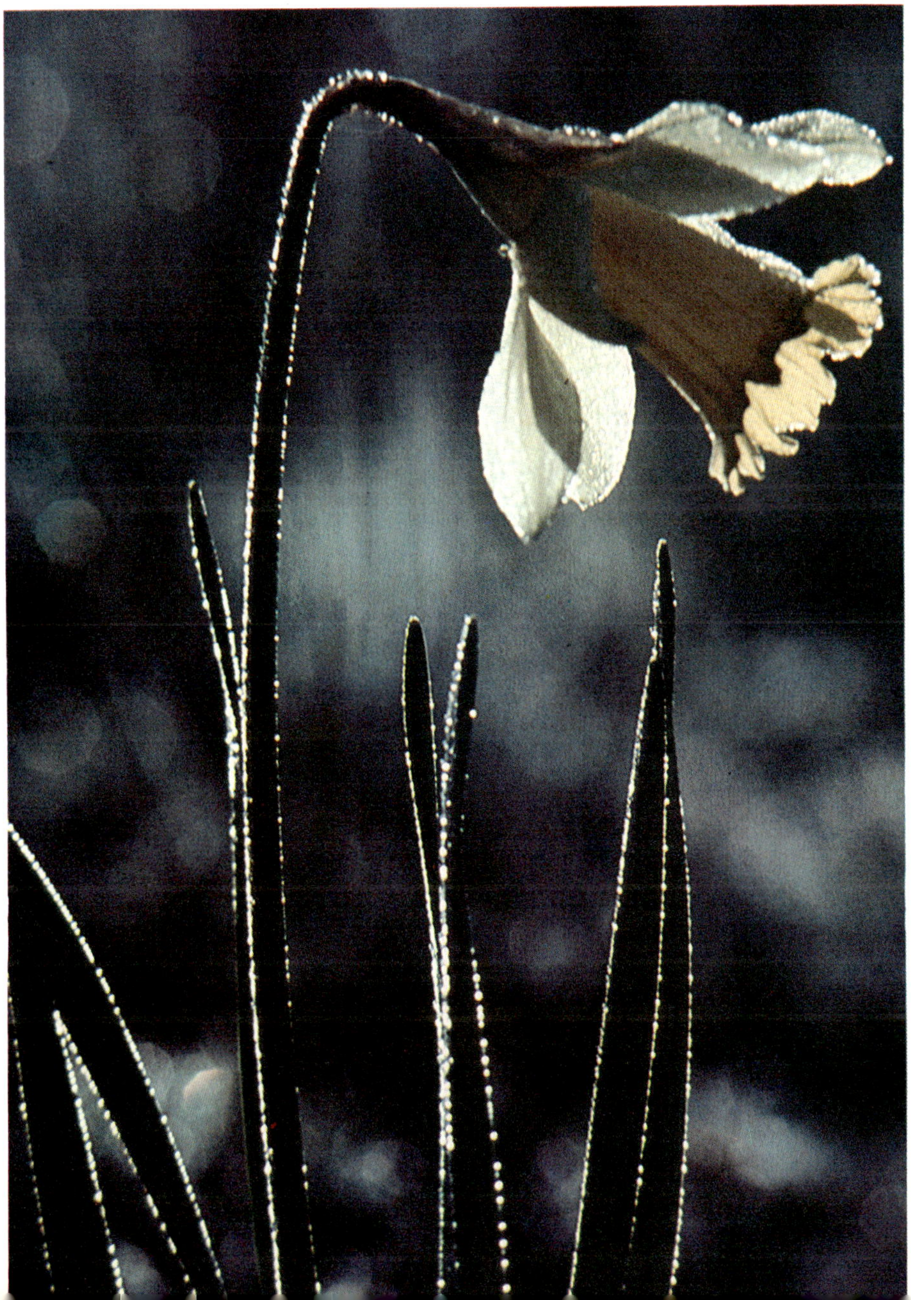

Top left: Back light, a slight haze and high contrast printing create a high-contrast image. Negative exposure needs to be enough to keep the light areas clean without unwanted detail in the foreground. Photo by Bob Kauders.

Above: This low-contrast image is the result of very soft light and a slight mist. Use a soft grade of printing paper to accentuate this effect. Photo by Jonathan Bayer.

Left: The high contrast resulted from exposing for the very strong back light. Photo by Richard Tucker.

Below: This is an example of low contrast in color. The brightness range here is actually lower than it seems because there is so much color contrast. Photo by Michael Busselle.

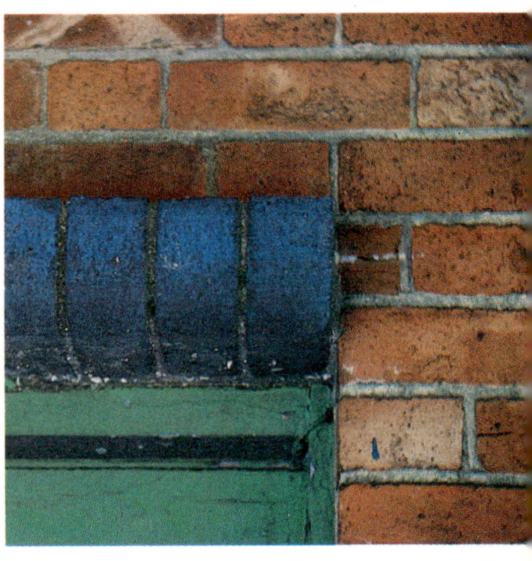

Seeing in Black & White

Many photographers prefer to use b&w. Although nothing beats color for realism, b&w is often more expressive. Color may be a distraction in certain circumstances, such as in documentary photography, or when the natural colors of the subject are not very pleasing. Without color, the image is simplified, allowing the shape, tones and texture to be emphasized.

COLOR AS B&W

To produce good b&w photographs, the world of color around us has to be seen as shades of gray. The change of approach is so marked that many experienced photographers find it difficult to shoot both b&w and color pictures at the same time.

One of the main problems is that colors of the same intensity, which may look very different in color, appear as the same tone of gray on b&w film. For example, a boat with a bright orange sail against a blue sea has strong contrast in color, but in b&w it may appear as gray on gray and look flat. When you start viewing the world in shades of gray, you will see that what makes a good color picture is very rarely as good in b&w.

If you have difficulty visualizing a scene in b&w, there are filters that will help you judge its tonal values. The Kodak Wratten No. 90 is a dark filter made specially for monochromatic viewing. You can place this gelatin filter in a transparency mount for protection and easier handling.

LIGHT AND B&W

Light changes tonal values and is of course vital to all photographic processes, but it has a special importance in b&w photography. The example of the orange-sailed boat on the blue sea, which looks flat and gray in b&w, can easily be converted into an exciting b&w image by a change of lighting. For example, if you aim into the

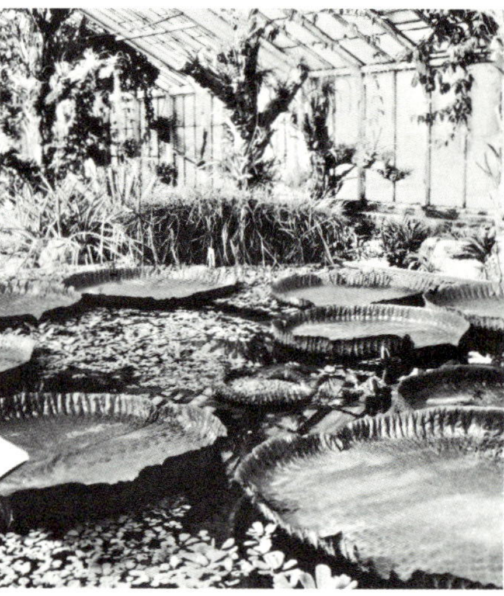

Right and below: When shooting b&w, look carefully at a scene's tonal values without regard to color. These radishes show what can happen to colors when imaged on b&w panchromatic film. The red and green give a strong contrasting image in color, but in b&w, the contrast disappears. Photos by Michael Newton.

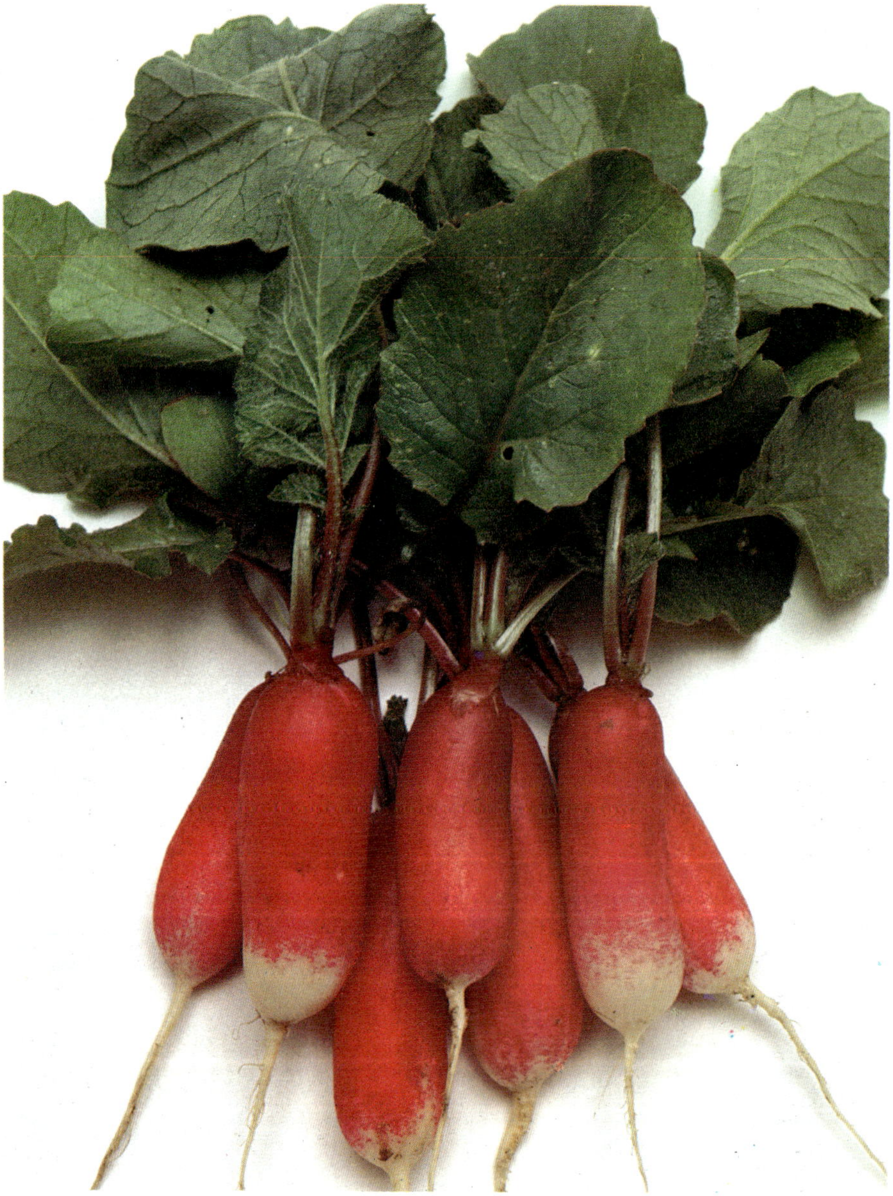

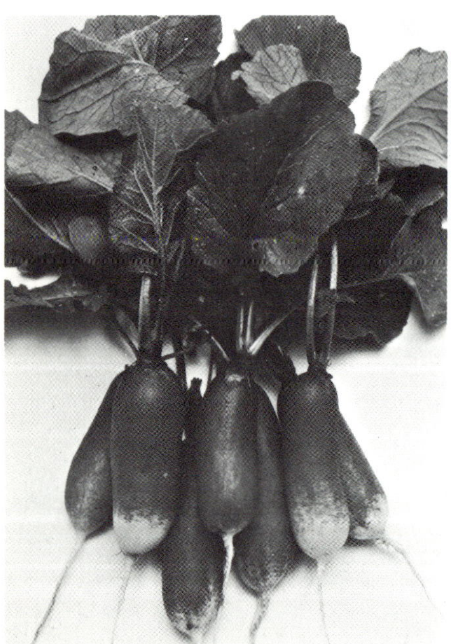

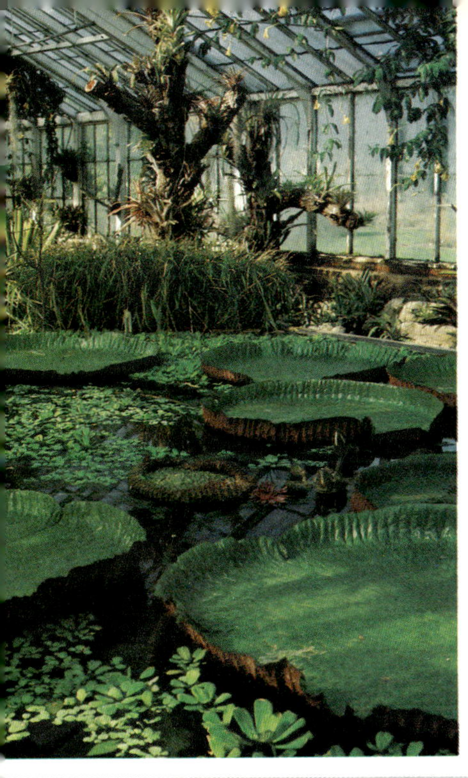

Left and far left: This garden is a busy scene that depends on color to separate the elements. These colors work well together but there is not much tonal contrast. In b&w the tonal values emerge as a rather distracting arrangement of details. Photo by Gunter Heil.

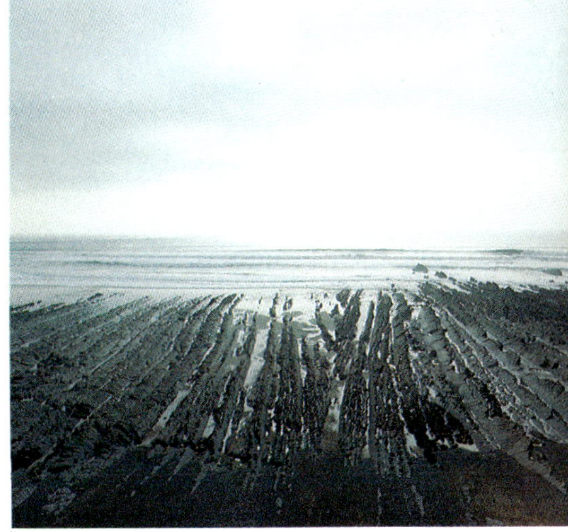

Right and below: This picture works better in b&w; in color it is rather flat. Increasing the contrast in the b&w print by using high contrast paper, and giving the sky extra exposure, resulted in an image rich in contrast. Photo by Michael Busselle.

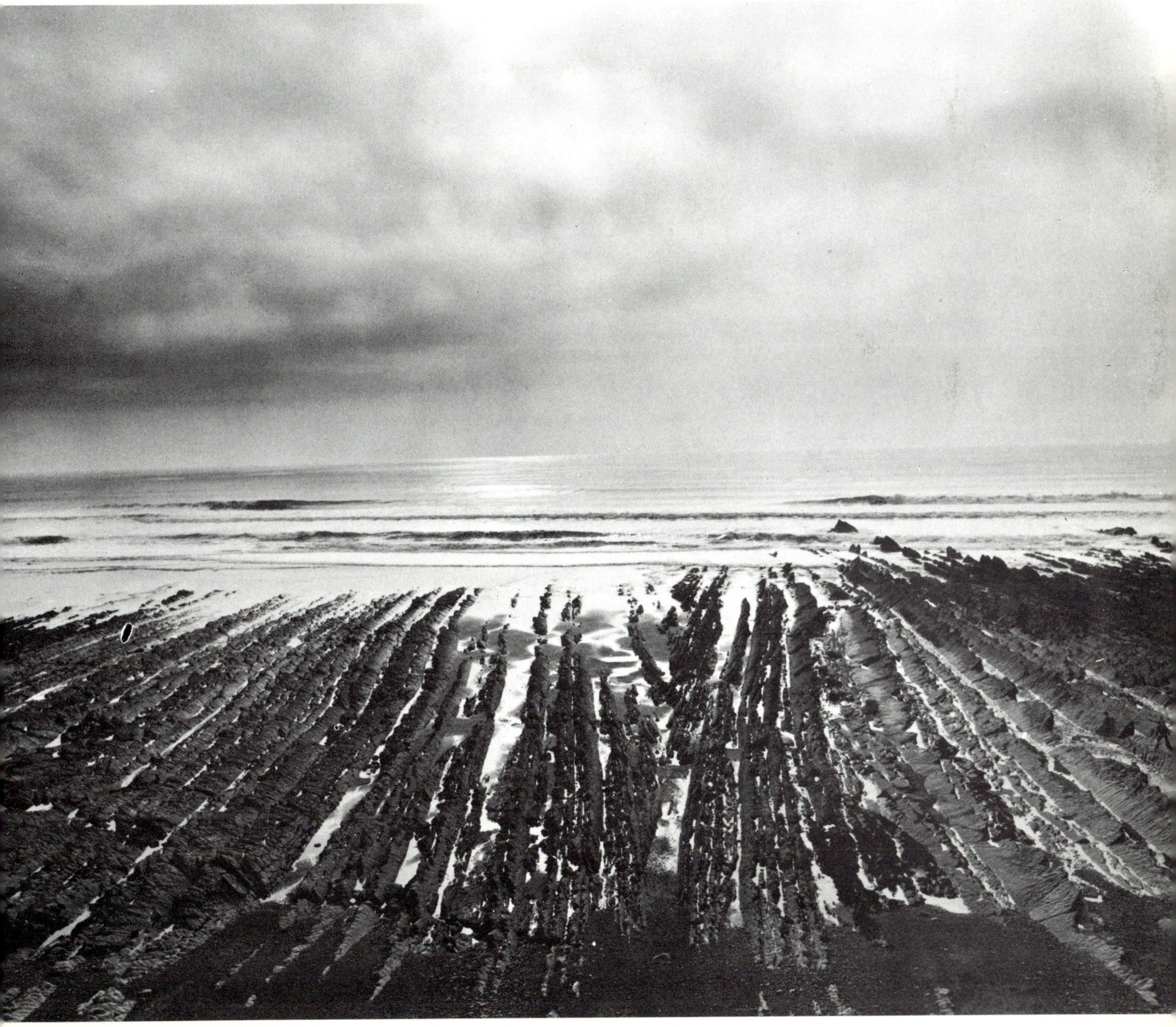

sun so the gray sea is highlighted and recorded as a much lighter tone, the sail will become silhouetted and record as a much darker tone. The resulting image will have impact and contrast.

Thus, tonal range of a scene becomes important. To a large extent it is the light that creates the tonal quality of a picture. Taking photographs in b&w is an excellent way of learning how to understand and use light.

FILTERS

Modern panchromatic b&w films have practically the same sensitivity to each color. This is why colors of the same brightness record as a similar gray tone. You can change the film's response to color by using filters designed to add tonal contrast in b&w photographs.

These filters are available as discs or squares of colored glass or plastic. They are mounted in front of the camera lens and work by passing light of the same color as the filter but holding back light of other colors. The effect depends on the density of the filter. For example, a dense primary blue filter passes blue light only and prevents all red and green light from reaching the film. A pale blue filter will hold back only part of the red and green light.

Color filters give considerable control over the response a b&w film has to color. Returning to the example of the orange sail and blue sea, you can use a strong blue filter to record the sea as a much lighter tone and the orange sail as nearly black. With a strong orange filter, the sail will record as nearly white and the sea as very dark gray.

Few of the colors around us are pure, so the red sail may reflect some blue and the sea some green. Even with a filter, the effect is rarely total.

Once you know how to "translate" the color you see into b&w images, you can create more powerful, dramatic photographs. You will see when b&w would be more effective than color. For example, in low-light situations where flash is out of the question, such as concerts, some sporting events or social functions, color would add very little. A fast b&w film would be best.

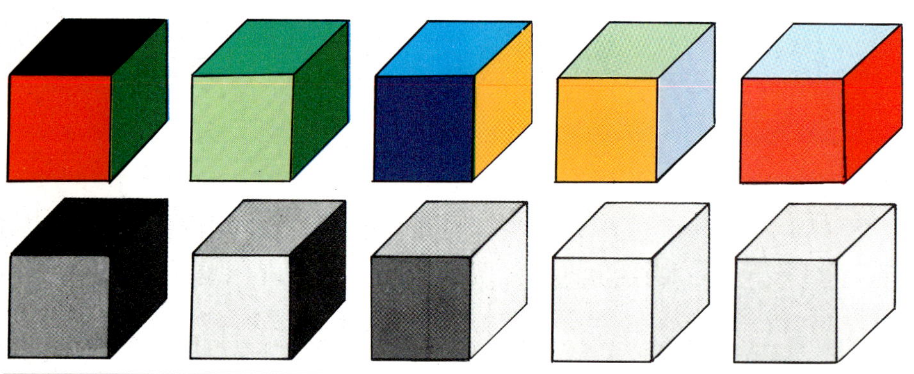

COLOR TO B&W
The two rows of boxes give an idea of how colors reproduce in b&w. Look at the tones that appear the same in the bottom row and then compare them with the color versions.

▶ News photographs such as this one by Don McCullin seldom gain impact from color because their effect depends mostly on the emotional content. Color tends to detract.

▼ The yachting scene is a strong composition as a color photograph, mainly due to the bold contrast between the orange sail and the blue sea. In the b&w at right, the sail becomes a medium gray and there is no longer a strong contrast. Below right: Using a blue filter with b&w film causes the sail to become darker and the sea lighter. Photos by Michael Busselle.

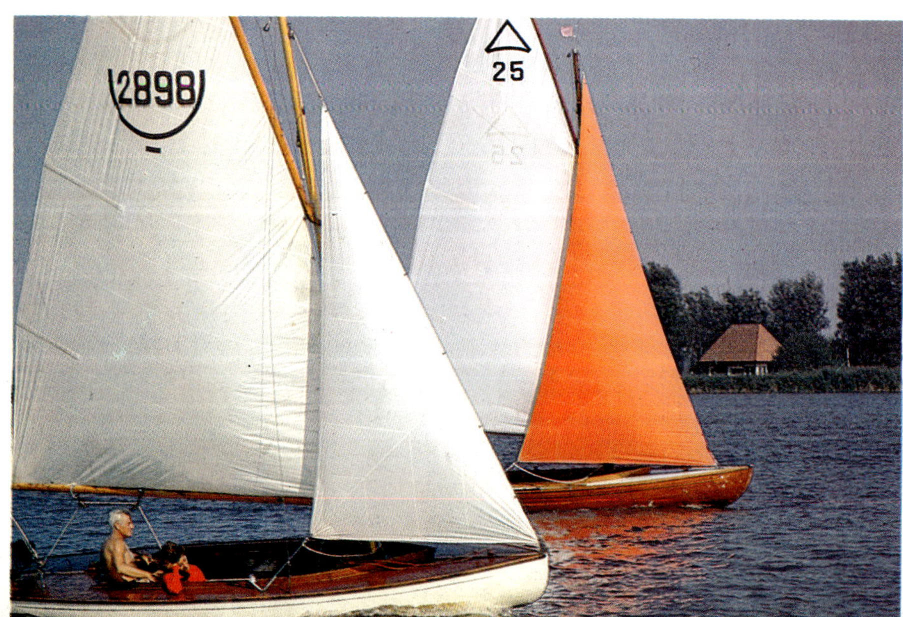

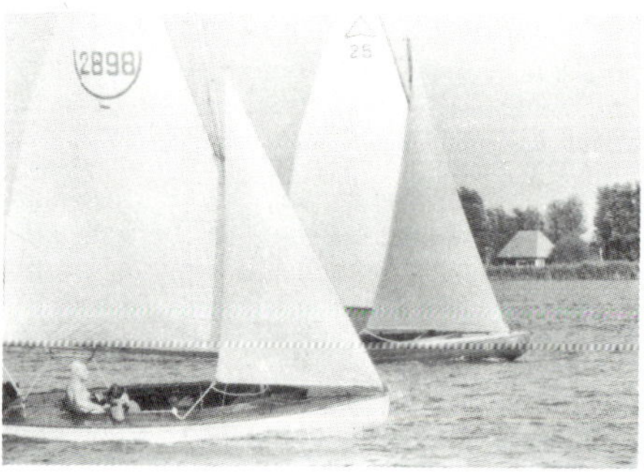

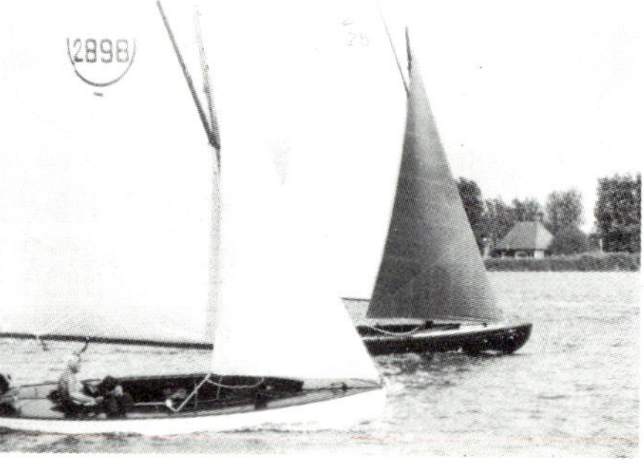

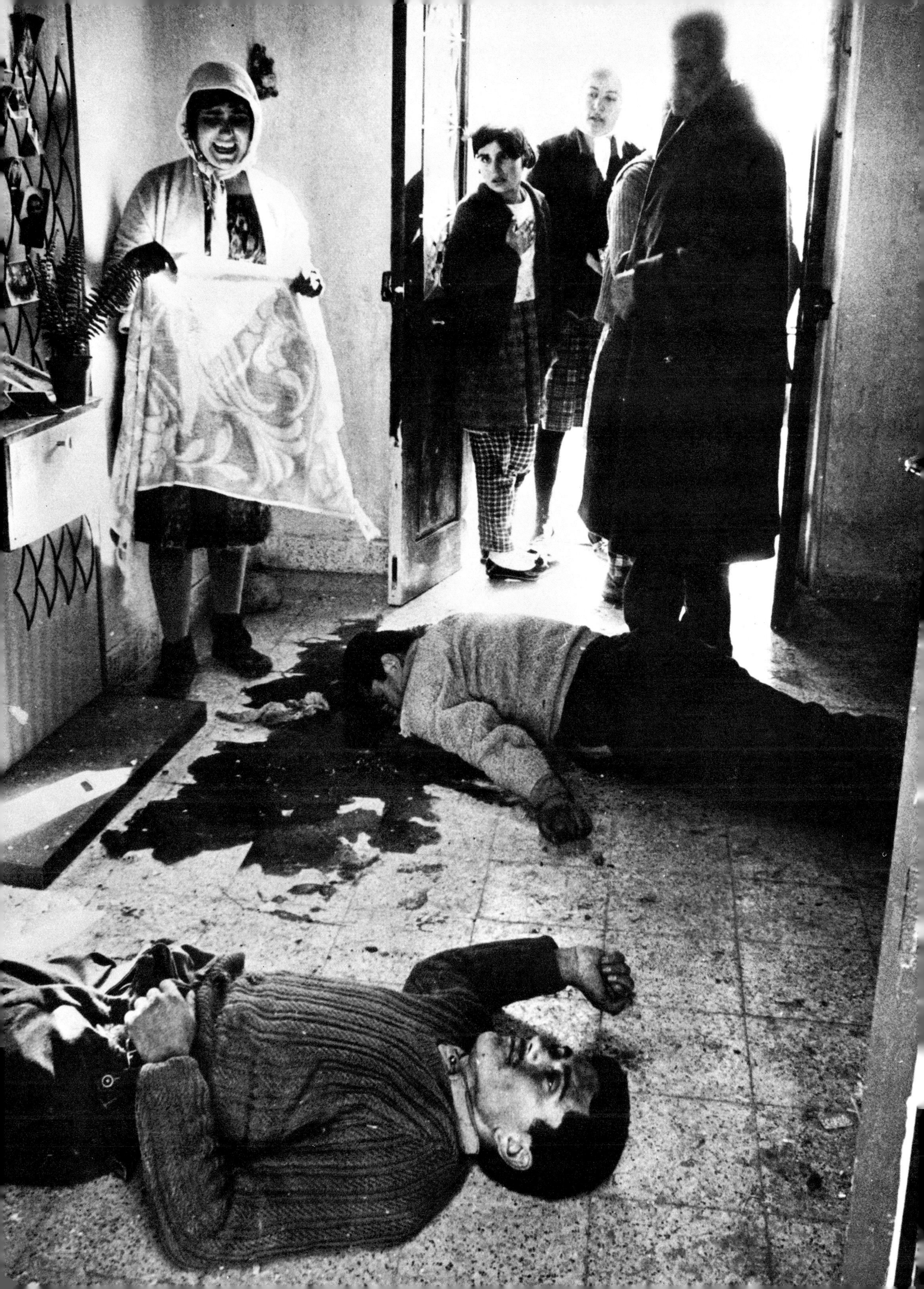

Scale and Depth

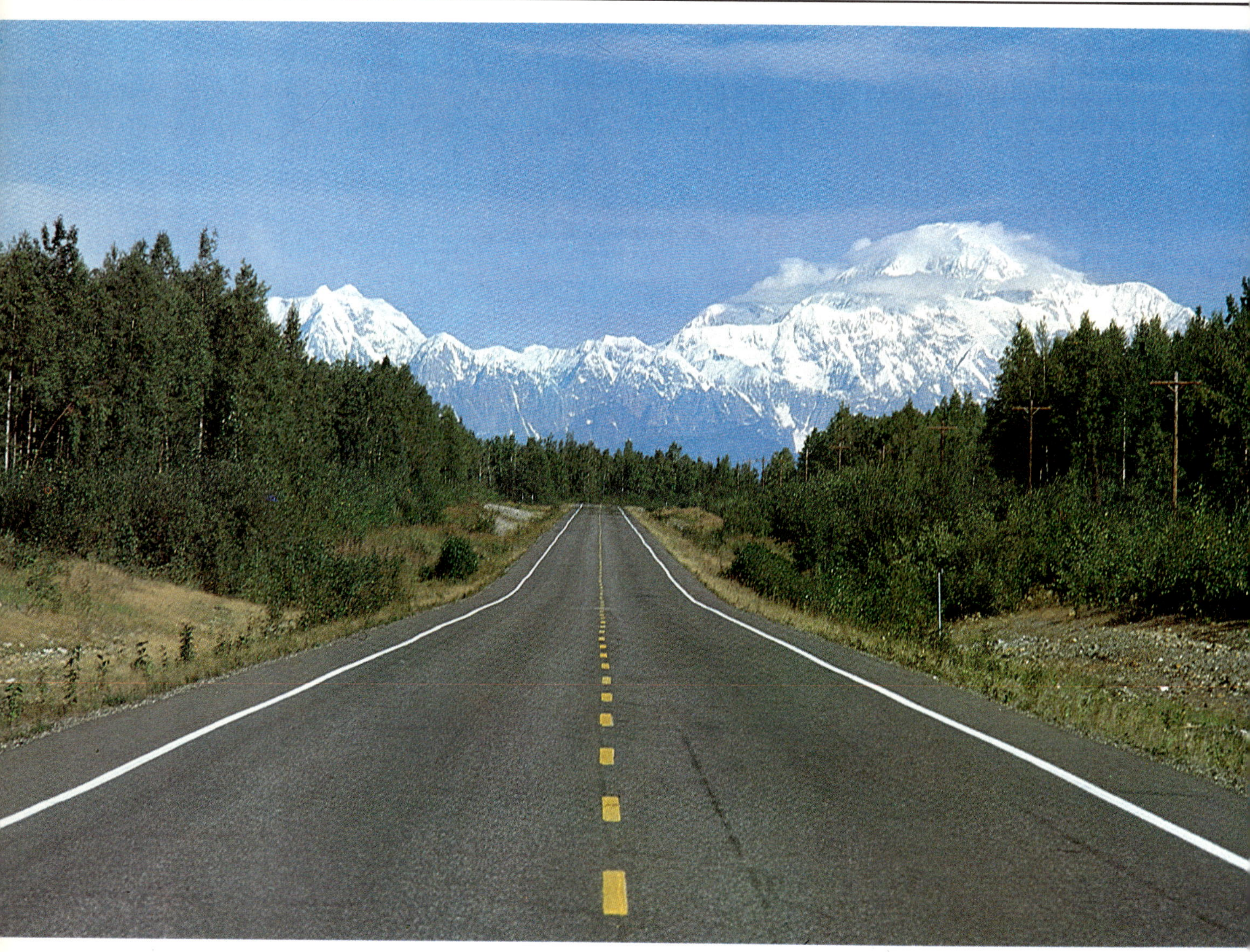

▲ Converging lines, which the eye accepts as an indicator of distance, is one of the most simple and effective ways to give a photograph the feeling of depth. Photographer Steve Herr dramatized the effect by standing in the middle of the road to take this picture.

One of the greatest limitations of photography is that it has to show a three-dimensional subject by using a two-dimensional medium—a piece of photographic paper or film. However, when you look at a photograph, it's not difficult to assess the depth and form of the objects in the picture. This is because there are clues to help you. One of the most important of these is *perspective.* It is perspective that shows the shape and size of objects in relation to their distance from the viewpoint.

As a photographer, the more you learn about the tricks of perspective and how to use them, the more you can create a sense of dramatic three-dimensional depth to suit the subject of your photographs.

CONVERGING LINES

Everyone knows that if you look down a railroad track, the rails appear to converge. They appear closer and closer together until, at a distance, they appear to touch. The ties also appear to get smaller and closer together. This apparent convergence is due to an effect of perspective—the fact that objects nearest to us always appear larger than identical objects placed farther away.

A railroad track is a simple and obvious example because we know that the lines are the same distance apart. But the effects of perspective are with us all the time. The buildings we see when looking down a street, even if they are not all identical, appear proportionally narrower and smaller the farther they are from us. Because your brain uses previous knowledge and experience, it modifies your eyes' accurate image and tells you that the buildings are the same relative size along the entire length of the street. You may *know* this to be true, but it is not the image actually received. Your brain has translated the information and decided to ignore perspective.

Having established that your brain has been tricking you all your life, as a photographer you must now start trying to see what is actually there. Because the camera does not have a brain, it will not ignore perspective. Learn to rely more on your eyes and less on previous experience.

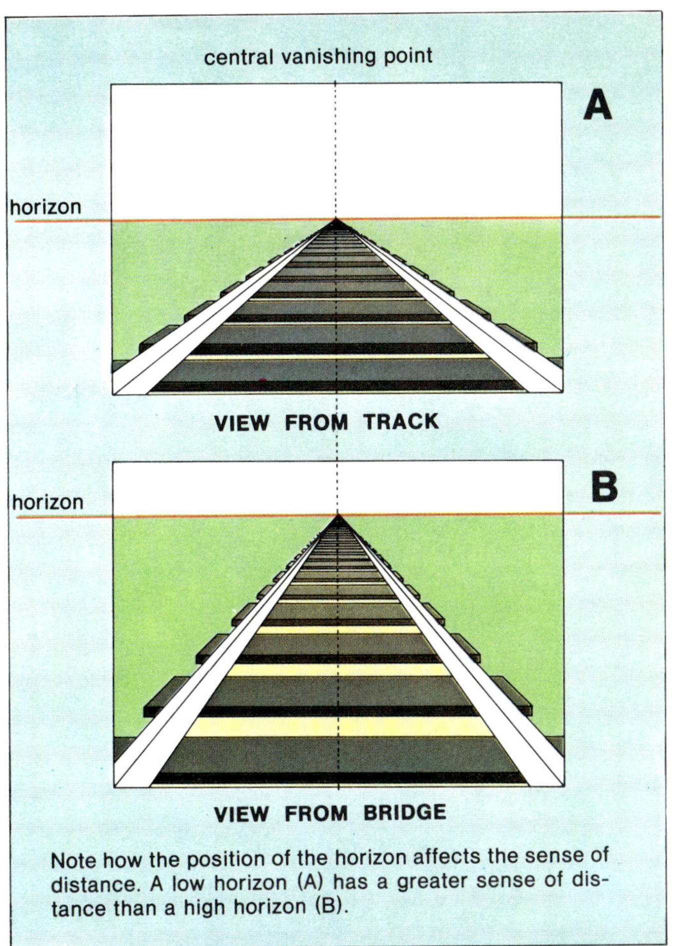

Note how the position of the horizon affects the sense of distance. A low horizon (A) has a greater sense of distance than a high horizon (B).

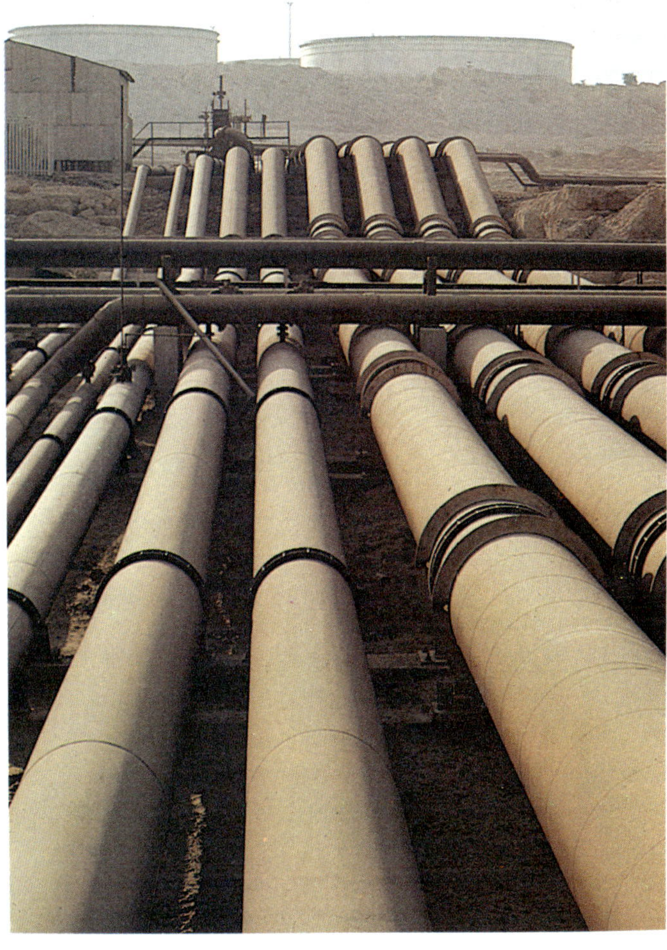

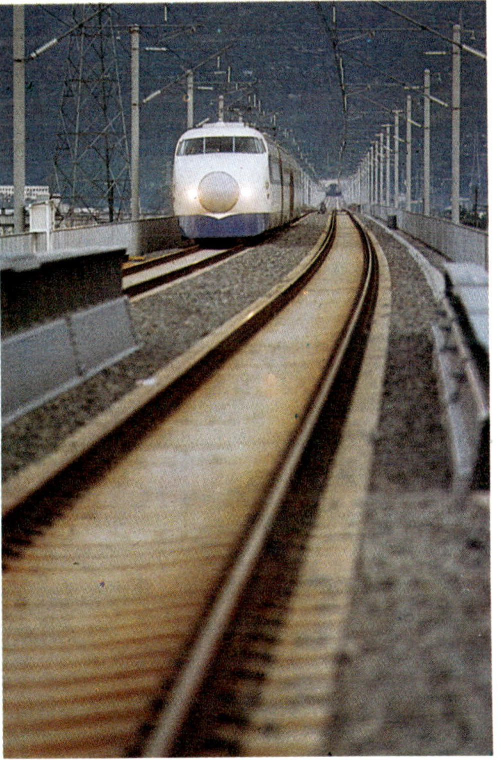

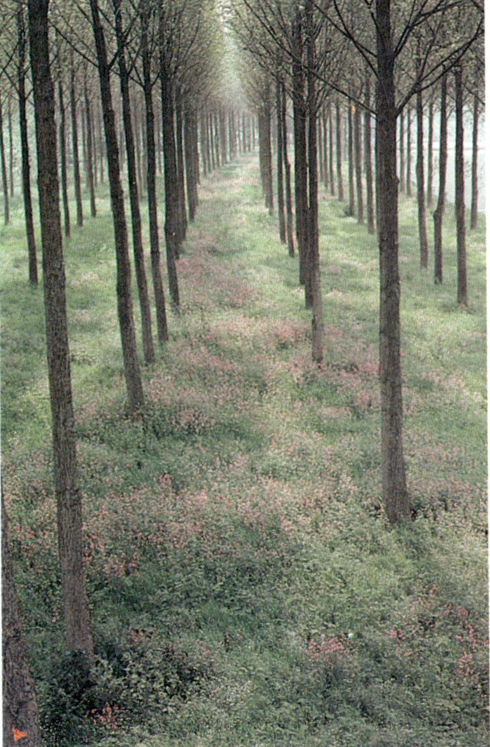

Including parallel lines that appear to meet in the distance is not in itself enough to make a good picture with good depth. You have to choose a viewpoint to best exploit the effect, thereby creating the mood you wish to convey.

Above: Paolo Koch's low, central viewpoint of oil pipes results in a feeling of power and order.

Lisa Mackson's high viewpoint at left draws the eye down into the quiet seclusion of the woodland scene.

Far left: John Bulmer stood slightly to one side to lead the viewer from the front of the photograph to the train, and then into the distance.

VANISHING POINTS

Vanishing points and the horizon are two essential elements of perspective. Taking the railroad track as an example, you can see that the lines appear to converge at a point as far as the eye can see, and then disappear. This is the *vanishing point.*

In any scene there may be more than one vanishing point. If you stand between the rails and look along the track, you will see that there is only one central vanishing point as you saw in Diagrams A and B on the preceding page. If you look at a building from one corner, as illustrated in Diagrams C, D, E and F, there are two vanishing points, one on either side. Whatever their number, and whichever direction you look, from the same viewpoint all vanishing points are on the same horizontal line. This line is the *horizon.*

VIEWPOINT

The position of the horizon, and of all the vanishing points along it, depends entirely on your viewpoint. By changing your viewpoint you change the position of the horizon, and alter the perspective.

The "normal" position of the horizon is at eye level, as in Diagram A. By moving higher up as in Diagram B, you extend your area of vision, and the horizon changes. The higher your viewpoint, the higher the horizon.

If you lower your viewpoint, objects appear to grow. A building appears larger because it towers above normal eye level, indicating that it is very tall in relation to your viewpoint.

Changing your viewpoint affects the position of the horizon and alters perspective, which, in turn, governs the visual impression of scale. With a very high viewpoint, such as from a helicopter, you could photograph a skyscraper so it would assume the scale of a cigarette pack in the resulting print. Your brain would adjust this image because it would recognize it as a building and because everything else would be in proportion. The building would still tower above its environment and stand out.

Similarly, you could photograph a cigarette pack from a very low viewpoint so it appears like a skyscraper.

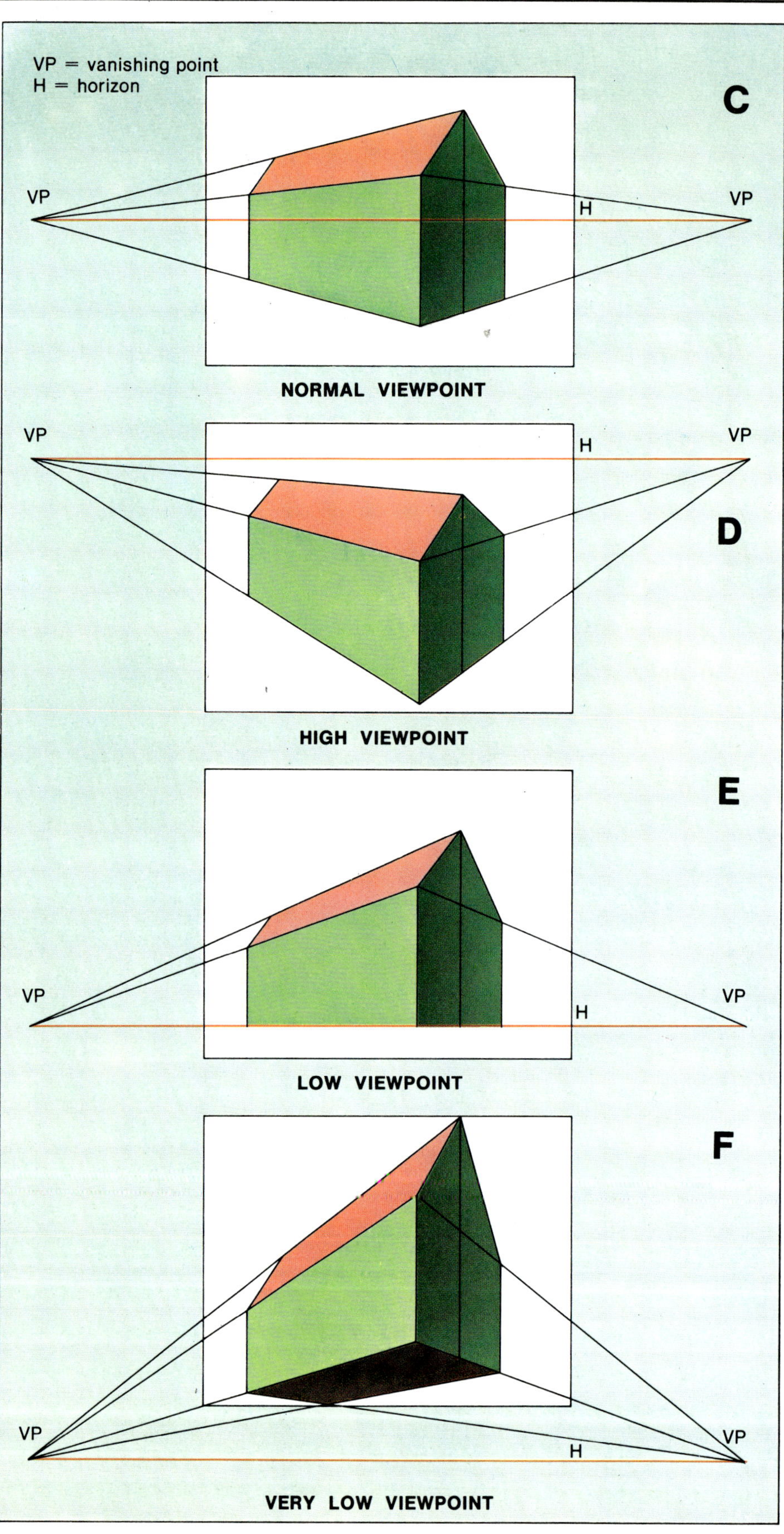

This series of diagrams shows how the effect of perspective becomes exaggerated by moving from a high viewpoint to a low one. When there are two vanishing points, the sense of depth can be further increased by moving closer to one side than the other.

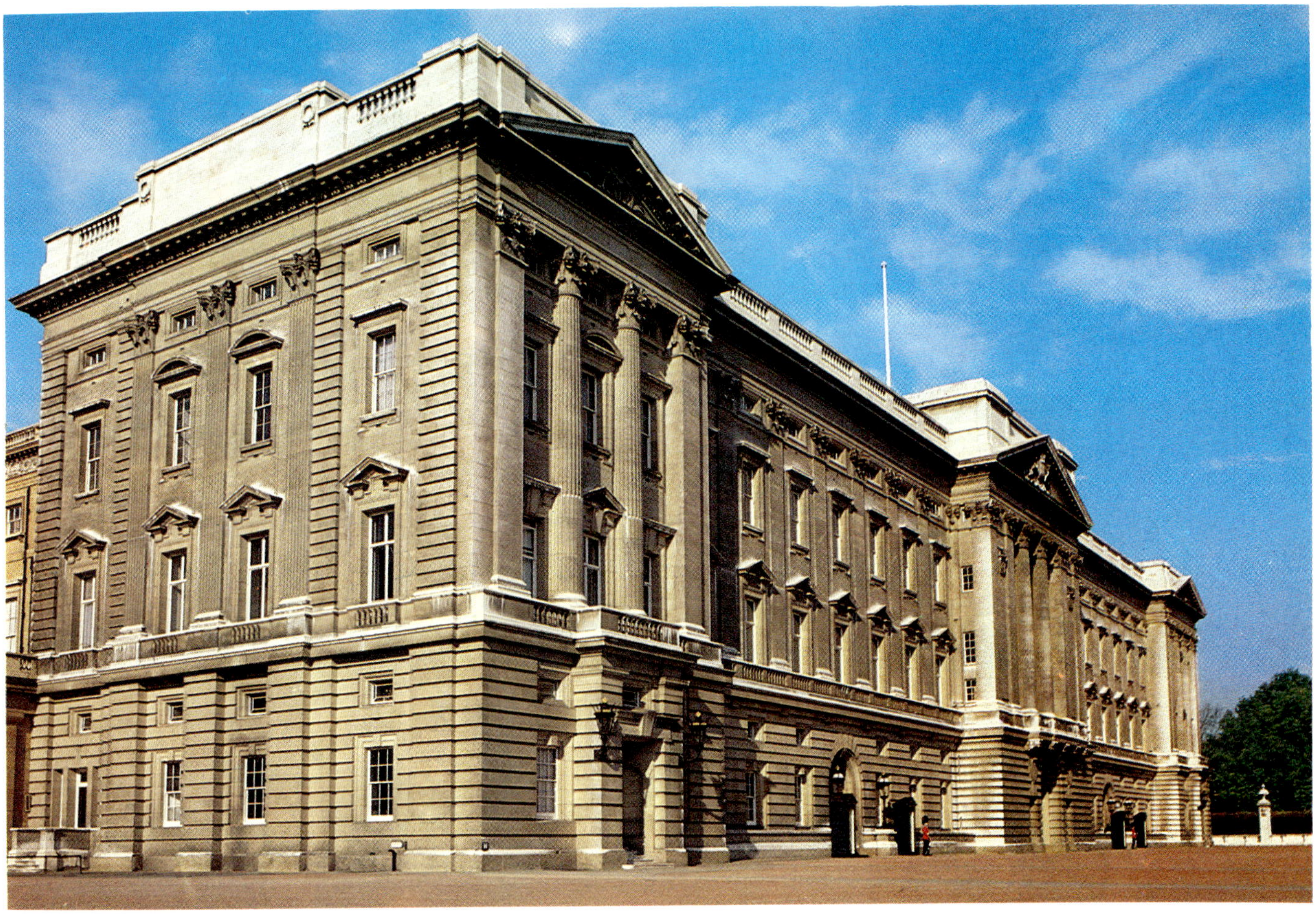

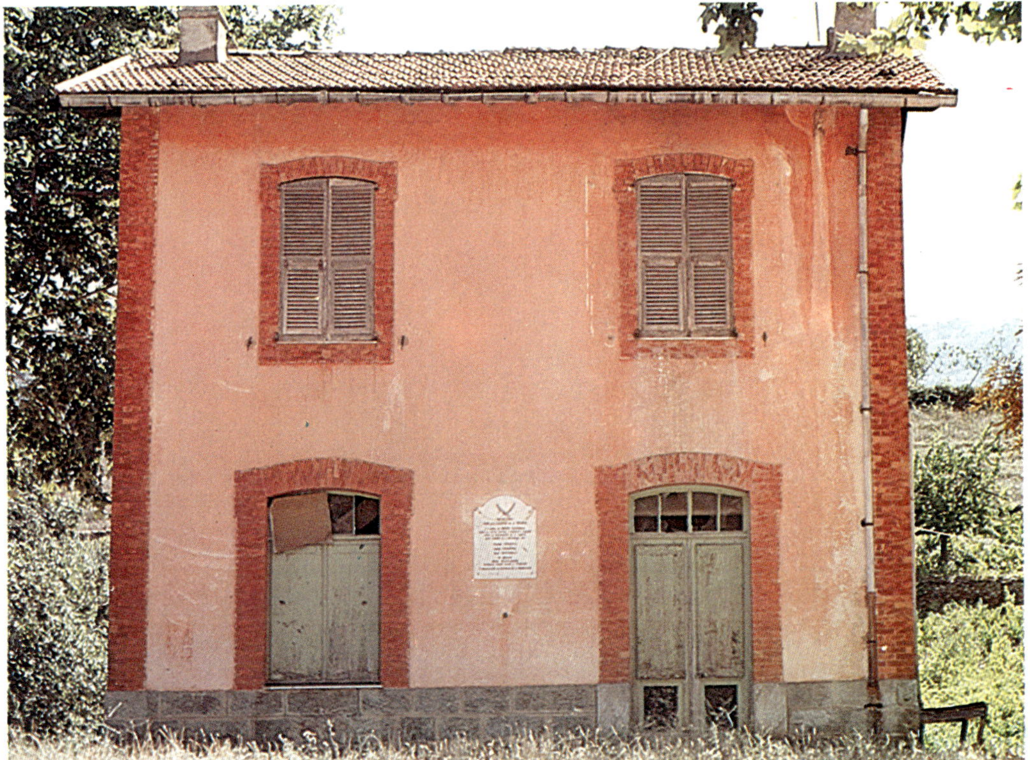

Two vanishing points are better than one, especially when you want to emphasize the subject's three-dimensional quality. For example, a building has two surfaces that meet at right angles to each other. This creates two vanishing points, one from each surface. You may not be able to include both, or even one, in the frame. But, by positioning yourself at the point where the walls meet, so both are seen at an angle (above), you can suggest vanishing points outside the edges of the picture. This will give a greater sense of depth than a shot made at a right angle to one surface, as illustrated at left.

USING PERSPECTIVE

Choose a photograph from a newspaper or magazine and draw a carefully measured grid over it. Better still, draw 1/4 inch or 1/2 inch (6mm or 12mm) squares on tracing paper. Overlay the grid on any picture. You can quickly see how perspective works with the aid of this grid.

You'll see how objects consistently appear smaller as they stretch into the distance because the grid has constant, equal squares. You should also find where the horizon is situated, and thus be able to plot vanishing points.

This will help you see the way three-dimensional scenes are depicted on the flat surface of a photograph or drawing. Try making better use of perspective as an element of design and composition in your pictures. Later, we'll outline a number of elements to help you create a sense of depth.

Incidentally, if you find yourself able to see the effect of perspective on the print but not through the camera viewfinder, consider using a focusing screen with a grid if your camera accepts interchangeable focusing screens. Such a screen may take a little time to get used to, but you should see a big improvement in your photographs. If you go back to using the original focusing screen later, this improvement should remain.

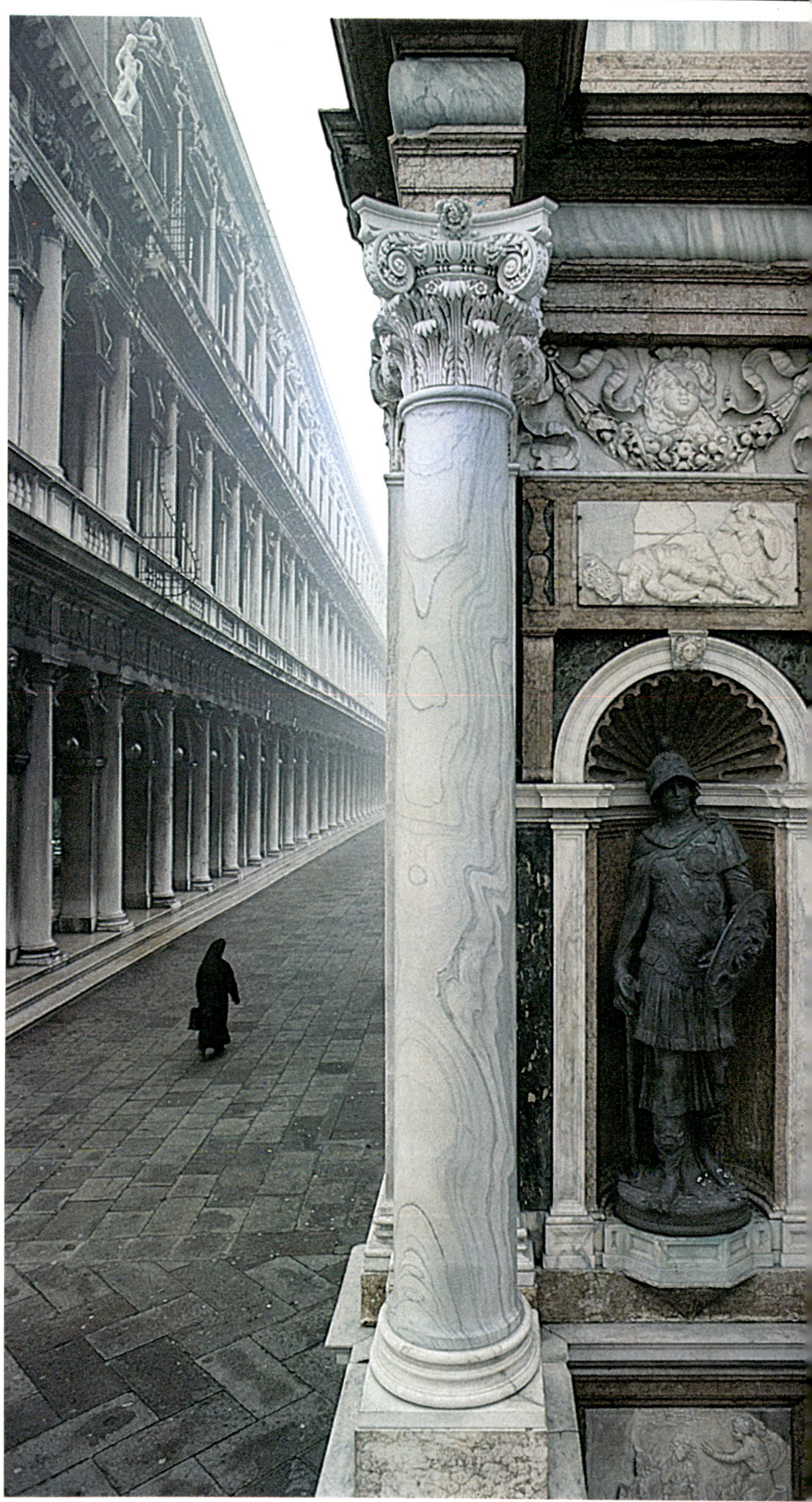

▶ For this picture, Adam Woolfitt found an unusual viewpoint that emphasizes the effect of perspective. The "flatness" of the head-on view coupled with the dynamic lines disappearing into the distance makes a striking contrast, emphasizing both elements.

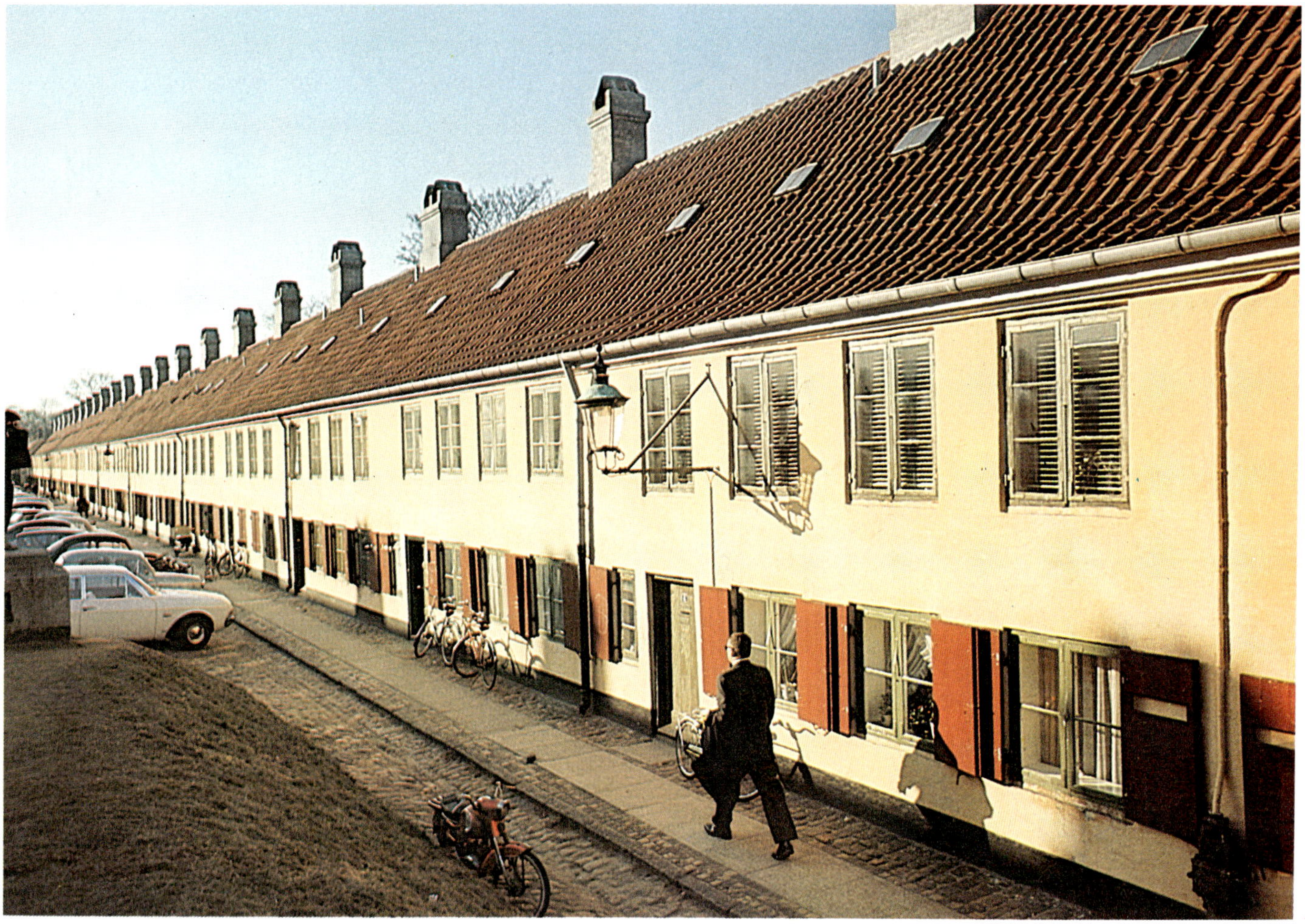

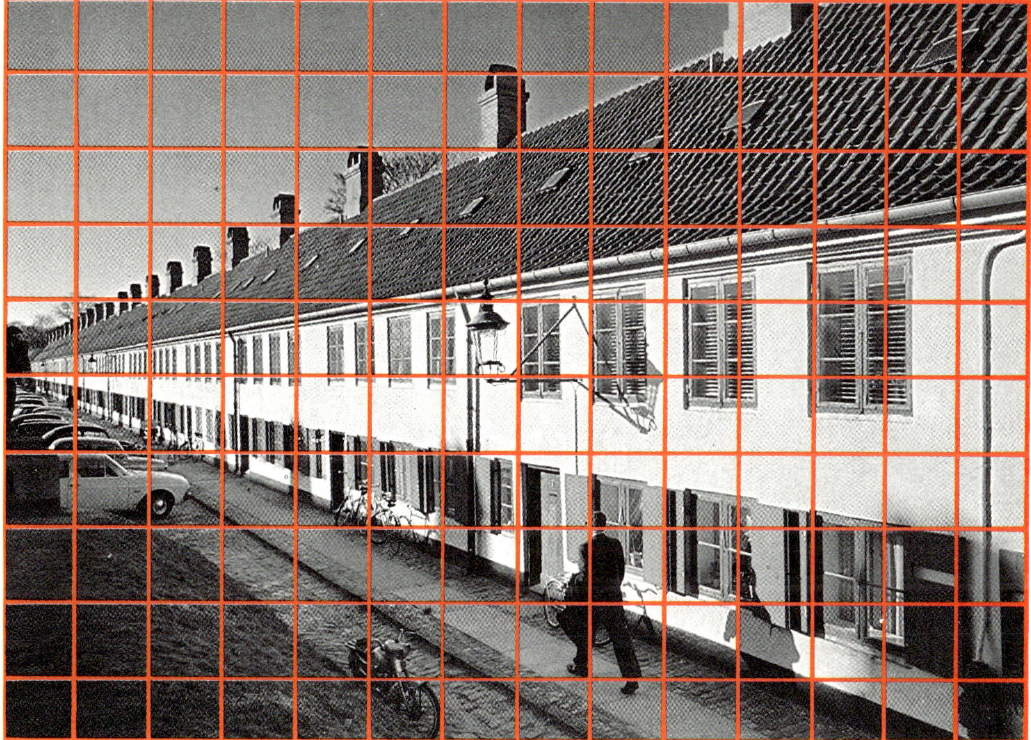

The essential part that perspective plays in showing depth and distance is obvious when you look at a print or transparency. It is not as easy to judge through the camera viewfinder. Placing a grid over printed photographs is one way of becoming more aware of the visual effect of perspective. This should help you think and "see" more carefully when perspective is an important part of a scene. Photo by Michael Busselle.

Creating Depth

A feeling of depth is not an essential requirement of every good photograph. A telephoto lens, for instance, compresses distance and can make an impressive two-dimensional picture that is arresting because of its flatness. The subject appears to be on the *surface* of the photograph like a flat, drawn design instead of a three-dimensional scene.

For many subjects, a flat image would be disappointing, and it is vital to create an impression of depth. Landscapes often appear to come to life only when the viewer's eye is drawn into and around the scenery, exploring the image. Look at successful photographs—still-lifes, landscapes or people—and observe how composition benefits from this strong three-dimensional effect.

Thus, one of the first decisions to consider every time you take a picture is, do you want to create a flat design or a three-dimensional effect?

There are many basic elements that can combine to give a sense of depth in a photograph. These are subject qualities such as scale, contour, tone and texture. In addition, you can use camera controls such as selective focusing. No matter what camera you have, you can exploit most of these. Start by looking for each element, described on the next four pages. Then see if you can make photos based on one or more of these elements. As with other areas of composition, the first step is to look carefully at the subject and recognize the opportunities.

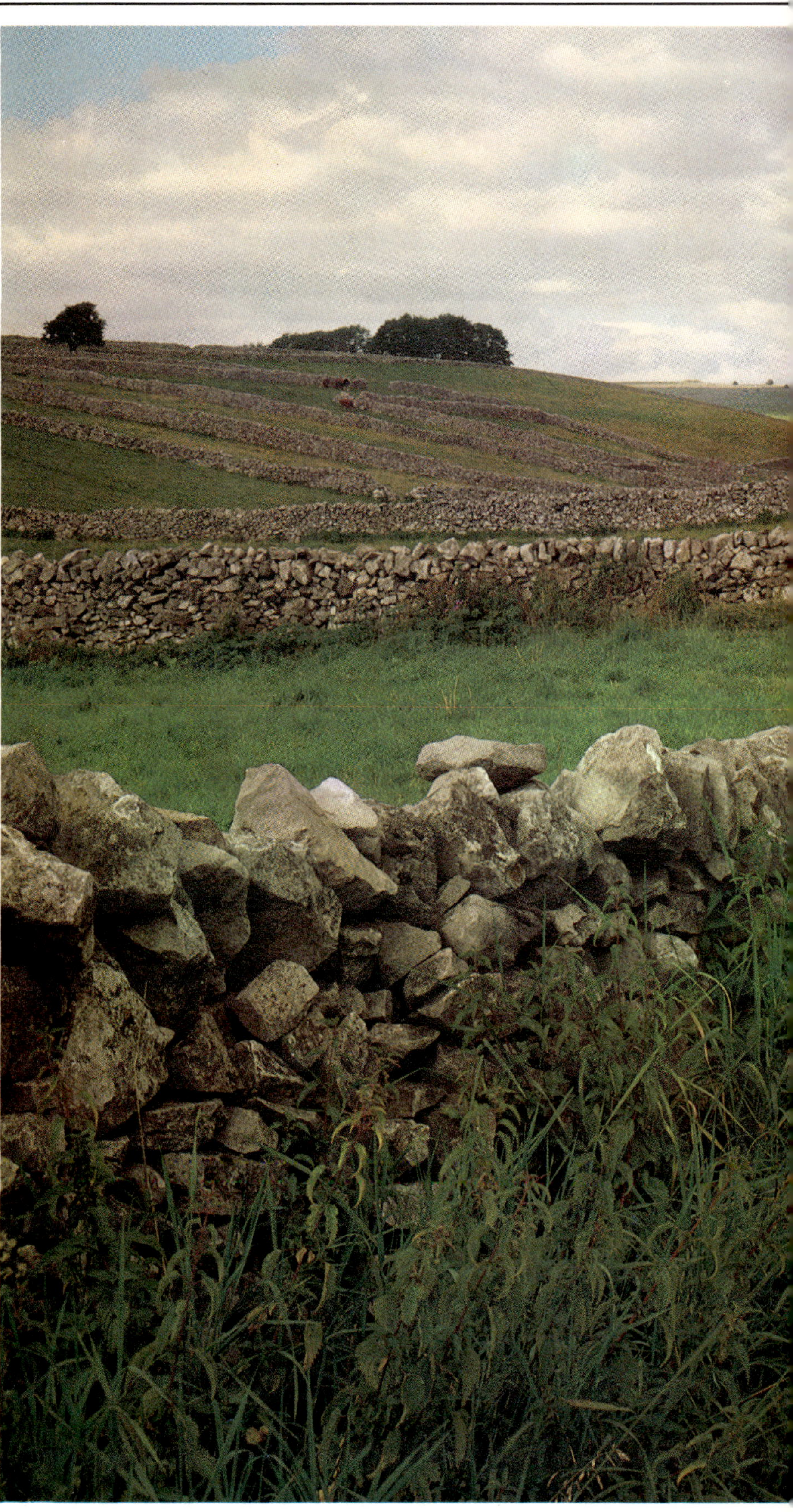

▶ There are times when a flat, diagrammatic representation of a landscape can look very impressive. The strength of this image, however, lies in its tremendous feeling of depth. The countryside seems to stretch on and on into the distance. Kenneth Griffiths carefully composed the picture so the viewer is drawn from the foreground on the left to the main subject on the right. The lines of the road and walls then lead you into the middle distance, almost in the center of the scene, and then on to the horizon. Including the low layer of clouds as a ceiling further increases the sensation of depth.

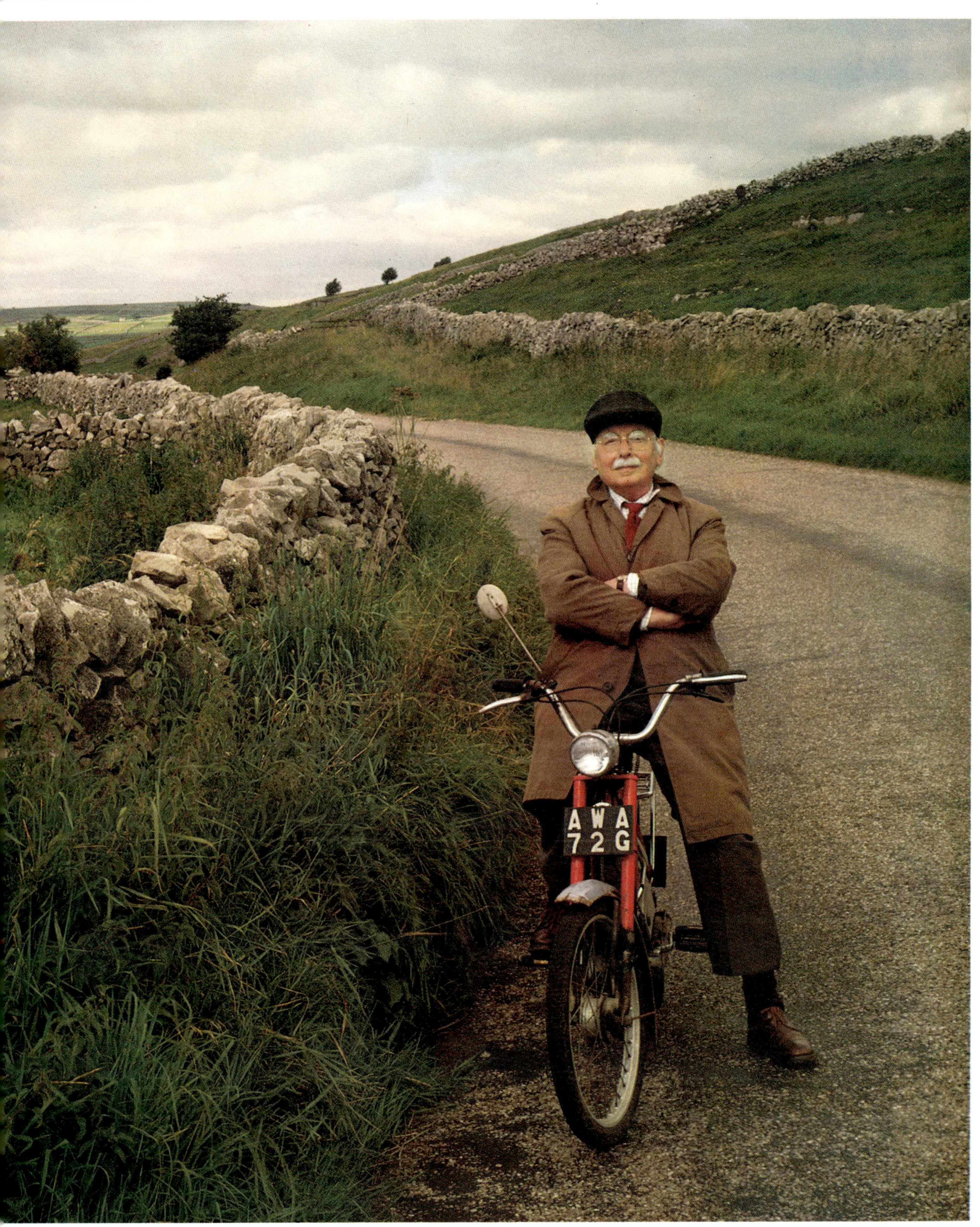
AWA
72G

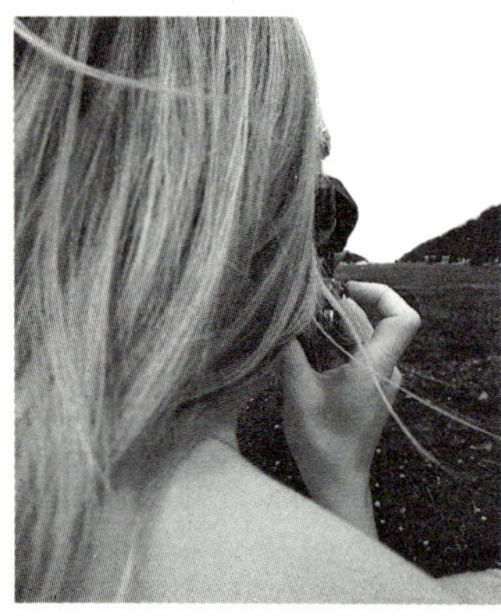

▶ SCALE: A picture that gives little indication of the scale of the elements within it can be very deceptive. Mountains, for example, may look like small hills unless there is something in the photograph to compare them with. Notice how the sense of distance here depends to a great extent on the Eiffel Tower relative to the figure in the foreground. When the tower is removed, much of the feeling of depth goes with it. Photo by Bryn Campbell.

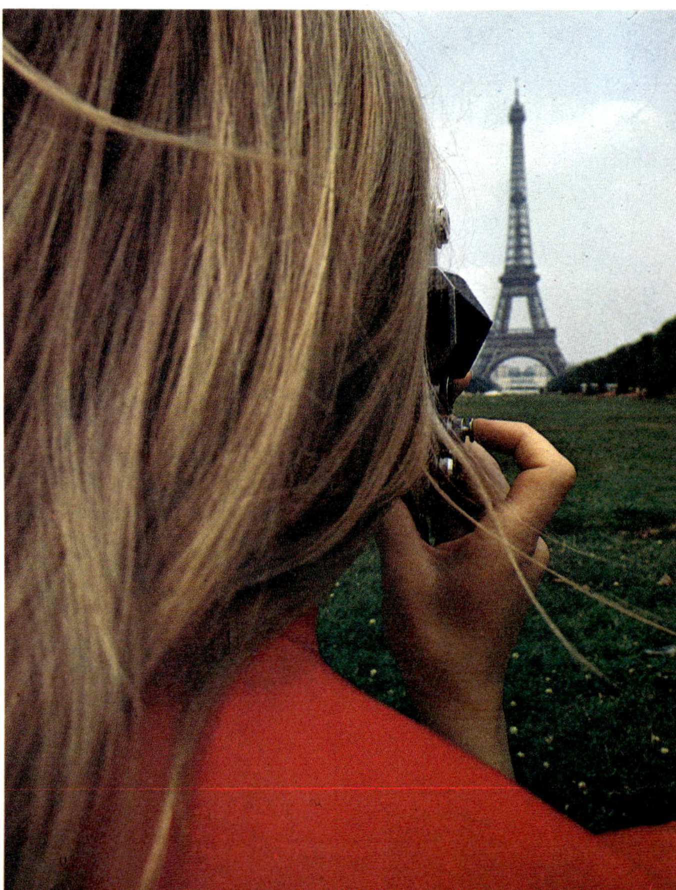

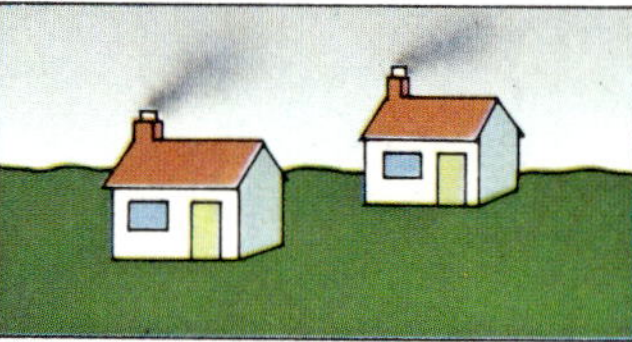

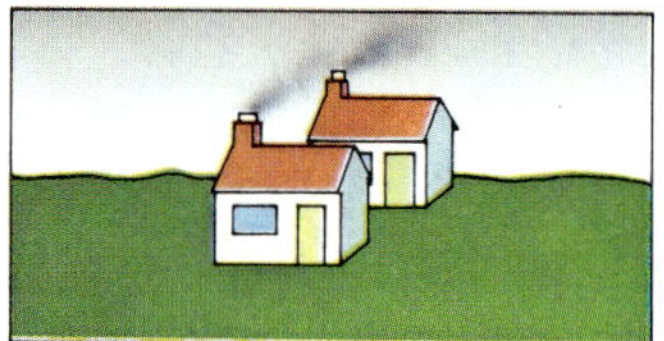

▶ OVERLAPPING FORMS: When one element partially obscures another, the overall impression of depth is greater than if the two are separated. This is illustrated by the simple drawings above. The photograph of the abbey shows how the principle works in practice. Had photographer Clay Perry moved closer so the wall in the foreground did not overlap the structure in the background, the final picture would lose depth and appear much flatter.

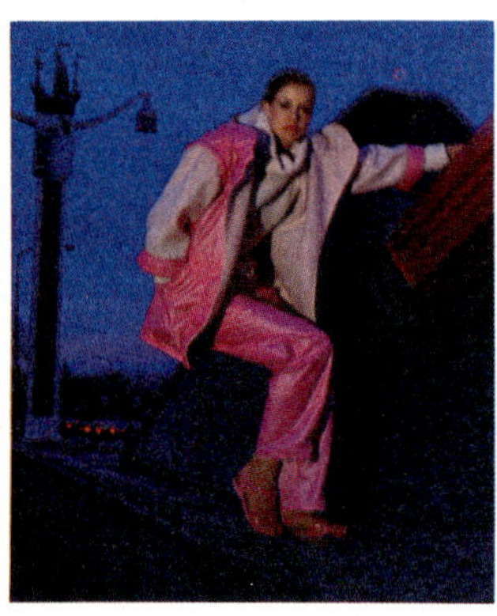

▶ LEAD-IN LINES: Lines that draw you into the image are a useful compositional device to create a feeling of depth. These lines can come from the bottom, the sides or the top. Compare the effect at right with the one above, in which most of the lead-in element has been cropped out. Photo by Tino Tedaldi.

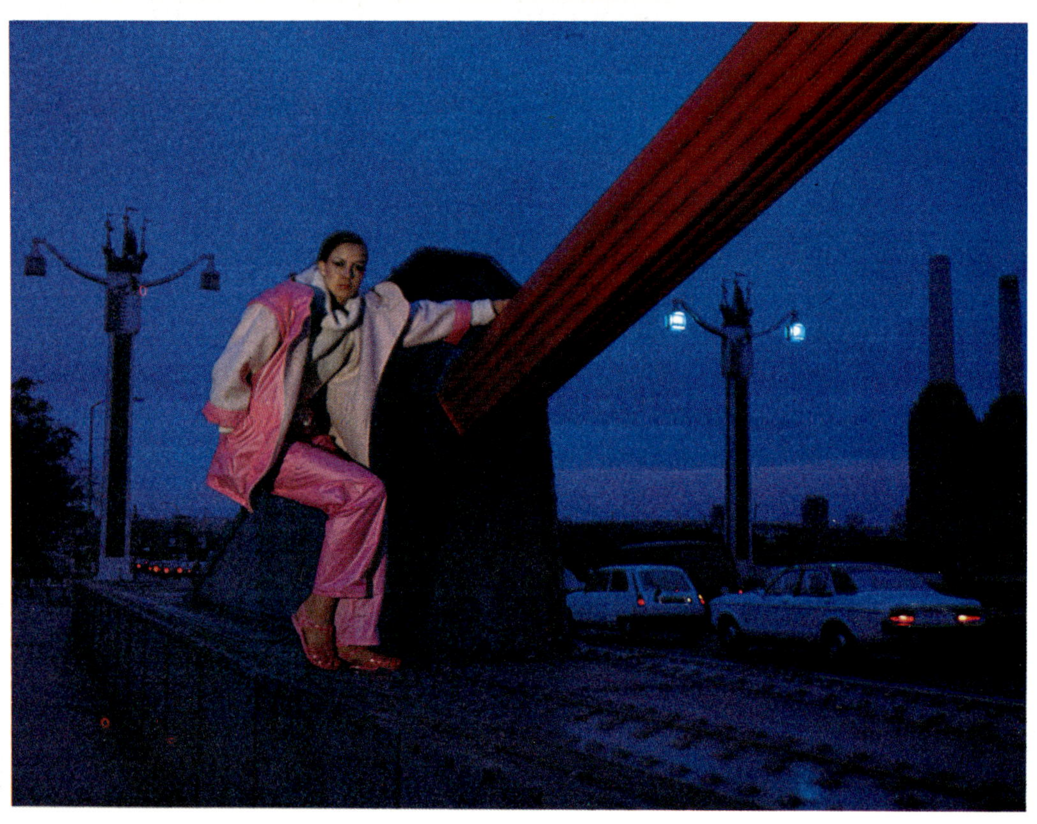

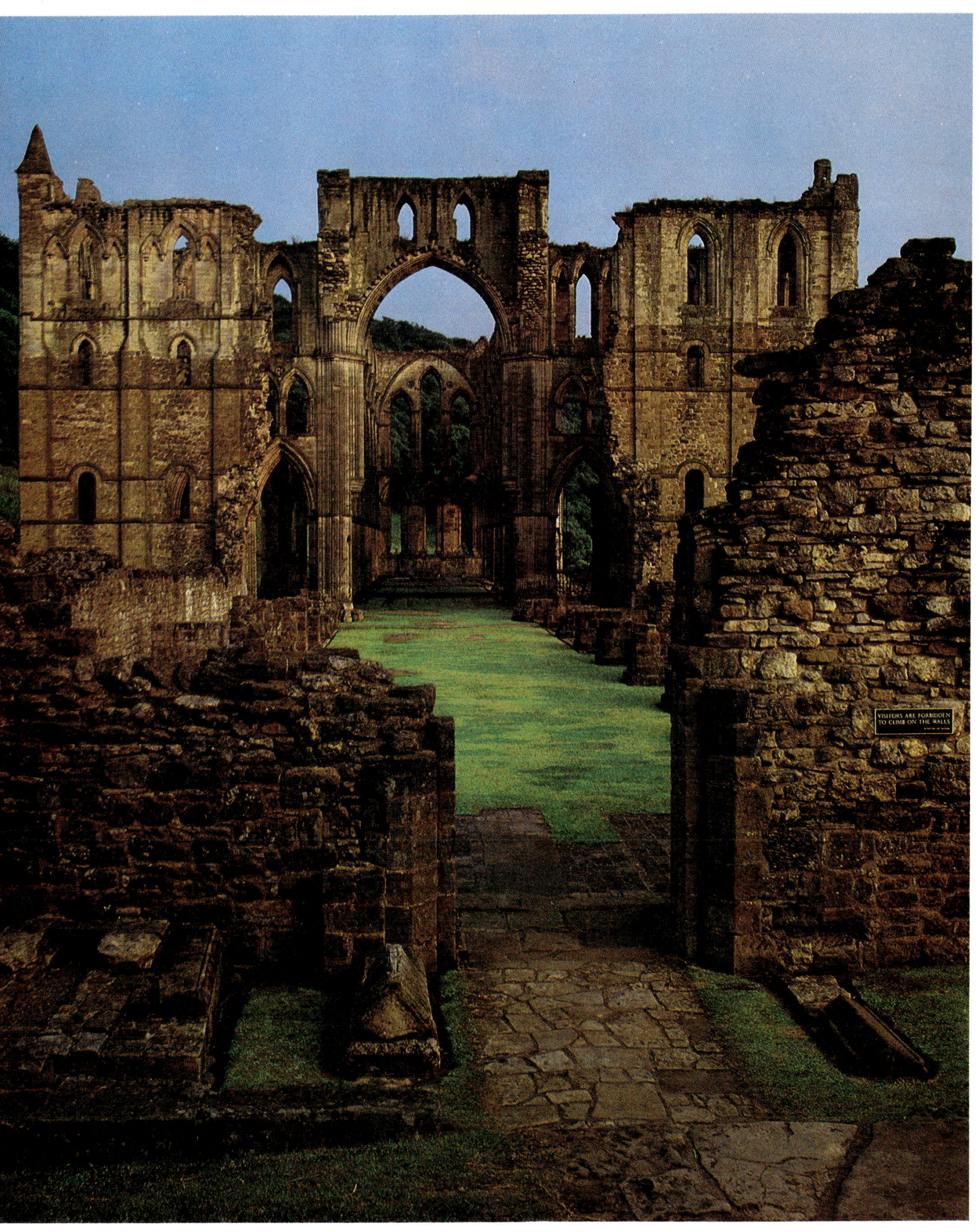
VISITORS ARE FORBIDDEN
TO CLIMB ON THE WALLS

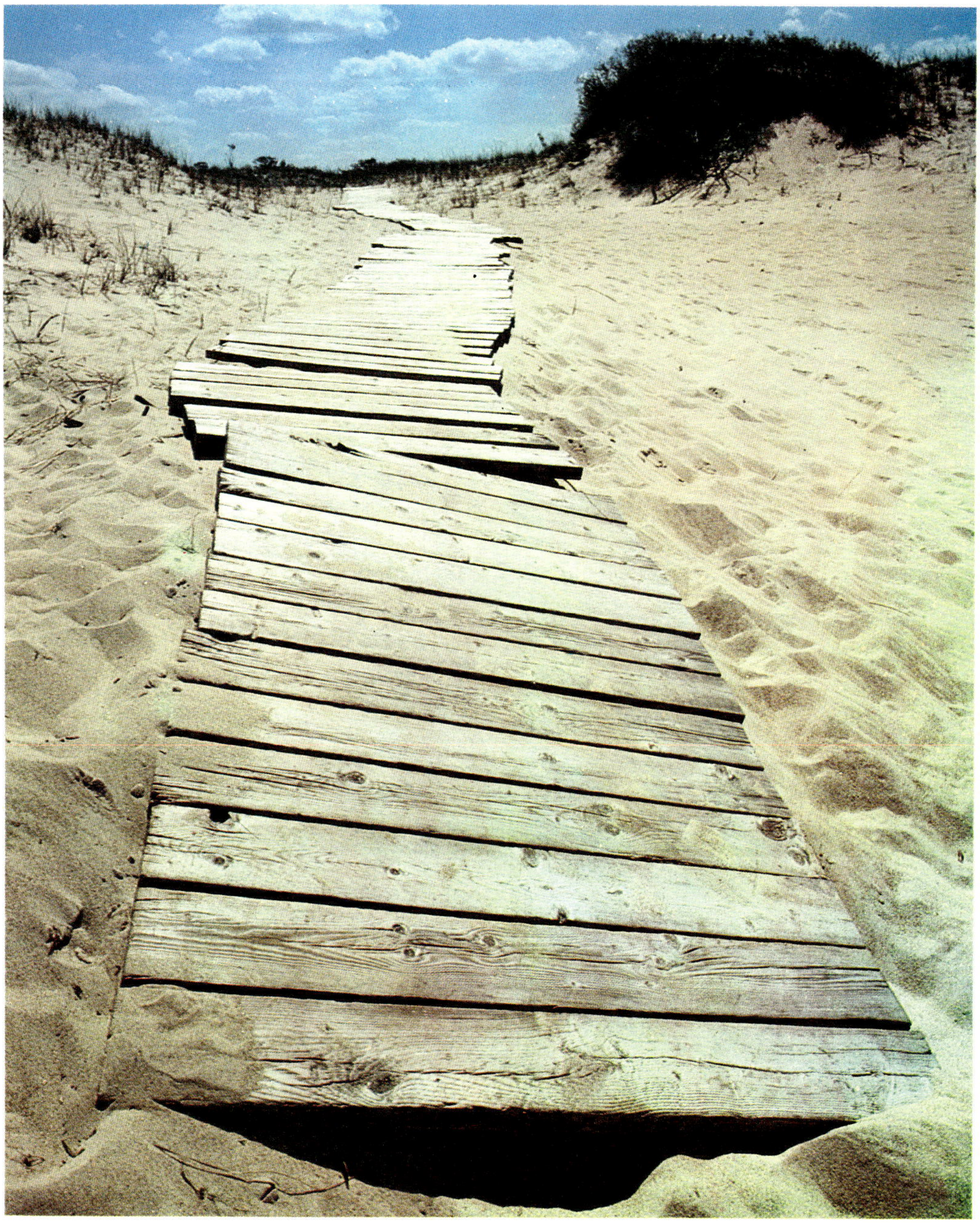

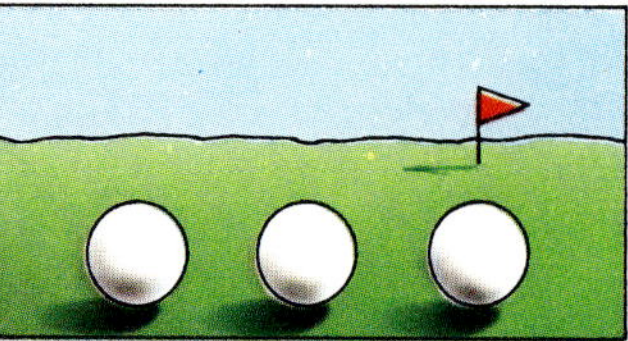

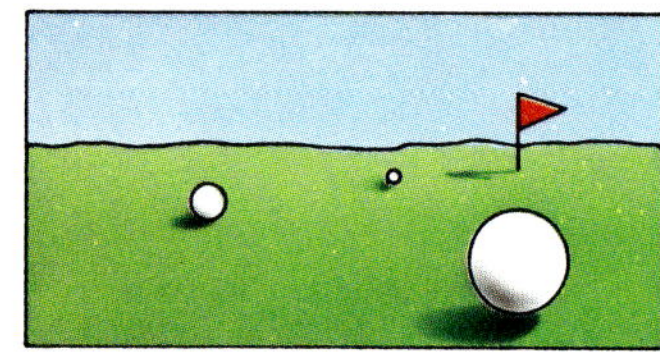

▶ DIMINISHING SIZE: Objects of the same or similar size appear to become smaller as they get farther away, as shown above. Using a wide-angle lens, Robert Estall emphasized this for a greater feeling of depth in the photo at right.

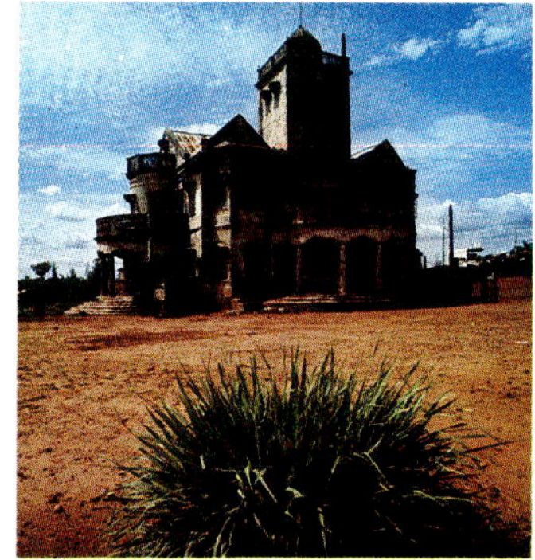

▲ FILLING THE MIDDLE AREA: Choosing a viewpoint that places the main subject in the middle area is an effective way of drawing you into a photograph, thus strengthening the feeling of depth. Photo by John Goldblatt.

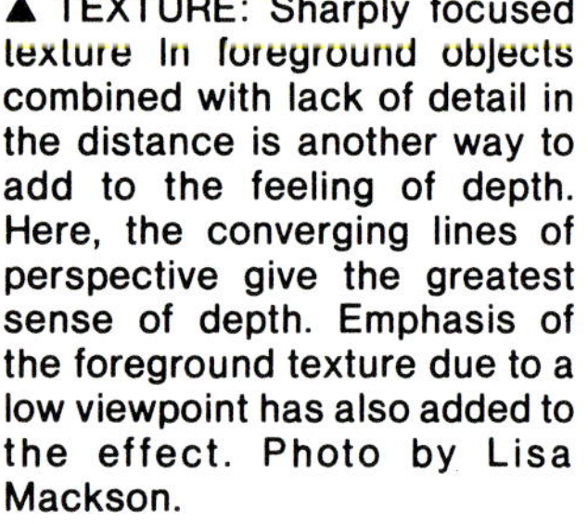

▲ TEXTURE: Sharply focused texture in foreground objects combined with lack of detail in the distance is another way to add to the feeling of depth. Here, the converging lines of perspective give the greatest sense of depth. Emphasis of the foreground texture due to a low viewpoint has also added to the effect. Photo by Lisa Mackson.

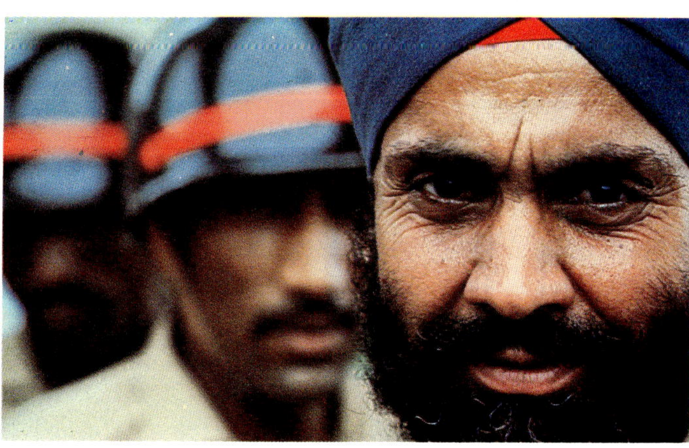

◀ SELECTIVE FOCUS: This technique is especially useful for producing good depth in close-up shots and in subjects with a confusing background. By throwing the background out of focus, you can make a sharply focused main subject stand out from the rest of the photograph. The lack of detail in the background makes it seem farther away from the main subject than it actually is, giving the illusion of depth.

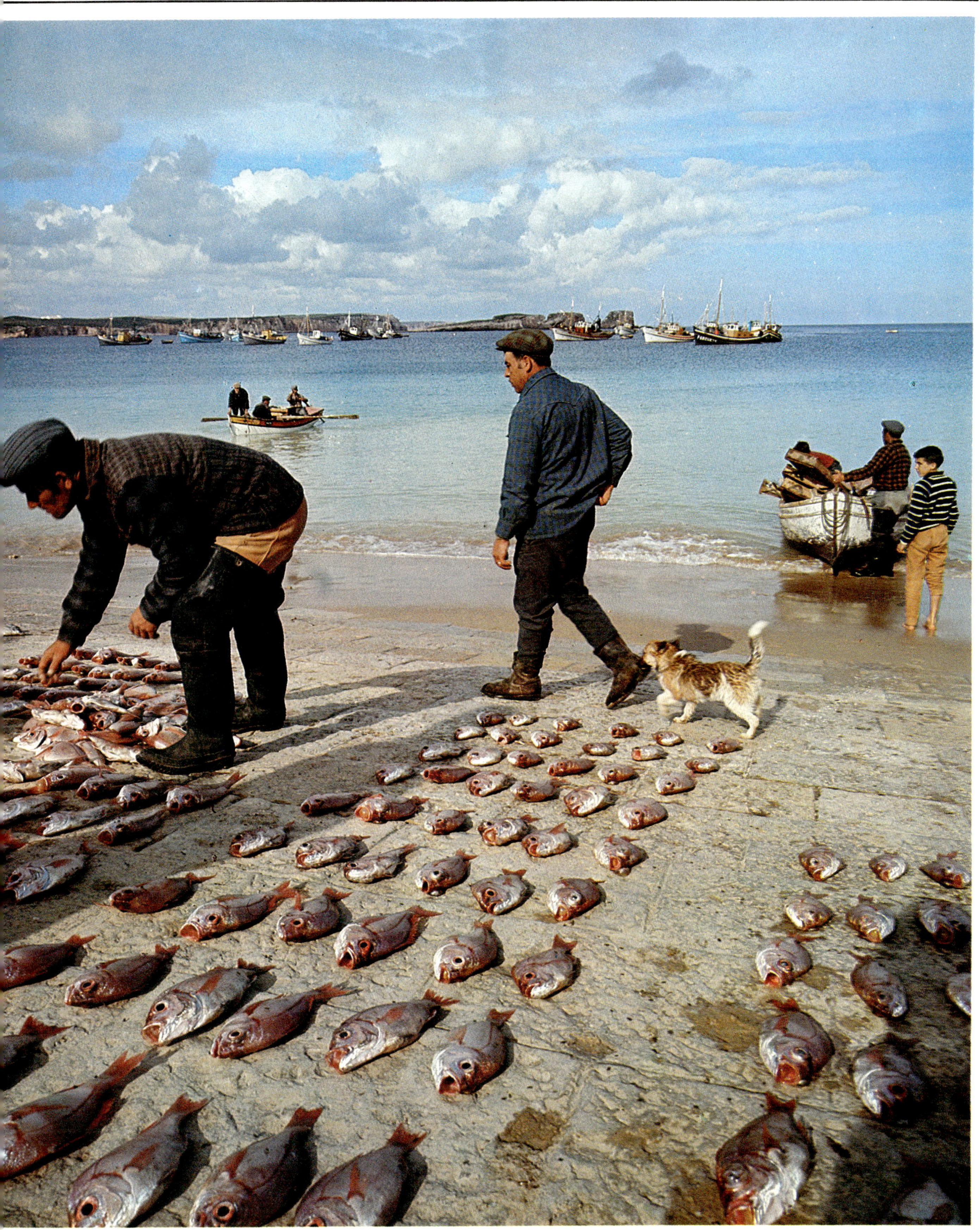

Exploiting Depth of Field

When making a photograph with anything but the simplest camera, you must make several decisions before pressing the shutter release—where to stand, what lens to use, which part of the subject to focus on, and which shutter speed and aperture to select. Each of these affects the final image in a different way, but all of them have a bearing on one very important aspect of photography—depth of field, or how much of the picture is in focus.

Traditionally, good pictures had to have extensive depth of field. For certain subjects this is still true, but it is now recognized that by controlling depth of field, the emphasis in a picture can be altered. This gives you control over the way the subject is portrayed. With creative use of depth of field, it is possible to manipulate the various elements of the composition.

THE APERTURE

To increase or decrease depth of field, change the size of the lens aperture—the smaller the aperture, the greater the depth of field. As a rough guide, closing down two stops on any lens will double the depth of field.

If you do stop down, you must use a slower shutter speed to compensate for the reduction of light. This may not always be possible, particularly when you are handholding the camera. A general rule for preventing camera shake and blurred images is to use a shutter speed that is the approximate reciprocal of the lens focal length; for example, with a 135mm lens on your SLR, set the camera to 1/125 second or faster.

With a 500mm lens, you should use 1/500 second or faster when hand-holding. This can force you to use a large aperture for correct exposure, which reduces depth of field. Solve this problem by using a firm camera support, so you don't have to hand-hold and use fast shutter speeds.

CAMERA-TO-SUBJECT DISTANCE

The farther you are from the subject, the greater the depth of field. With a 50mm lens, a distant view will show everything in focus, unless you include close foreground detail. For a portrait, you get closer to the subject to fill the frame. This will give a much shallower depth of field.

INTERCHANGEABLE LENSES

Lenses of different focal lengths appear to have different depth of field characteristics. *As we normally use them,* lenses

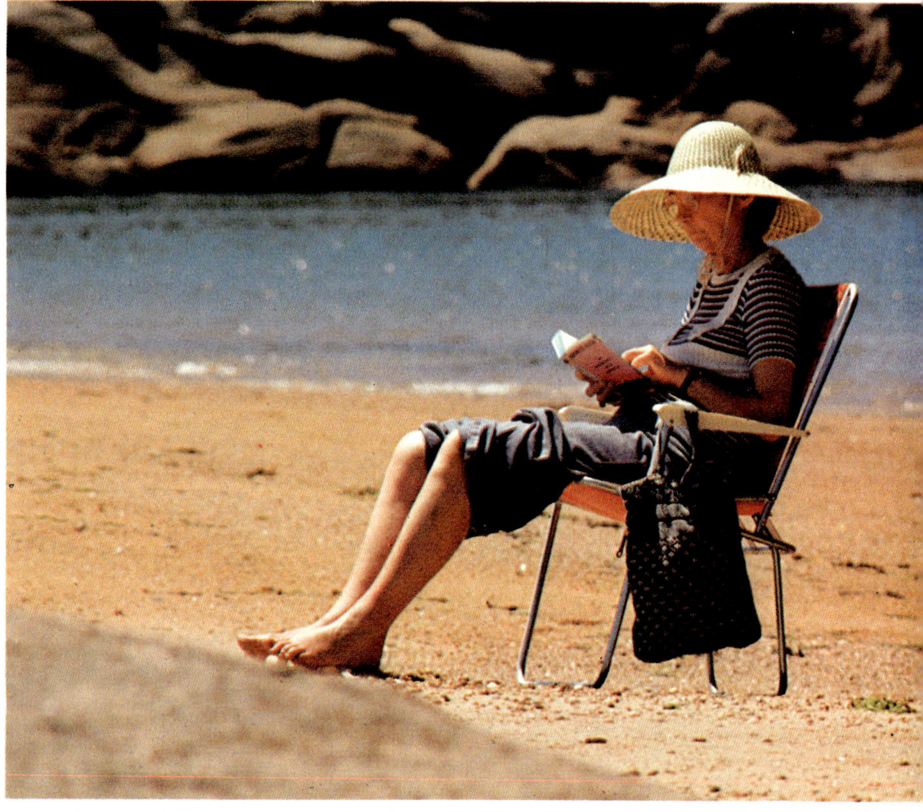

▲ Generally, the longer the lens, the shallower the depth of field. For this shot, Ed Buziak used a 300mm telephoto lens at an aperture of *f*-5.6. Depth of field is extremely limited. If you look closely at the sand, you will see the zone of good focus.

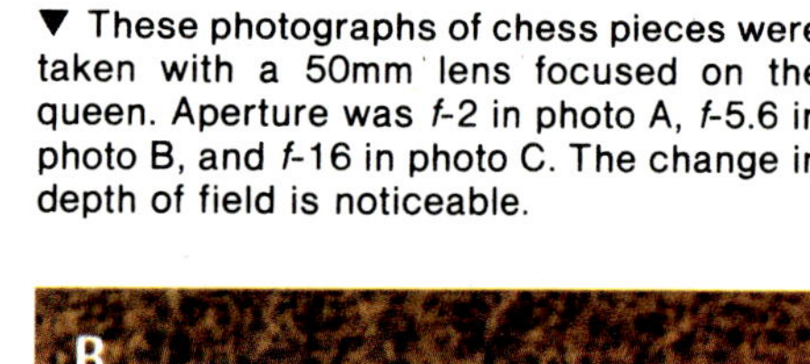

▼ These photographs of chess pieces were taken with a 50mm lens focused on the queen. Aperture was *f*-2 in photo A, *f*-5.6 in photo B, and *f*-16 in photo C. The change in depth of field is noticeable.

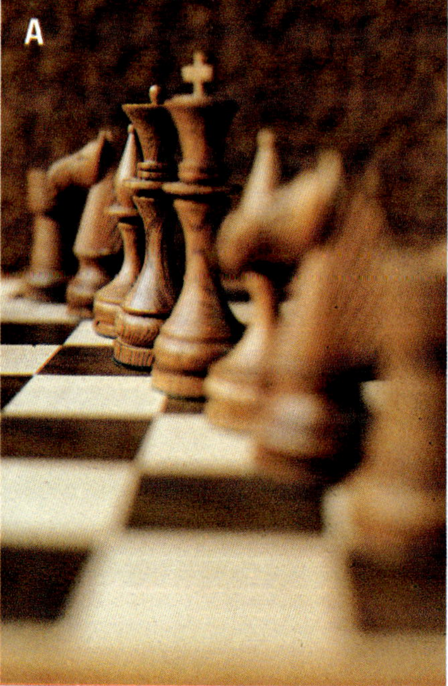

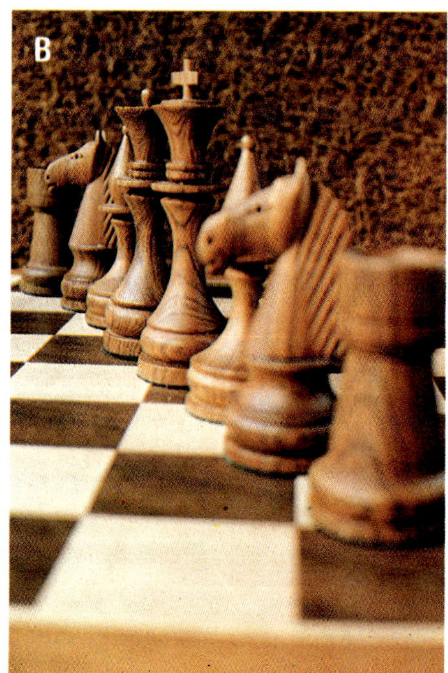

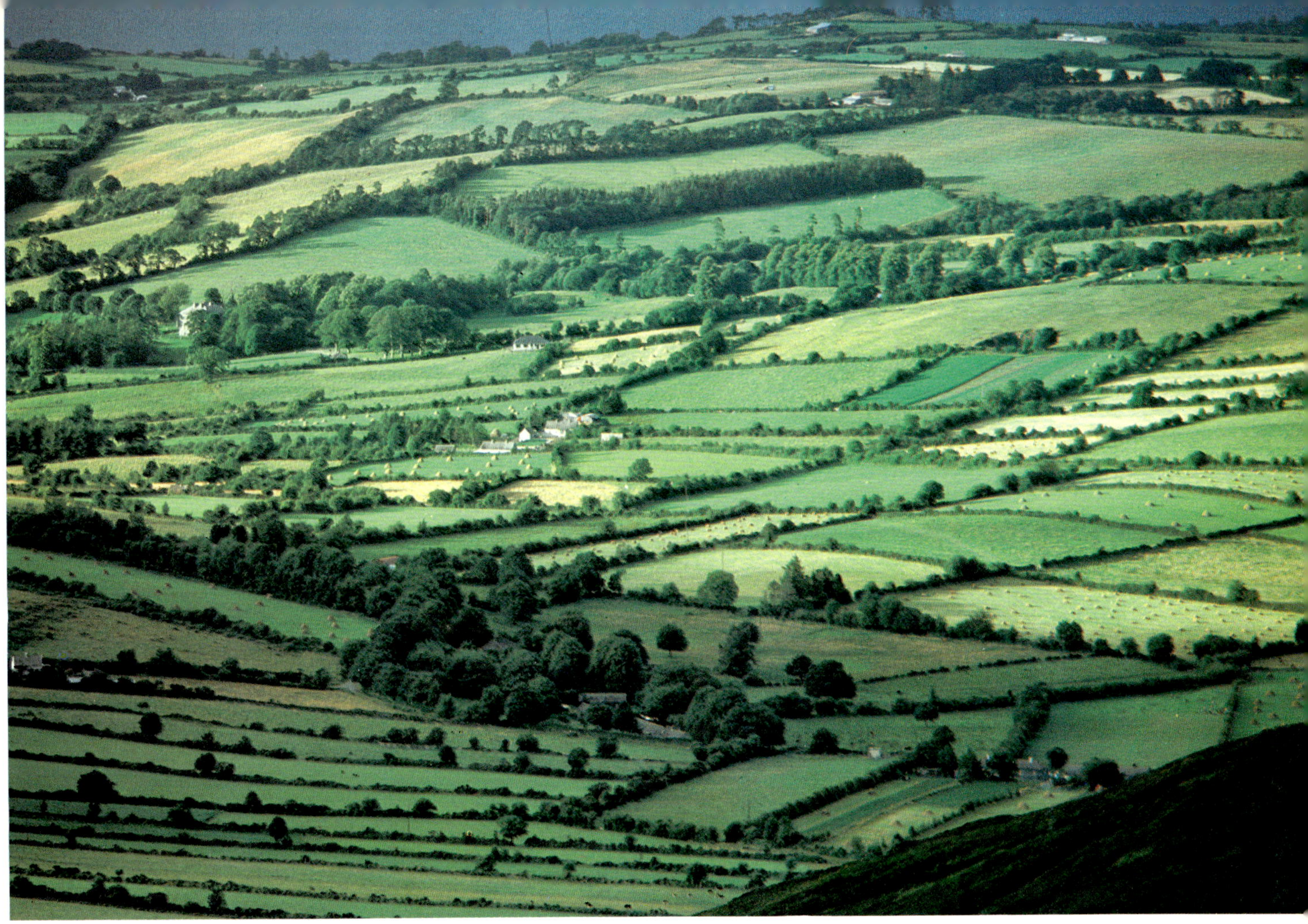

▲ The farther the subject is from the camera, the greater the depth of field—even when using a fairly long lens. For this picture, Adam Woolfitt was on a hill about 1000 feet (300m) away. He used a 200mm lens and an aperture of *f*-8, but because he was so far away the whole picture is sharp.

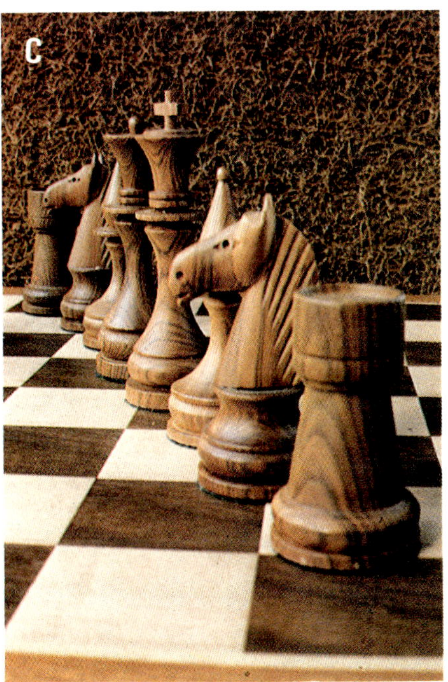

with short focal lengths, such as 28mm, exhibit more depth of field than "longer" lenses such as 200mm or 300mm.

This subject is technically complex because several factors determine depth of field as seen by *the viewer* of a photograph—aperture size, lens focal length, distance between camera and subject, amount of enlargement in printing and the viewer's distance from the print. We can eliminate the complexity by considering that we normally print the entire frame or nearly so, we don't make unusually large prints and the viewer holds the print at a comfortable distance.

For this "average" set of circumstances, you can use short-focal-length wide-angle lenses to record both more of the scene and more depth of field in the scene. Long focal lengths take a narrower view and have reduced depth of field that often puts foreground and background out of focus.

TRYING ALTERNATIVES

One of the important advantages of many SLR cameras is that you can preview the result of changing lens and aperture and see depth of field in the viewfinder.

Here's an exercise. Select a subject that is either static or easy to control, such as a landscape or a still life. Be sure the subject is well lit or you will not be able to see it clearly in the viewfinder as you stop down to the smallest apertures. Then try combinations of apertures and lenses to see the effects you can get and which subjects they suit best.

Once you are familiar with these options, expose some film at small, medium and large apertures, varying the shutter speed to keep the exposure constant. Then study the effects of a change in depth of field.

SHALLOW DEPTH OF FIELD

This is used to isolate objects or people from their surroundings. The subject, which is sharply focused, contrasts strongly with the background and foreground, which are out of focus. It is commonly used in photographing flowers, where the natural background is often distracting.

HYPERFOCAL DISTANCE

The hyperfocal distance is a special focusing distance that all photographers should know about. This applies to any lens at any aperture, and it provides an easy way to obtain maximum depth of field. The calculations to determine the hyperfocal distance are complex and are not discussed here. The shortcut method is to read it off the lens.

First, focus on infinity (∞). At any aperture, the depth-of-field scale on the lens shows the near limit of good focus. The far limit is beyond infinity. The near limit is the hyperfocal distance as shown in Diagram A. Then turn the focusing ring so the lens is focused at the hyperfocal distance. Infinity is at the far limit on the depth-of-field scale as shown in Diagram B. Depth of field is from half the hyperfocal distance all the way to infinity.

By focusing at the hyperfocal distance, you obtain the maximum possible depth of field for any lens at the chosen aperture. It will increase with smaller aperture settings.

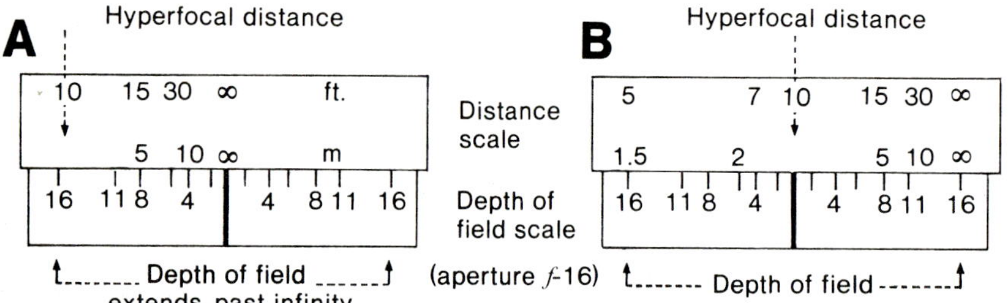

Using shallow depth of field is also a particularly effective way of drawing attention to one person in a crowd or street scene. It helps to isolate an expression or gesture that would otherwise be lost in a mass of detail. Be sure to focus exactly on the subject of interest.

When using shallow depth of field, you can't disregard out of focus background and foreground. Strong colors or highlights can be just as intrusive when blurred as when they are in sharp focus. Check point of view and composition carefully even though some objects are out of focus.

EXTENSIVE DEPTH OF FIELD

If the entire image is sharply focused, a completely different approach to composition is necessary. With shallow depth of field, composition can depend on part of the image being out of focus. When the entire image is sharp, you must place the camera precisely in relation to the subject. The frame edges must be used to eliminate unwanted objects and distracting details.

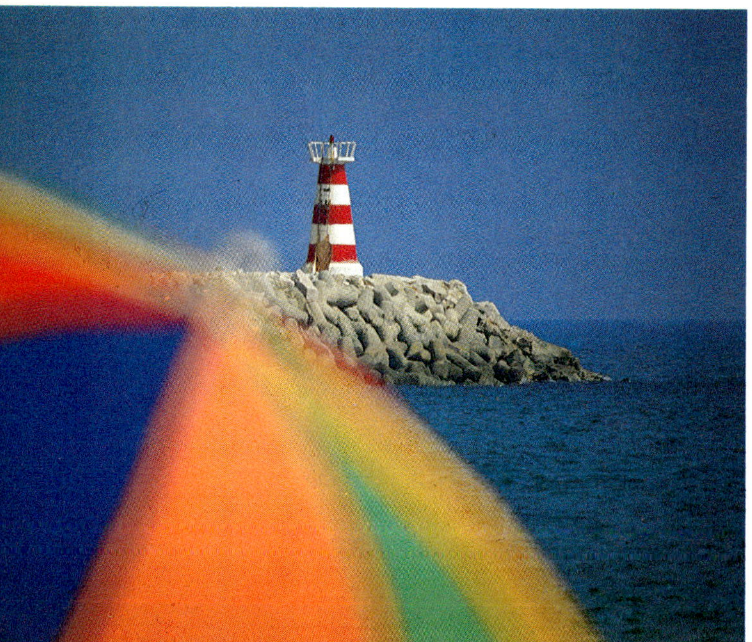

▲ To put the umbrella out of focus and emphasize the lighthouse, Raul Constancio used limited depth of field.

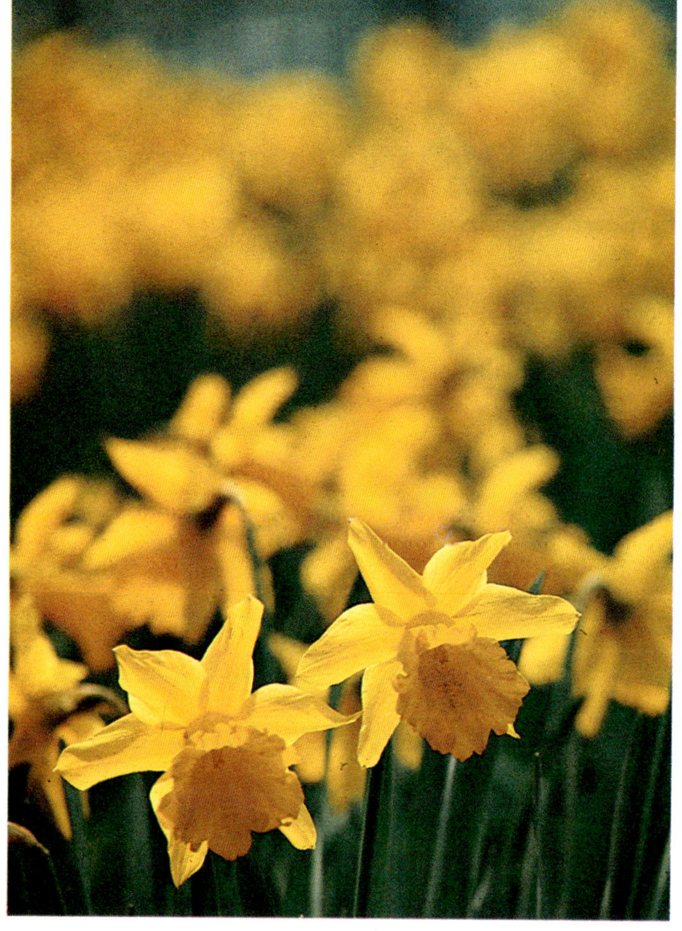

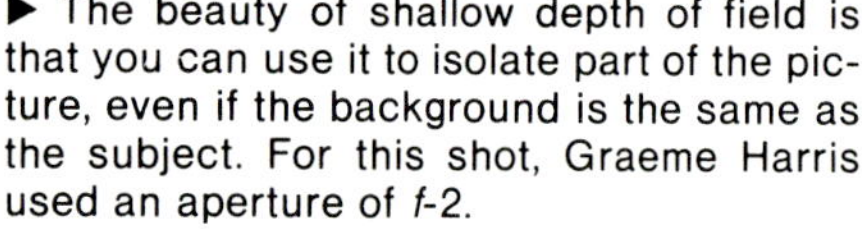

▶ The beauty of shallow depth of field is that you can use it to isolate part of the picture, even if the background is the same as the subject. For this shot, Graeme Harris used an aperture of f-2.

The fineness of detail in the image will allow you to use textures and shapes in a more subtle way than with shallow depth of field. Rounded stones can be contrasted with slender, spiky patches of grass, for example. Or the solid, regular shape of a building can counterpoint the fine lines of some leafless trees.

Portraits take on a different dimension when using extensive depth of field. Instead of concentrating on the lines and features of the face, you can photograph the person in an appropriate environment. Pose a gardener against a background of flowers, for example, but be careful to avoid confusion. The details of the surroundings must be well organized to complement the central character.

SOME HELPFUL RULES

With cameras using interchangeable lenses, these rules will help you control depth of field:

- Short-focal-length lenses give more depth of field than long lenses.
- Any lens has more depth of field when focused at greater distances from the camera.
- Any lens has greater depth of field when it is stopped down to a smaller aperture.
- To maximize depth of field, use the hyperfocal distance when focusing.

Therefore, if you need more depth of field, you can use a smaller aperture, move back or change to a shorter focal length lens. If you want less depth of field, you can do the reverse—use a larger aperture, move closer to the subject or change to a lens of longer focal length.

If you want everything in the picture to be sharp, follow the rules and take extra care with composition. To separate the subject from the background for more emphasis, follow the rules for narrow depth of field, but remember that the subject itself must be interesting enough to stand on its own.

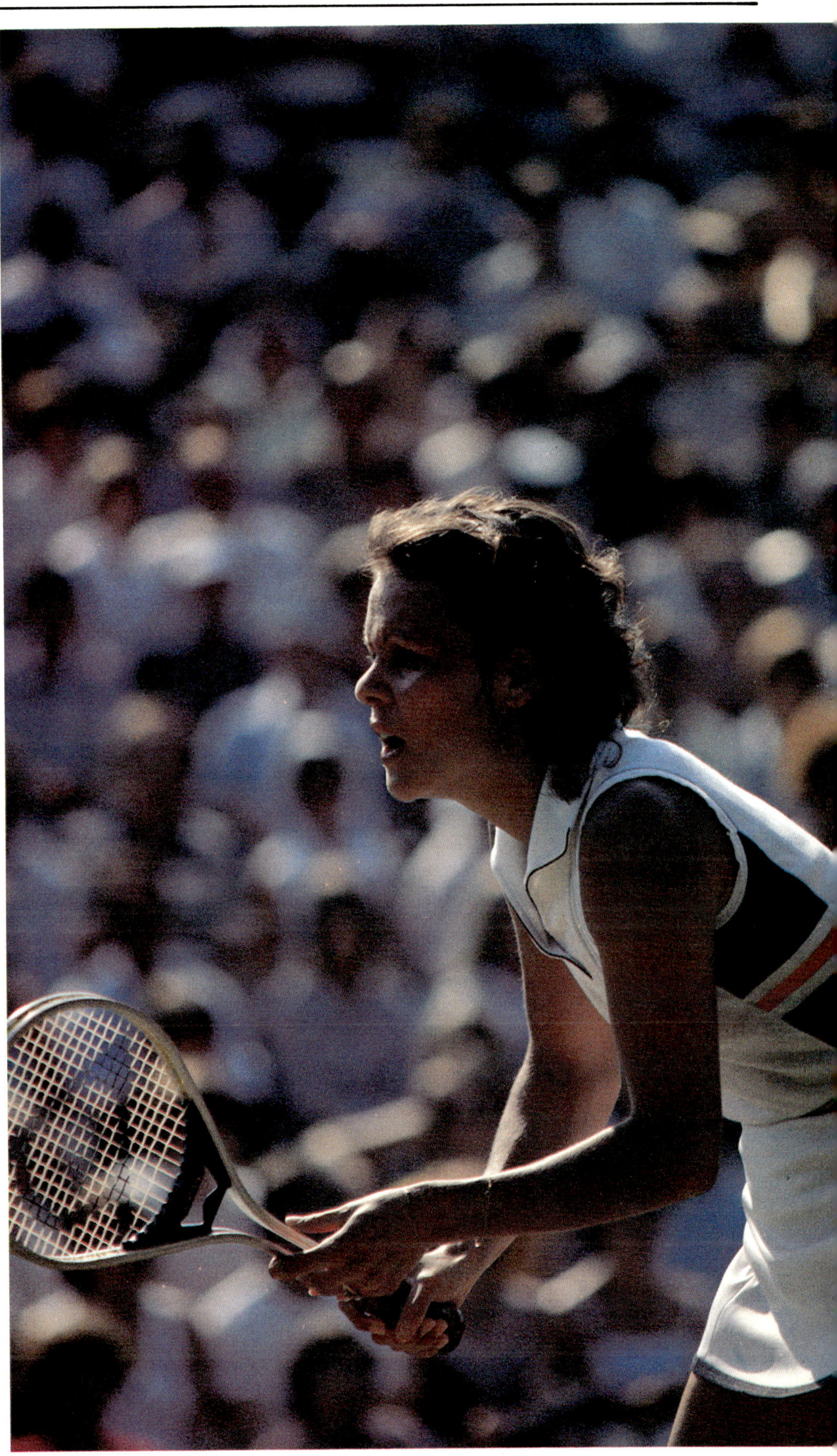

▶ The creative use of shallow depth of field is known as *selective focus.* You select the part of the image you want in focus. By using a telephoto lens for this shot, Nigel Snowdon not only managed to separate the subject from a confused background, but also got a close-up without disrupting the action.

Abstract Images

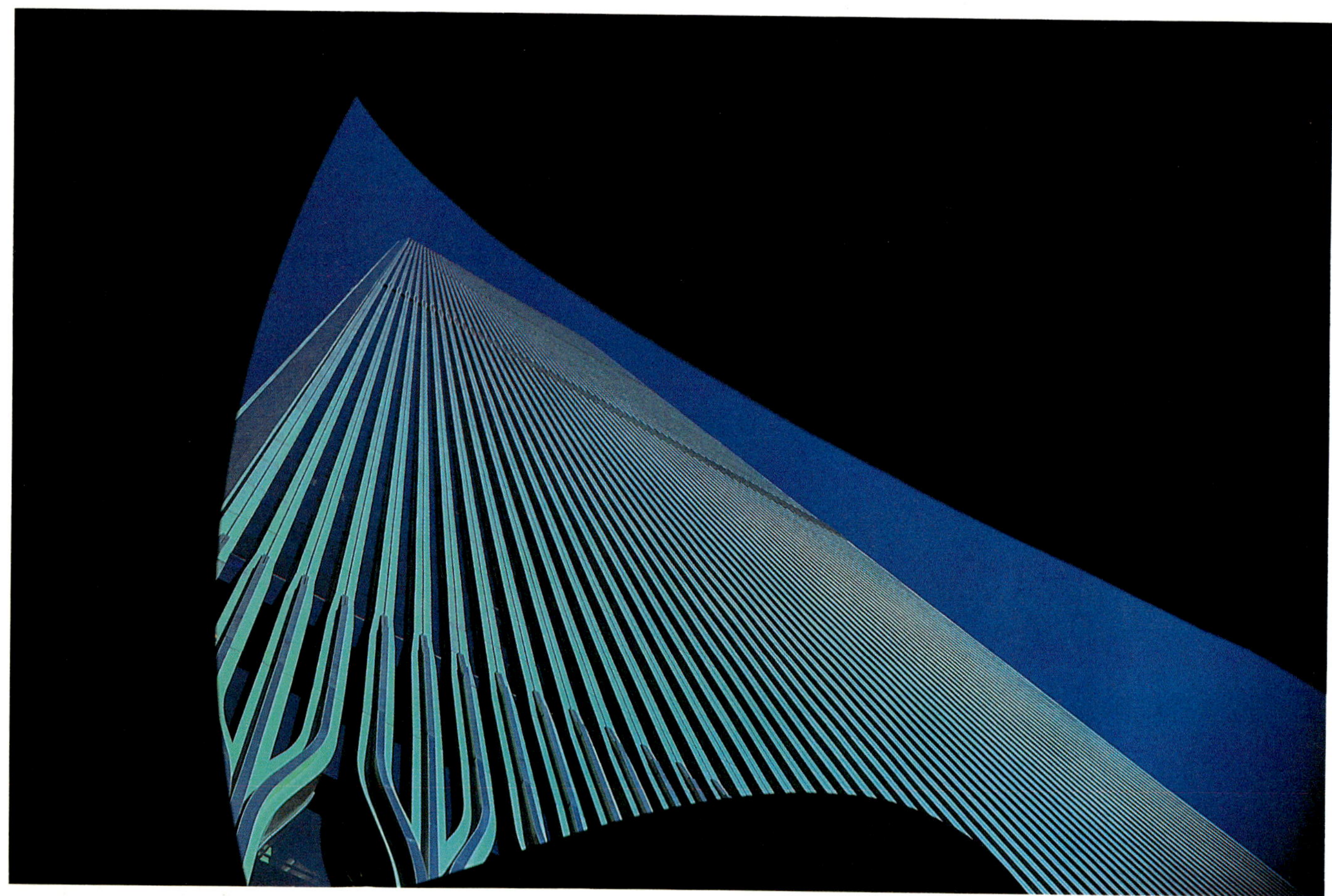

▲ An unusual viewpoint can transform an ordinary subject into an abstract image. This photograph of the World Trade Center in New York City shows a low viewpoint with unusual framing by a foreground object. Photo by Richard Laird.

▶ By breaking the accepted rules of composition and dividing this image in half diagonally, Ed Buziak made a striking photo of a cobblestone path.

One of the most common beliefs about photography is that the camera cannot lie. This idea is so strong that we are often surprised when a subject in reality does not match up to how it appears in a photograph. In fact, the camera does not lie, but there are "tricks" you can use to make the camera "exaggerate" reality. These are especially useful when taking abstract pictures.

Most photographers, like painters, want to do more than just record reality. We want to express our personal feelings and place a particular interpretation on what we see. We want to explore the medium and not be governed by rules and conventions. By breaking the rules, or by using them in a new way, we become more creative. One of the most rewarding areas of creative photography is making abstract or semi-abstract images.

You can create abstract pictures by manipulating basic elements of composition—viewpoint, perspective, pattern, shape and movement. You can also create abstract images in other ways, by using special lenses, multiple exposures, and different films and filters.

VIEWPOINT

Generally, photographs are taken from eye level. This is due mainly to the popularity of SLR and rangefinder cameras with eye-level viewing. However, viewpoint is one of the most flexible aspects of composition. By altering the viewpoint you can dramatically change the whole meaning of the picture.

When composing an abstract image, the choice of viewpoint is very important. By moving higher or lower, closer to or farther from the subject, you alter scale and perspective, and can rearrange the subject in a way that seems more interesting. With close-ups especially, you can capture a tiny part of a subject or isolate a small but dominant area of color so the subject becomes unrecognizable.

Alternatively, a subject can form an abstract image from a distant viewpoint. A landscape taken from the air, for instance, can appear so diminished in scale that it is reduced to an abstract series of lines and patterns.

PERSPECTIVE

Perspective and viewpoint are inseparably linked. The effect of perspective depends entirely on viewpoint—a close viewpoint will "exaggerate" perspective, a more distant viewpoint will diminish the effect.

Exaggerating perspective by using a low, close viewpoint can produce spectacular or weird abstract images. Perspective can be manipulated to produce an abstract image of a series of hills. A long focal-length lens will add to the abstract effect by compressing distance.

PATTERN

A pattern is the orderly or disorderly arrangement of elements, natural or man-made, in some form of repetition. It can be

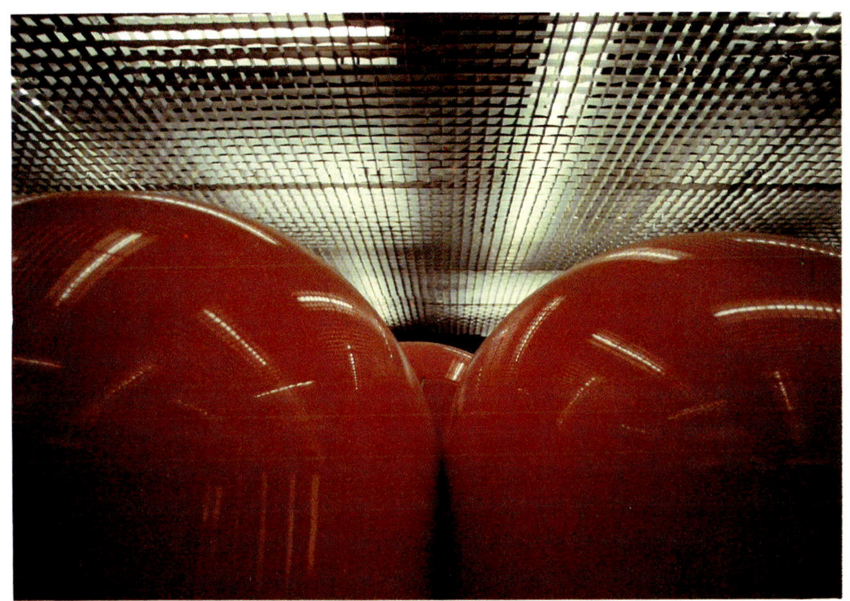

▲ Balls in a bowling alley? Crash helmets? By excluding familiar elements from the image area, John Sims eliminated scale of the objects in this composition, creating a totally abstract photograph with strong color and line.

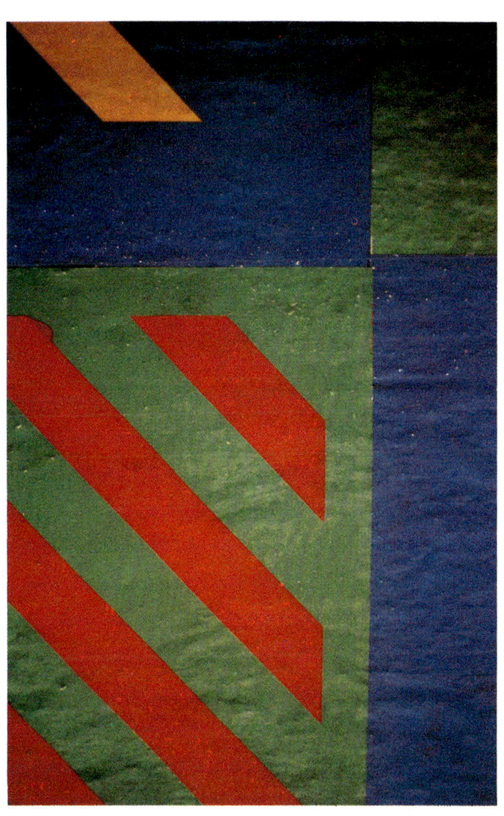

▶ An abstract image usually works best when the colors and shapes are kept simple. A close viewpoint, used here for an abstract of a wall painting, helps exclude distracting detail and give the colors impact. Photo by Ed Buziak.

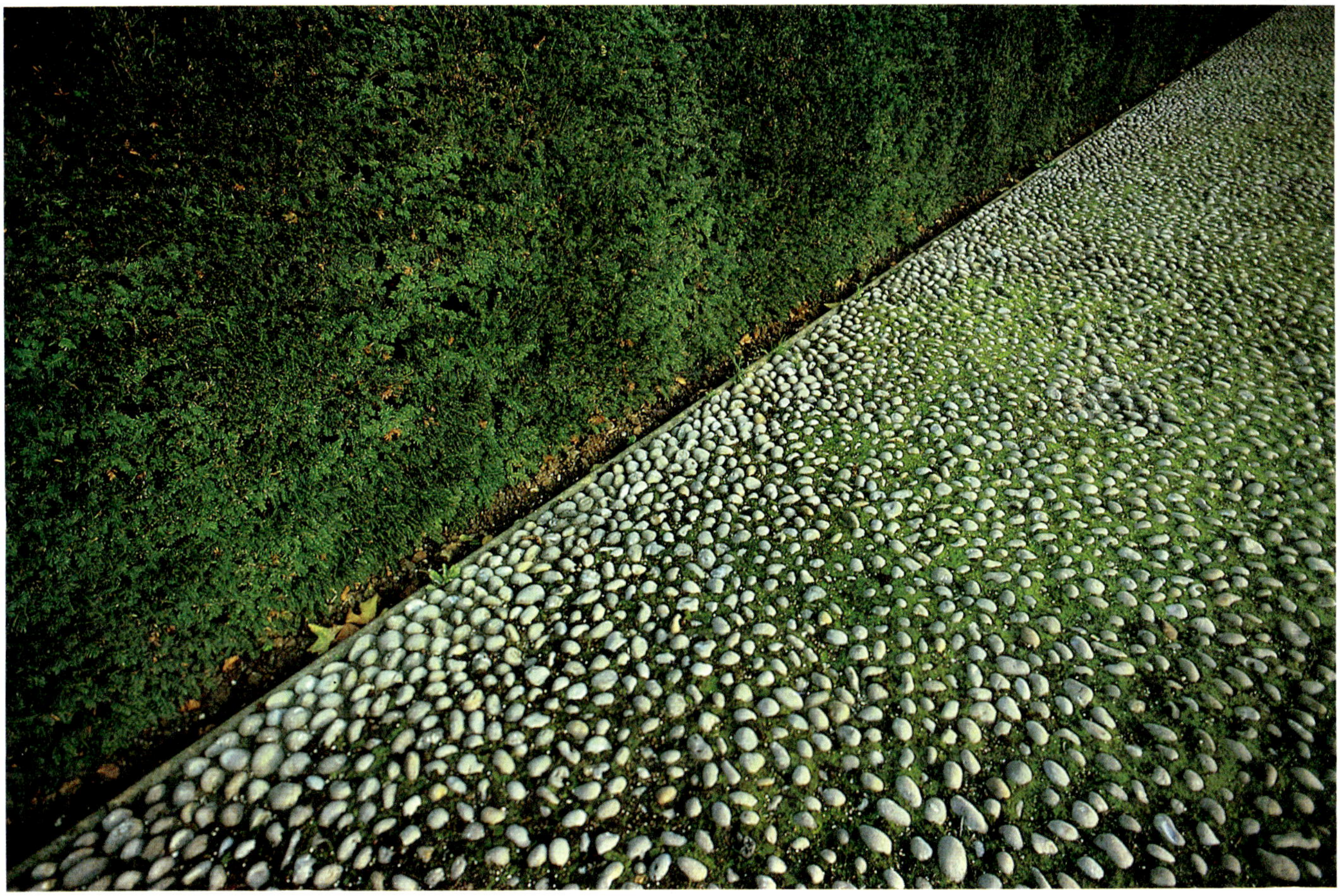

▼ Pattern is one of the most natural subjects for abstract photographs. Light is a vital element in this pattern formation. Adam Woolfitt's abstract is simply the pattern created by light from a swimming pool.

two-dimensional, as in brickwork or a cross-section of a piece of wood, or it can be three-dimensional, where light and shadow reveal a texture or repetitive shape.

For abstract pictures, pattern can be explored from all angles and distances. Its abstraction is apparent in itself when isolated from non-patterned elements, or when put into contrasting situations with other repetitive forms.

Care should be taken when creating abstracts from patterns. Too much of the same pattern can look monotonous. Good, tight framing is usually needed, coupled with a close viewpoint.

SHAPE

Normally, it is the shape of a subject that enables us to recognize it. You can make abstract pictures by disguising or distorting a previously recognizable shape. An unusual viewpoint, reflections, shadows or refraction through glass can make interesting abstract shapes.

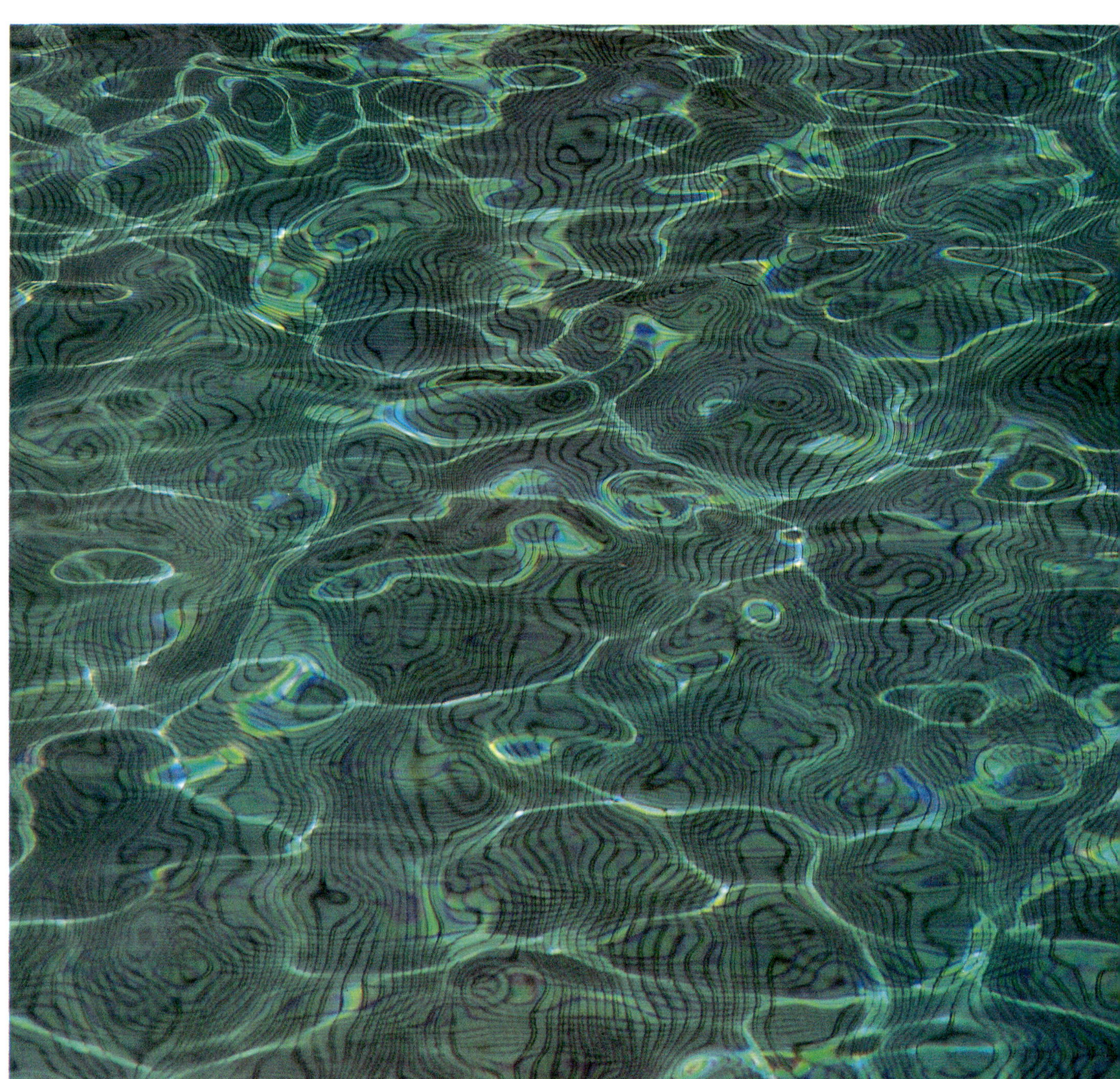

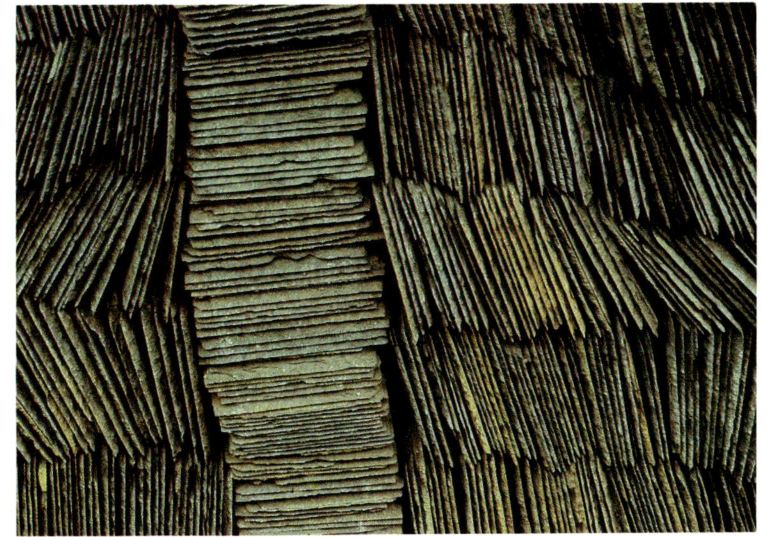

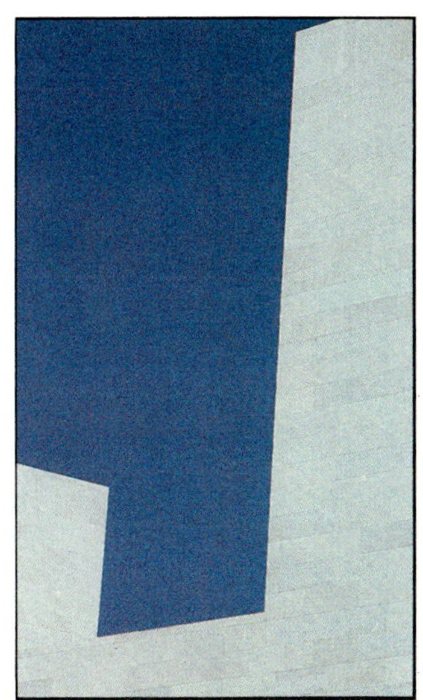

▲ A break in the pattern can add an important element of variety to an abstract, especially if the colors are subdued as they are here. For this abstract photograph, Michael Busselle chose a point where the rhythm was disturbed.

Above right: Shape can be disguised by careful framing. This bold abstract image was helped by strong, flat light on the building's surface. Photo by Anne Conway.

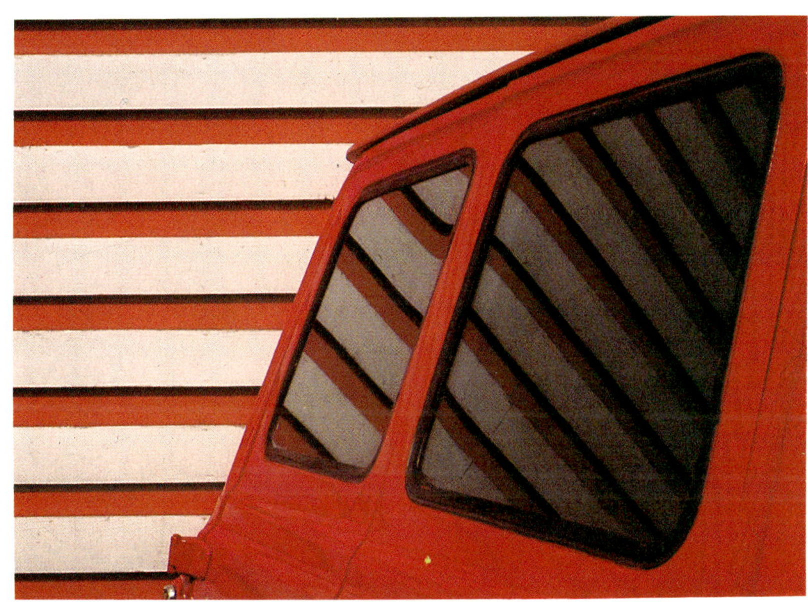

▲ Reflection and the repetition of colors give this photograph its abstract quality. If the van were blue, for example, the composition would have assumed a greater sense of reality. Photo by Ed Buziak.

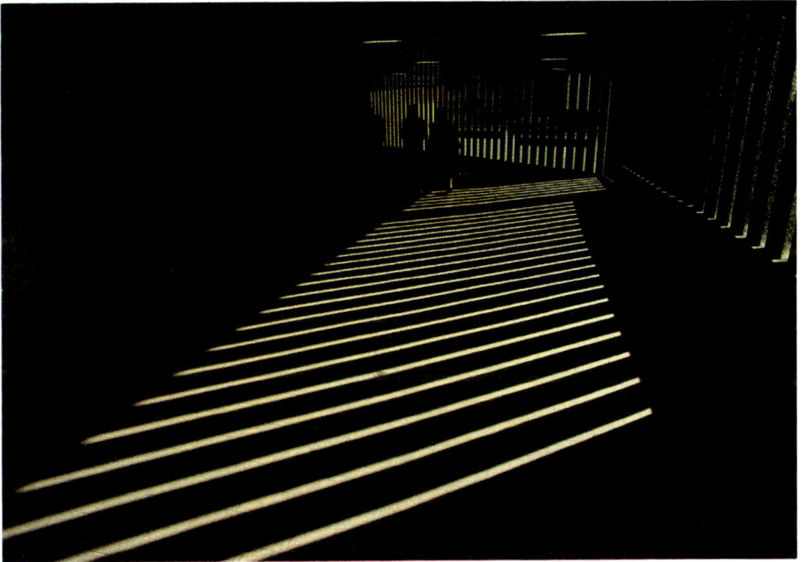

◀ The shapes and patterns formed by shadows are often a good subject for abstracts. This is especially true when all detail in the shadow areas is lost and only the shapes remain.

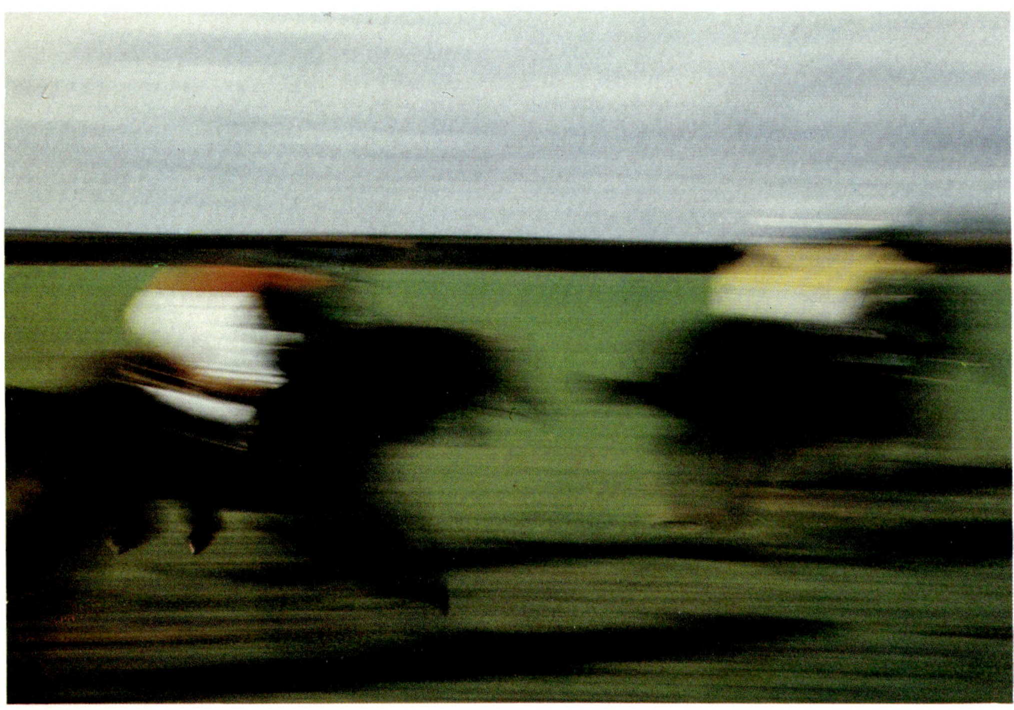

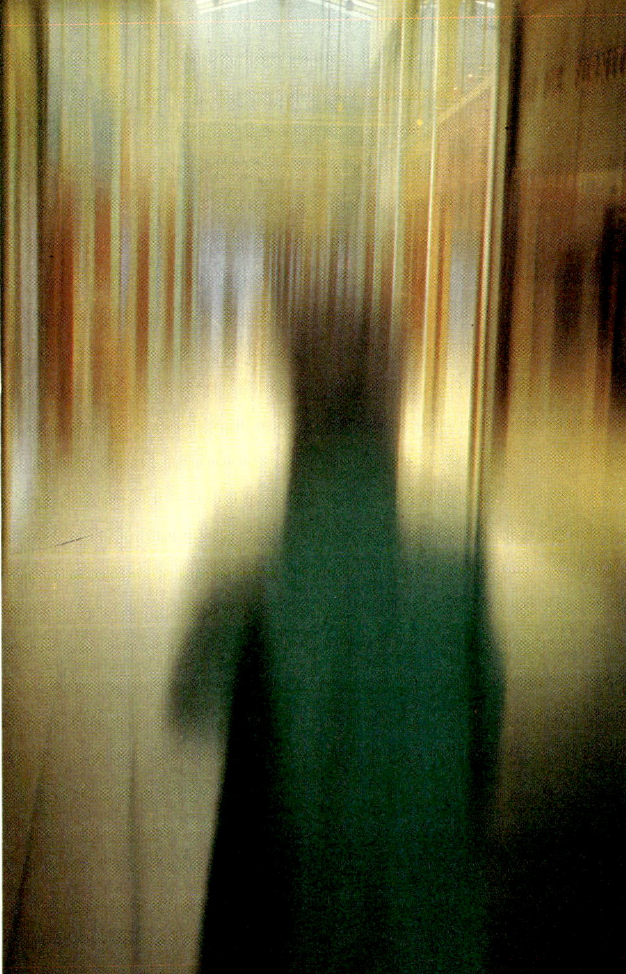

▲ Panning the camera with a moving subject can create an abstract image. When you pan at the same speed as the subject, only the background is blurred. Pan faster or slower, and both subject and background become blurred. The complete image forms an abstract of lines in the direction of the pan. Photo by Richard Tucker.

◀ Straight movement of the camera, even if the subject is static, will produce a strongly linear abstract.

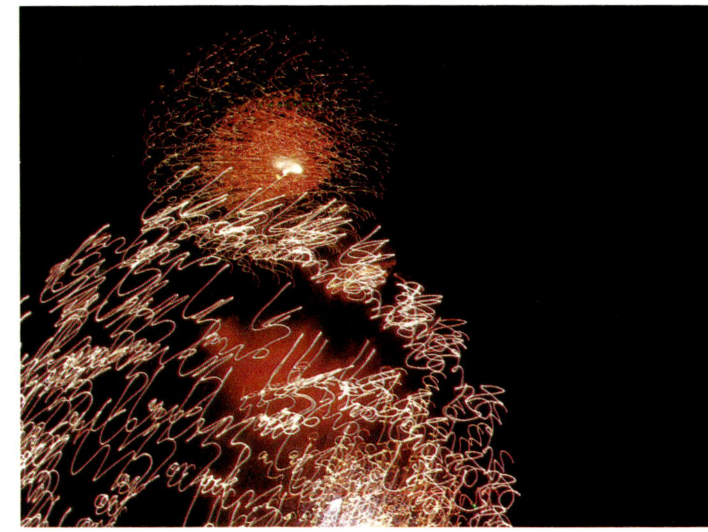

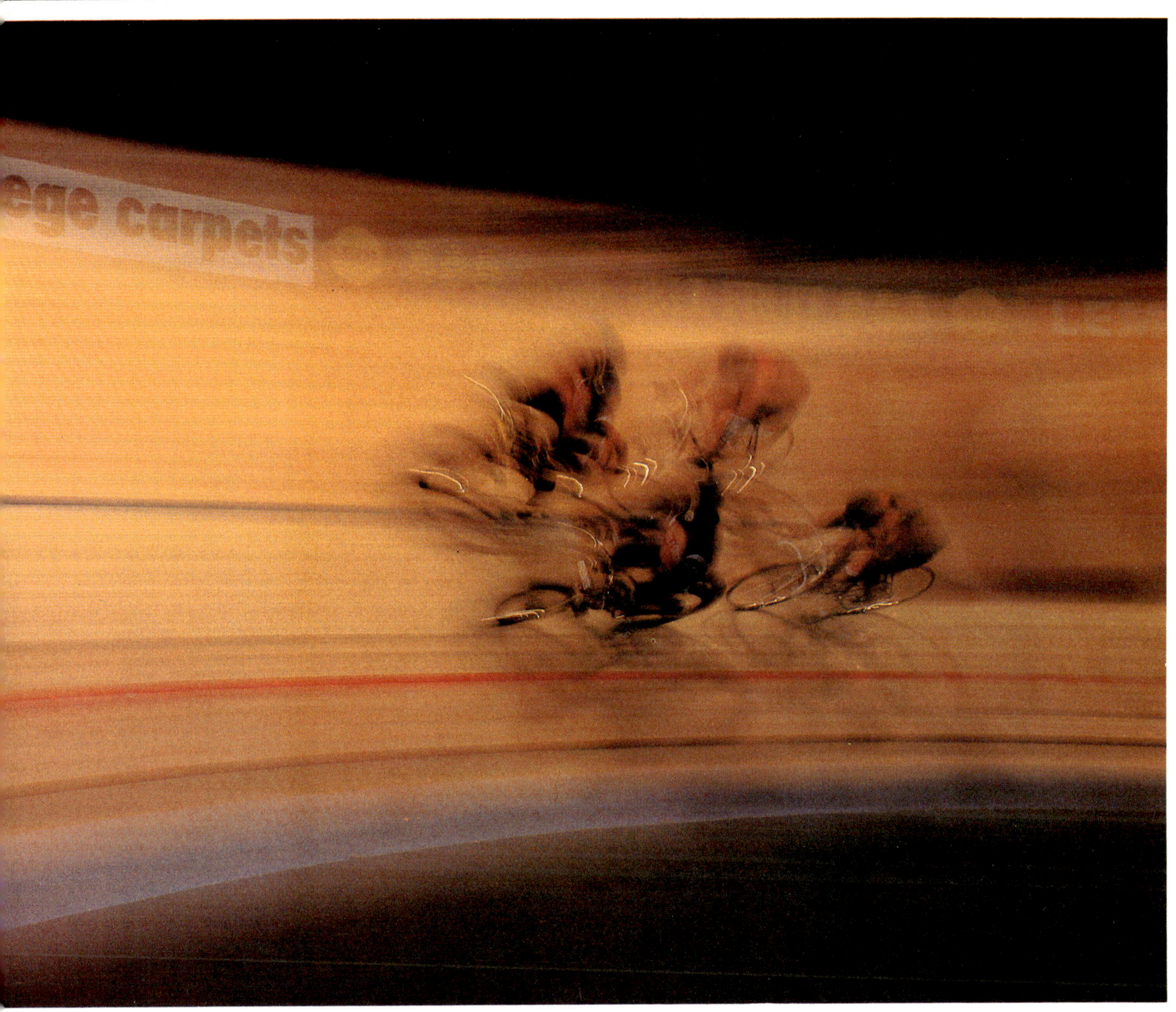

▲ A certain amount of abstraction is helpful when you are trying to convey the impression of speed, but it is useful to retain some degree of reality if the subject is to remain recognizable. Notice how the parts of the subject that move in a different direction from the camera make a separate abstract pattern—the wheels in this photograph.

◀ Moving lights will record an abstract pattern during a long exposure with the camera on a tripod. Moving your camera will produce an abstract image of non-moving lights. Here, Ed Buziak shook the camera during an exposure of several seconds. Every tiny light has traced a similar pattern.

MOVEMENT

Photography is sometimes used to take sharp, frozen pictures of moving subjects. In abstract photography, you seek the opposite effect—creating and controlling blurred images. You do this by moving the camera, choosing a moving subject, or both, while making a long exposure.

There is almost no limit to the abstractions you can create with image blur, but you must first do some experiments. Start simply, and then move on to more complicated images as you become more skillful. Too much blur will result in confusion, so don't overdo it. Also, don't keep the shutter open too long—overexposures can wash out the colors.

Daytime color blur is easy to practice with slow film and slow shutter speeds, combined with a small aperture. If the light is too bright for a long exposure, use a neutral-density (ND) filter over the lens. Ordinary crowded streets can become a wonderful blur of color with the mood of a carnival. A horse race can become a striking abstract of straight lines.

As a rule, daylight abstract shots of movement are most suitable for color film. The tonal contrast is normally not great enough for b&w photos. At night, either color or b&w is suitable for abstract pictures of lights. Neon lights especially create a good effect, because of their intensity.

Glossary

A

Afocal Lens: A lens accessory that attaches to a camera lens to decrease the focal length.

Angle of View: The largest angle between the two rays that form the diagonal of the film frame. Angle of view increases as focal length decreases.

Aperture: The adjustable opening in a lens that controls the brightness of the image exposing the film.

Aperture Priority: See *Automatic Exposure.*

ASA: An abbreviation for the *American Standards Association,* the organization that devised a film-speed rating for general-purpose films. In this system, as the ASA number doubles, film speed increases by one exposure step. Also see *DIN* and *ISO.*

Automatic Exposure: Camera metering system that sets shutter speed, lens aperture, or both after metering. There are three types: *Aperture priority* means you set aperture, camera sets shutter speed; *shutter priority* means you set shutter speed, camera sets lens aperture; *programmed* meters set both shutter speed and aperture.

Autowinder: Motorized unit that automatically advances film and cocks the camera shutter after exposure. This is an accessory with some cameras; built into others.

B

B (bulb) Setting: The shutter remains open as long as the shutter button remains depressed.

Barn Doors: A lighting accessory used to restrict the light beam. Usually composed of three or four swinging doors.

Bayonet Mount: A quick-locking and quick-release fitting between the camera and lens or lens accessory.

Bracketing: Making a series of frames having different exposures. This technique is typically used when you photograph a nonaverage scene. By making the metered exposure and frames with more and less exposure, you have a good chance of getting one picture that has "perfect" exposure. Bracketing is typically done in half- or full-step increments.

C

CC Filters: Also called *color-compensating* filters, these are filters available in a variety of colors and densities. They are usually used for fine color control of color film exposure.

Catadioptric Lens: See *Mirror Lens.*

Color Negative: Film that yields reverse tonalities and colors after exposure and processing. Used to make color prints. Negative has an orange cast that does not appear in the print.

Color Reversal: Color film or paper that yields correct tonalities after exposure and processing. Also called *color positive.* Color reversal films and papers usually have the suffix *-chrome* in their name.

Color Temperature: A scale of values that represent the relative amounts of red, blue, and green light in a light source. Values are represented in degrees Kelvin (K), in which the higher the number, the bluer the light source. For example, midday sunlight has a color temperature about 5500K. Candlelight, which looks much redder, has a color temperature about 1800K.

Composition: The arrangement of parts to form a unified whole.

Conversion Filter: Any colored filter designed to change the color temperature of the light to match the sensitivity of the film. Also called a *light-balancing* filter.

Cool Colors: Violets, blues and greens.

Cropping: Selecting the framing of the image. You do this when viewing a scene through the camera viewfinder. Some photographers also crop the image later during printing.

D

Daylight-Balanced Film: Color film designed to give best color reproduction when exposed with 5500K light. See *Color Temperature.* Daylight-balanced film is available as color negative and reversal film.

Depth of Field: The distance between the nearest and farthest points of acceptable focus. Increase depth of field by decreasing image magnification, using small lens apertures, or both. Decrease depth of field by doing the opposite.

Depth-of-Field Preview: A control on the lens or camera that you use to manually stop down the lens aperture, allowing you to see depth of field through the viewfinder.

Differential Focusing: The technique of using large lens apertures, long-focal-length lenses, or both to create a narrow depth of field. This separates the focused subject from the out-of-focus foreground and background. Also called *Selective Focusing.*

Diffuser: Any material that scatters a beam of light.

DIN: An abbreviation for *Deutsche Industrie Normen,* a German organization that devised the European film-speed rating for general-purpose films. In this system, as the DIN number increases by 3, film speed increases by one exposure step. DIN and ASA speed ratings agree at a film speed of 12. Also see *ASA* and *ISO.*

E

Electronic Flash: Light created by ionization of xenon gas due to rapid discharge of electrical energy. Color temperature of typical flashes is about 5500K. See *Color Temperature.*

Enlargement: Photographic print made from a negative or transparency that is larger than the original image.

Exposure: The amount of light that strikes a film—the product of illuminance and time. Exposure is determined by shutter speed and lens aperture.

Exposure Meter: See *Meter.*

F

False Attachment: Compositional mistake that makes a background element appear to be connected to a foreground subject.

Fast Film: General classification of films with ASA speeds of 400 or higher. See *ASA.*

Film Speed: A numbering system that compares the relative sensitivity of films to light. As sensitivity increases, so does film speed. See *ASA, DIN, ISO.*

Filter: Any material that absorbs light. Filters can be made of glass, plastic or gelatin. They can be used over the camera lens or light source.

Fisheye Lens: An extreme wide-angle, small focal-length lens with an angle of view greater than 100°. A fisheye produces distorted images by curving lines that do not pass through the center of the image.

Flash Sync Speed: Fastest camera shutter speed that works with electronic flash. With electronic flash and focal-plane shutter this is 1/125, 1/90, or most commonly, 1/60 second. With leaf shutters, electronic flash sync occurs at all shutter speeds.

Floods: See *Photofloods.*

Focal Length: Distance between the film plane and the *optical* center of a lens measured when the lens focuses rays from infinity to a point on the film plane. Focal lengths are used to classify lenses according to image effect they create. See *Angle of View.*

Focusing Screen: Piece of plastic or glass that intercepts the image formed by the lens and reflected up by the mirror of an SLR camera. It is what you see when you look through the camera viewfinder.

***f*-stops:** Series of numbers marked on lens aperture ring that represent the size of the lens aperture. Common *f*-stops are *f*-1.4, *f*-2, *f*-2.8, *f*-4, *f*-5.6, *f*-8, *f*-11 and *f*-16. Larger numbers represent smaller openings, and vice-versa. Each number represents twice as much area as the next larger number, and half the area of the next smaller number.

H

Highlights: Brightest areas of a subject or image. The opposite of shadow.

Hot Shoe: Flash holder on a camera that automatically connects to flash's circuitry when flash is attached. External sync cord is not necessary.

Hyperfocal Distance: The near limit of depth of field when the lens distance scale is set to infinity. If the lens distance scale is set to the hyperfocal distance, the far limit of depth of field is infinity, and the near limit is half of the hyperfocal distance.

I

Incident Light Reading: A meter reading made by measuring light illuminating the scene. This is a method done with a hand-held accessory meter called an *incident light meter.*
Infrared: Invisible part of the electromagnetic spectrum that has wavelength longer than that of red light. We sense it as heat.
Interchangeable Lens: A lens that detaches from the camera, allowing another interchangeable lens to be attached. See *Bayonet Mount.*
ISO: Abbreviation for *International Standards Organization,* which uses ASA and DIN speed ratings to indicate film speed. For example, an ASA 100 (DIN 21) film is also rated ISO 100/21°. See *ASA* and *DIN.*

L

LED: Stands for *light emitting diode,* which is a small electronic device that glows. LEDs are used for exposure displays that are visible in camera viewfinders.
Lens Hood: A conical or rectangular tube of metal, plastic or rubber that attaches to the front of a lens. It blocks stray light from striking the front element of the lens. This preserves good image contrast.
Light: Visible part of the electromagnetic spectrum. It is the colors we see and photograph.
Long-Focus-Lens: A lens with a long focal length, typically greater than 150mm in 35mm photography. Also see *Telephoto Lens.*

M

Meter: Device that measures light and, based on the measurement and film speed, recommends camera exposure-control settings for good exposure.
Mirror Lens: A lens that uses mirrors in addition to conventional lens elements to focus light rays.

N

Neutral-Density (ND) Filters: Gray-colored filters available in glass or gel form that absorb light without changing its color balance. Used to reduce the light striking the film.
Newton's Rings: Multicolored lines created when two transparent surfaces make non-uniform contact with each other. Sometimes occurs with glass-mounted slides.

P

Pentaprism: An optical device used in a camera viewfinder to make a laterally-reversed image read correctly from left to right.
Perspective: The relative sizes, shapes and distances of three-dimensional objects reproduced in two dimensions. In photography, you control perspective by camera location.
Photoflood: A photographic lamp using a tungsten filament. Yields 3200K or 3400K light.
Polarized Light: Light that vibrates in only one plane along its line of travel.
Polarizing Filter: A filter that absorbs polarized light. Used to accentuate colors or reduce reflections from materials other than unpainted metal.

R

Reciprocity Law: This law states that exposure is the product of illuminance (aperture) and time (shutter speed). For a certain exposure, a variety of shutter-speed and lens aperture combinations can be used as long as their "product" yields the same exposure.
Reciprocity Law Failure: This occurs when shutter speeds are very long or very short. Film appears underexposed even though the calculated exposure should give good results. When using general-purpose films, this occurs with speeds longer than 1/2 second or shorter than 1/10,000 second.
Red Eye: The phenomena of flash light reflecting from blood vessels in subject's eyes so the retinas reproduce bright red on color film. Happens only when flash is very close to lens-to-subject axis. Avoid the problem by having the subject look away slightly, or move the flash away from the lens-to-subject axis.
Reflected Light Reading: A meter reading made by measuring light reflected from elements in the scene. This is the method used by most built-in camera meters.
Reflector: Any material that bounces light. Smooth silver or white materials reflect the most light without changing its color balance.
Retrofocus Lenses: Lenses designed with the optical center behind the rear lens element. This design makes interchangeable wide-angle lenses possible.
Reversal Film: Color film that yields correct tonalities after exposure and processing. Also called *color positive* or *slide film.* Color reversal films usually have the suffix *-chrome* in their name.

S

Selective Focus: Using reduced depth of field to place the subject of interest in sharp focus with the rest of the scene out of focus.
Shutter: The camera mechanism that controls the duration of the exposure.
Shutter Priority: See *Automatic Exposure.*
Single-Lens Reflex (SLR): Classification of cameras that use one lens for viewing and taking the picture. During viewing, a mirror reflects the image to the viewfinder. During exposure, the mirror moves out of the way of the image, which strikes film behind the open shutter.
Skylight Filter: A filter that absorbs ultraviolet (UV) radiation and some blue light, reducing the excessive blueness in color images. No exposure compensation is necessary.
Slave Cell: Device that senses flash light and almost instantly creates an electrical impulse to trigger another flash connected to it.
Slide: Image on film that has correct colors or tonalities. Used in projector for viewing an enlarged image. See *Color Reversal.*
Slow Film: General classification of films with ASA speeds of 64 or lower. See *ASA.*
Snoot: Lighting accessory that limits a beam of light to a small area.
Spectrum: The range of electromagnetic radiation organized by wavelength or frequency. The visible part of the spectrum (see *Light*) includes wavelengths of blue light from 400nm to red light of 700nm. Ultaviolet radiation is invisible and has wavelengths shorter than 400nm. Infrared radiation is invisible and has wavelengths longer than 700nm.
Standard Lens: Lens with angle of view between 40° and 59°. With the 35mm format, this is a lens with a focal length between 45mm and 55mm. Many cameras are sold with a lens in this range.
Stopping Down: Selecting a smaller lens aperture (bigger *f*-number). Increases depth of field, cuts down light illuminating film.

T

Teleconverter: Lens accessory that fits between the camera and lens to increase lens focal length, thereby increasing image magnification. A *2X teleconverter* doubles lens focal length. A *3X* triples it.
Telephoto Lens: A lens designed with its optical center toward the front of the lens. This allows interchanging various long-focal-length lenses on a camera body. This expression is also used to describe any lens with a focal length longer than standard. With 35mm photography, this includes lens focal lengths longer than 55mm.
Tone: The shade of a color. Most often used in b&w photography, when a neutral color, such as white, gray or black is described.
Transparency: An image with correct tonalities or colors on film. Used in a slide projector for enlarged viewing. Also called a *slide.* See *Color Reversal.*
TTL: Abbreviation for *through-the-lens* used when referring to a camera with a built-in meter that reads the light through the lens.
Tungsten-Balanced Film: Color film designed to give best color reproduction with 3200K or 3400K light. Also called *Tungsten Film.*
Tungsten-Halogen Lamp: Light source using a tungsten filament in a halogen gas. This type of bulb has a long life.

U

Ultraviolet Radiation (UV): Invisible radiation that can expose film. Reproduces as blue with color film, as low-contrast haze in b&w. Most prevalent at high elevations or when you photograph distant scenes. Effect removed by using a UV filter. See *Spectrum.*

V

Variable Focal Length Lens: Lens with more than one focal length. Change focal length by adjusting a ring that moves lens elements. Also called a *zoom lens.*

Viewfinder: Part of the camera you look through to see the image on the focusing screen. On most 35mm cameras, the viewfinder is a pentaprism that shows the focusing-screen image right side up and laterally correct.

Viewpoint: Location of camera relative to subject. Changing viewpoint changes *perspective.*

Vignetting: Image cutoff due to light rays being intercepted before they can expose film. Typically occurs in the corners of the image.

W

Warm Colors: Yellow, reds and oranges.

Wide-Angle Lens: Classification of lenses with angles of view smaller than that of the standard lens. With the 35mm format, this term used for any lens with a focal length smaller than 40mm.

Z

Zoom Lens: Lens with more than one focal length. Change focal length by adjusting a ring that moves lens elements. Also called a *variable focal length lens.*

Index

A-5.5747527071